# ROOT BEER
# FLOATS

*Story of a Boy, a Time, a Town*

MW00943858

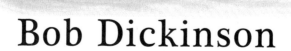

# Bob Dickinson

Published by Exit 8 Publishing
Author email - exit8pub@yahoo.com

Book Design and Printing by Createspace

Copyright 2012 Bob Dickinson

Second Printing

All rights reserved.

ISBN:  1478194847
ISBN 13:  9781478194842

Library of Congress Control Number: 2012912465
CreateSpace Independent Publishing Platform
North Charleston, South Carolina

*For Maya and Giada*

*Tickle me Dear,*
    *Tickle me here,*
        *Tickle me Love, in me Lonesome Ribs!*

"The Lugubrious Whing-Whang",

**James Whitcomb Riley**

# Table of Contents

# Introduction

In writing this book, I quickly discovered a couple of things I hadn't considered at first. One was, unless you keep at it day-in and day-out, a book can take a long time to write—a bad thing. Second was, with today's electronic marvels, the technical process of writing and publishing is nearly a whiz—a good thing. And so, with an ancient version of a software program called Microsoft Word, a seven-year-old computer with the word COMPAQ embossed across its face, and a little cubby hole just off our master bedroom, I set off to write my story.

I planned to take about a year to write it. My kids would have a copy for Christmas that same year. As it turned out, I thought about it for a couple of years before I even began, then was able to whip it out in, oh, say four more years give or take. Thankfully however, in support of my second discovery, if I'd used the same typewriter I learned to type on in Miss Schwin's typing class back in 1958, I suppose it would have taken me another four years, or more likely it would never have been finished. As it was, I was able to make changes to this story a thousand times without ever using a messy little gizmo called a typewriter eraser or even that marvelous invention for the hunt-and-peck specialist called Whiteout. I didn't even have to use what must have been one of the last typewriter-age improvements, correction tape. I never ran my ink ribbon dry in the middle of the night and didn't need carbon paper to make copies. By self-publishing it, there were no publishers to reject it and no editors to change it.

Given the amount of time it took, you might ask yourself why an old guy like me spent so many years sorting through his thoughts about growing up in Covington, then finally sitting down and writing it. Who would want to read it anyway? Who would care? Good questions, both, and after some serious introspection I guess I've accepted the fact that there will never be more than a handful of people who will ever be the least bit interested in reading this fine labor of love. In other words, I can live with the proposition that my book ain't gonna end up on anyone's bestseller list. So the question remains, why did I write it?

For the money? Are you kidding! This little baby's going to be a losing proposition all the way. For posterity's sake? Okay, maybe, at least partly. My wife and daughter have both encouraged me to write it for that reason.

"You're such a good writer," my wife, Alinda, often tells me. "This would be a story that could be passed down for generations."

"It'll be something we'll all want to read, Dad," my daughter, Heidi, encourages me. "The girls will want to read it when they get older," she says, referring to my precious granddaughters, the very ones to whom this book is dedicated.

All right! All right! At least that's two I can actually count on. My son, Lincoln, doesn't read for pleasure. He studies technical manuals at work, and that's only because he must. But just maybe, since his old man wrote it, he might humor me and actually suffer through it. Same with my son-in-law, Corey. As for my granddaughters, by the time they get old enough to be interested in how their grandfather spent his youth, they'll have grandchildren of their own and will remember their grandfather as the one who gave them coins for the gum-ball machine and passed along that horrible Jewel Tea china to them.

My brothers and sisters might read it just to see how much better I was treated than they were. "Yeah, he was the oldest and he was born while Dad was off to war. Of course he was Mom's favorite."

Then there will be a few of the town's people interested in it just to see if their names or someone they know, or more likely someone they knew, are in there. One book donated to the public library should take care of that group.

So, I guess posterity did play a part. And if I thought someone would walk into the Covington library 200 years from now, pick the book up, and enjoy reading about life in 1950's Covington, Indiana, hey, that would be great. Having that happen would be worth every bit of the effort and expense I put into it. However, I imagine about ten years from now, when the librarian sees that the book hasn't been checked out since the year it was donated, into the book sale it will go for 50 cents.

And so, with money being a losing proposition and posterity being only marginal, just what reason could be left?

Well of course, there is more to it. I've been writing short stories, poetry, and unsung song lyrics for most of my adult life. Much of it was written with family or friends in mind, for a birthday or a holiday, to commemorate a birth, to celebrate a memory. None of it has been published. Some of it is pretty good according to Alinda, and a lot of it is pure crap and not worth the paper it's written on according to me. But, it was all done because I enjoyed it. So, when it came to writing this book, I found that I was having fun, a real pleasure from beginning to end. Besides that, I was at that point in my life when I had the time and the tranquility that I needed to do this story justice.

Let me tell you a little more about this tranquility business. Alinda and I have done a little yoga in recent years. It's one of several activities that's both fun and healthy all rolled into one. And even though many do yoga for its meditational and harmony-of-life aspects, I'm in it strictly for the stretching and exercise. There is a position in yoga called the corpse pose. As its name implies, it is performed by lying on your back with your arms out beside you, palms turned up and eyes closed. It comes at the end of a yoga routine, and the idea is to be perfectly relaxed in order to bring complete tranquility to both body and mind. During this pose, all of your tensions, your stresses, all of your troubling thoughts are to be put aside. I recently shared a little secret with Rachel, my yoga instructor, when I told her that if I were to relax any more than I already am every day of the week, I would have to be in a state of unconsciousness. That's exactly how unburdened I feel these days.

That hasn't always been the case of course. Like everyone else I've ever known, there have been rough spots and pitfalls all along that proverbial narrow path. And now to find myself in a world of peace seems strange. I've wondered recently at what point in my life that subtle transformation began to take place. It probably had a lot to do with retirement, because almost immediately I began to feel very familiar with terms like "kicked back," "taking it easy," and "don't sweat the small stuff". Today many of the decisions Alinda and I are faced with concern such serious issues as whether to eat leftover meatloaf or to scramble up some eggs for supper. A particularly rough night might involve a full-blown discussion over whether we should watch *Jeopardy* first or *Wheel of Fortune*. It's what I call the ultimate in simplicity, and at this point I'm finding life very pleasant indeed.

I think it's because of this newfound peace that my thoughts are free to linger in those good and wonderful days of my childhood, days that were spent laughing, living, playing, working just a bit, and then laughing and playing some more. Every time I go for a walk, and Alinda and I walk Covington's sidewalks almost every day, those memories come flooding back. Every neighborhood, every street, the turn at every corner, and every season elicits a host of fond and cherished memories from my youth. And in these thoughts, I always contemplate my good fortune. Because in order for me to have experienced the wonderful childhood that I remember, there had to have been so many things come together at just the right time and in just the right place. As fate would have it, darned if they didn't.

This is the story of my childhood and early adolescence. I was born in 1943, so the time period I'm speaking of falls between 1945 and 1961, and even though that's a long time ago, luckily for me, most of it is still well remembered. Thanks to my loving parents, who made life so simple, those were very happy years for me, easy to live, and uncomplicated. It was simple but it was fun, and since we always had to consider one major element in any Dickinson household decision, it was inexpensive.

Now I choose the word "inexpensive" out of deepest respect for my wonderful and now deceased parents, for in my opinion they were never "cheap". To me cheap connotes an unwillingness to share, and my folks were always willing to share, they simply didn't have enough money to spend freely. They were frugal, lived within their means, always paid their bills, and always wanted to pay their way. When Dad's aunt Myra and her husband Warren Myers built the Illiana Drive-In Theater in Danville, they gave my Dad a free pass each year. That meant we could get in free all summer long. But, it was a real effort to get Dad to use it. He had nothing to give them in return and felt that he was freeloading whenever he showed that pass at the ticket booth. Consequently, we ended up seeing fewer movies than we would have if we had had to pay. So I guess you'd say discretionary spending was seldom a problem. It made life much simpler.

Also, there were very few rules in our home, at least rules that needed to be discussed. Mom and Dad set examples by the way they lived their own lives, and it seems that I liked what I saw. If my parents observed something in me they didn't approve of, they didn't put their foot down, but more than likely made a very innocuous suggestion. For example, Dad asked me one evening after he and Mom had been to the city park watching the roller skaters at the skating rink, "Was it cold out there tonight Bob?" I'd been playing tennis just a few hundred feet away and saw them drive through just about the time I exhaled a puff of cigarette smoke.

"No Dad, it wasn't cold," I replied, knowing I'd been caught.

"Oh," Dad said, "I thought I saw your breath."

"Well, it wasn't because it was cold," I replied meekly, not giving him any more information.

That was all he said until the next day when he simply told me that even though he was a smoker, he wanted me to know that smoking wasn't good for you and he hoped I wouldn't start. I said I understood. That was the end of the discussion. We never discussed it again. Sorry to say I didn't listen to him. The point is, there were never any long-winded lectures, no yelling, no threats. I was given the freedom to make my own way, to make my own decisions, to make my own mistakes.

The timing of my birth in 1943, and the hopeful atmosphere that prevailed in America over the next two decades, was also a big influence on my childhood. It was that period after World War II when America was just waking up to a future of endless possibilities and great opportunities. There was a sense of new beginnings and expectations, a complete turnaround from the hopeless feelings left by the great depression of the 1930's. The troops were home and times were exciting. Opportunities for work and play were abundant; in Covington a kid had only to look across the dining room table, out his front door, and certainly no further than the end of the block to find plenty of fun. So I don't think there was a better time in American history for a kid to be growing up.

Then there's the place of my story, one of the earliest loves of my life, Covington, Indiana. It's hard to paint a picture of Covington and the countryside that surrounds her in so many words, but if I were asked to name the top ten most beautiful places I've ever seen, I could honestly include the panoramas revealed to me every time I go right up Covington's Pearl Street and out past the point.

The fact is, unless you were born and raised here, you may never have experienced the visual pleasures that can be derived from Indiana's simple rural wonders. And even for those who have taken nearly every breath of life in this town, maybe it takes a special vision to see the unique beauty that has always surrounded you. Certainly, that is not without reason. The fact is, Indiana is essentially mile after mile of vast and empty space, interrupted by the occasional farm house, a distant barn here, a cowshed or a silo there, and of course, for a few months out of the year, mile after endless mile of tall waving corn, of haygrains rippling in the hot summer breeze, or those still blankets of soybeans, thigh high and turning brown by mid September.

As for myself, I find that I'm overwhelmed by the sight of the distant horizons, the flat stretching prairies reaching up to touch the beauty of a cerulean sky. It's very much like standing on a sun-lit shore and looking out across the endless ocean. You can see forever, and for some reason, in me at least, it brings a sense of joy.

Of course Indiana is more than empty spaces. It is the home to some 6.5 million Hoosiers, of whom over a million live in, or within commuting distance, of our state capitol, Indianapolis. Besides the Indianapolis metropolitan area, there are some 30 communities of 25,000 or more population and hundreds of smaller cities, towns, hamlets, unincorporated areas, and bends-in-the-road where people call home. It is in one of these small towns perched above the banks of the Wabash River that my story takes place.

Indiana is not famous for her waterways. When compared to such giants as the Ohio, the Colorado, or the mighty Mississippi, the Wabash is a definitive small-fry. In fact, during the summer she becomes little more than a trickle in many spots along her 450-mile length where giant sandbars rise up like lost islands. In some places the water becomes so shallow that she can easily be waded across without getting one's hips wet. I have read that in the days of the early settlers to this area, the river was beautiful and clear. Fish were abundant, and it provided food, transportation, and a livelihood for many who chose to settle on her banks. And even though time has had its deteriorative effect on this once pristine river, people far and wide still recognize her name. She is Indiana's official state river and her praises can be heard in Indiana's official song, *Back Home Again in Indiana*. At one time, she was an integral part of the long defunct Wabash and Erie Canal that ran parallel to her course.

Her size notwithstanding, the Wabash is still well embraced by the many who live along her twisted and muddy banks. And, most importantly to me, it is upon these banks that sits my beloved town of Covington.

Sprouting above the river's bank like a volunteer patch of corn amid Indiana's vast prairie lands, Covington is, in a word, "rural". Compared to the larger towns within an easy hour's drive—Lafayette, Indianapolis, Terre Haute, or Champaign-Urbana in Illinois—there is little doubt that Covington is pretty much small-town in every way. If it weren't for a lonely number-8 exit sign announcing her presence along lightly traveled I-74, most people would pass by without ever knowing of Covington's existence.

And even though "rural" would be an apt description for many to use, to me it is a word that never really fit, a word pulled from some bannered headline and used out of context. To me this Indiana town of my youth was always a giant and for many reasons has found its way into almost every stitch of my life's fabric.

In today's world, Covington is still graced with quaint tree-lined streets leading to an old-fashion town square, centered by a courthouse whose magnificent wall murals depict her early settling. Covington has beautiful churches, a century-old Carnegie Library, and a large and much beloved city park. To me Covington really is picturesque and is, after all, the epitome of what that colorful term is meant to describe. And, even though I could go on and on about the beauty I find here, what I am about to write is not simply a story about Covington, but more about the true symbiosis of the town, the life of a boy, and a time. And although I may not always point out every influence this town has had on my life, for at times I may not have understood that relationship myself, I truly believe that

Covington was such an integral part of my childhood that it has in some way affected almost every breath I have ever taken.

But things change over a 60 or 70 year period, and as sad as it makes me, there is no stopping it. It is, after all, history taking its natural course. Many of those things that had such an influence on my youth in Covington no longer exist, which leads me to believe that capturing those days in the bounds of this book might actually be significant. Hopefully, if I have done a proper job in writing this book, some of you will be able to experience at least a slight glimpse into those wonderful days of my past.

Just a couple of final words. Before publishing this book I discovered that professional editors can be very expensive, a fact I considered long and hard. As an alternative, I have opted for the editing services of "friends and family". Consequently, if you should find a grammatical, punctuation, or spelling error, consider yourself lucky and immediately yell out, "Ah-ha, look here Ethyl, I found one!"

Secondly, even though this is a book derived entirely from my memories, some of which have lain dormant for over 65 years, I have still done my best to achieve accuracy. All the events I have written about are just as I remember them. However, I have asked a few people about dates and names and a few other details that simply weren't important enough to stick with me when I was a kid. If there are still minor inaccuracies, please accept them with my apologies, but please know, I refuse to call them senior moments.

# Chapter 1

## *Winter*

I really loved my winters, which is to say that I loved the one season that my dad hated with a passion. Many a winter's day Dad would moan and groan about the lousy weather then follow up by saying he wished we lived in Hawaii where it never snowed and you didn't even need a "damn" furnace. I always blamed his cursing of that wonderful season on the fact that he had to carry mail in it for 30 years.

Not only did I love winter, I loved all of Covington's seasons. From the long school-free days of summer, when those much maligned twins, heat and humidity, often settled down on Covington for weeks on end, days that brought me home from playing covered in dirt, stinking, and soaked through with sweat, to those cold and often bitter months of January and February, when the northern winds could chill you to the bone in a matter of seconds, I savored them all. An April thunder storm rewarded me with gushing puddles rushing along the curbs of Pearl Street, where I would send a maple twig sailing down its rapids, and those colorful months of September and October that brought winds to give me perfect days to let out my 100 feet of kite string wrapped around another maple twig, sending my kite up over the grade school playground, or better yet the football field, where I'd watch it dance at string's end for hours at a time high above the city park.

And yet, as much as I liked the outdoors, I wasn't the least bit averse to getting stuck inside from time to time. After all, my parents made a very happy and loving home for me and my brothers and sisters, making those few stormy-weather days spent inside more than tolerable. But there were so many great things to do in the out-and-about that I couldn't wait to get at it each day. I was often up and out the door while everyone else was still sleeping, not to return back home until dusk or later. Through each season, I guess I got about as much out of each day as there was to get. But at the same time, I was anxiously anticipating the next season. And even though my springs, summers, and autumns were always dear to my heart, there were many years when they actually took second place to those magical winters.

So why would a boy growing up in Covington find that coldest of seasons so special? Well, a lot of it had to do with that one thing that was so freely given to every kid in town. Rich or poor, big or little, smart and not so smart, it didn't matter who you were or what you were. It didn't matter if you were named Dickinson, Wigley, or Wallace; it was there for the taking. And at no charge either, which was a very important consideration in the Dickinson home. It was the stuff that covered the town several times each winter in a blanket of its white beauty. It was the same stuff that finally hid the leftover leaves of autumn until they were revealed once more as brown speckles ruin. the perfect whiteness of the huge balls I rolled up, stacked thr high, and topped off with my dad's old wide-brimmed fedora Adding a carrot for a nose, about six pieces of coal hauled up from the basement for his eyes and mouth, and there he was, a three-foot high man looking back at me with a smile, built from that free, white, and beautiful stuff called snow. And he had brothers and sisters standing in about half the front yards of Covington.

Because of this white magic, I would leave the house early in the morning in freezing, icy, blowing, miserable conditions with nothing on my hands but a pair of paper-thin Red Ryder gloves, so flimsy that within minutes my fingertips were numb. I often wore shoes with half-inch holes in the soles, a hat with pull-down earflaps that never quite made it to my earlobes, and a pair of corduroy pants so wash-worn and thin I could feel the wind against my legs on even the mildest of winter days. Of course, back then there wasn't such a thing as wind chill, so that was one thing Mom never had to worry about. I never had to meet inspection. If I went out in those deplorable conditions without enough clothing, so be it. I'd know better next time.

On a really good snow day, I wouldn't return to the warm comfort of home until late in the afternoon. And in all those hours of exposure to those numbing elements, I just hoped that once I got back to 601 Pearl, it wouldn't take too long for all the feeling to return to my body parts without a lot of painful tingling. I learned early in life that hot water was the worst thing you could use to thaw out your hands. Cool water was best, warm gave you a bite, but hot water felt like a thousand little needles pricking your hand all at the same time.

Of course, the first snow of the year was always the most exciting. After all, it seemed like forever since it had last covered

nd waiting for it to fall again was not only the
eat anticipation, but also the substance of my active
ion. And why not? Because not only did it become my
ound of white, but it was also the first sign that some-
g wonderful was on its way. It only took a few flakes to con-
rm that the holiday season was near and Christmas was just
around the corner. Santa Claus was making preparations and
there would be much hustle and bustle around the Dickinson
home. I loved it. I reveled in it, every bit of it.

Sledding, snowball fights behind quickly assembled snow
forts, the building of snowmen, snow angels, and duck-duck-
goose were all a part of the magic. Not only that, but as I got
older it meant getting out of school for snow days, ice skating,
scooting around town on an old car hood pulled behind a car,
and the fine art of car hopping.

I don't know if car hopping was just a local thing during
my freshman and sophomore school years or not. I've never
known anyone outside of my buddies and me who were dumb
enough to try it. That's because besides being fun, it could also
be dangerous, or so I was told by my parents. Of course, I never
saw it that way and thankfully never got hurt, at least not sig-
nificantly. Neither did any of my friends, so I think it might
have just been a parent's way of trying to kill a good time.

There wasn't much to car hopping as long as you remembered to wear the right shoes and a pair of gloves. Rubber boots,
crepe soles, and tennis shoes had too much traction, wouldn't
let you slide, and would most likely give you a bloody knee
or nose. You wanted older, slick-soled shoes that would glide
along without a drag. And of course, you had to wear a pair
of gloves because in ten-degree weather a car's bumper could
freeze your fingertips in a matter of seconds. So, with the right
equipment, car hopping was a fairly simple game. All we did

was wait for a car to stop at a stop sign, grab onto the car's rear bumper, get into a crouch and slide from one end of town to the other on the soles of our shoes. Of course, all this had to be done without the driver ever being aware of the thrill he was providing.

Car hopping was a way to fill a winter's day and it was always done with friends. Jim Bodine, Bill Huffman, Jerry Carter, and Bob Dicks were four of my closest, and from time to time, I think they all participated with me in this much-anticipated winter "sport". There was a knack to it of course. First, we had to find a stop sign near where we could hide behind a tree or bush. If it were a corner with no hiding place, one of us would stand on one side of the street and draw the driver's attention with a friendly wave while the rest crept up to the back of the car from the other side of the street. Once the car came to a stop, and preferably when it was just begin-ning to pull away, we quickly duck-walked up to the rear of the car while staying as low as possible so as not to be observed through the driver's rearview mirror. Then we grabbed hold of the bumper and remained in a stooped position with our soles flat on the snow-covered street. Occasionally one too many of us would grab on, and to the driver's dismay, he couldn't figure out why his car wouldn't budge when he tried to pull away. In those instances, we gave his car a little shove to get him going while staying crouched down and out of sight. Then we simply flew along behind the car, the soles of our shoes fairly humming over the snow. Of course, if the driver saw us, the game was up, and we ran away as fast as we could before we got a serious tongue-lashing.

If it was cold enough and the snow didn't melt into slush, it could be a daylong event, and often was. One of the dangers of course, or more accurately from our point of view, part of the challenge, was in avoiding dry spots or streets where the city had put down a load of cinders. That would stop you in your tracks and often resulted in a scraped knee. Of course, the drivers and our parents didn't appreciate our little game. Neither did the city cops, who we always had to keep an eye out for. They could be downright nasty about it too. Thankfully, I was only caught once, and after the, "You idiot, don't you know you could get killed," lecture I was let go with a warning that they would call my parents next time they caught me. I was sneakier after that.

As much fun as car hopping was, however, it didn't begin to compare to the thrill of hood riding. Hood riding was without a doubt the most exciting winter activity I'd ever, up to that point in my life, participated in. It was also the shortest lived. I discovered this little activity one snowy Saturday during my junior high years when I ran across a bunch of older boys down on, what I think was, Second Street. One of them was just old enough to drive and had a car at his disposal that day. This group had come up with the idea of taking an old car hood from the junk yard, removing the hood ornament from its top, flipping it upside down, and then with about a ten-foot piece of heavy rope, tying it to the rear bumper of the car.

Two to four kids, depending of their size, then sat down in the hood and grasped onto the upturned edge with one hand and onto the kid next to them with the other. When everyone was more or less settled, the driver gunned the motor, threw the gearshift into first, popped the clutch, and let the snow fly into our faces as the tires threw back buckets of snow. Off we went, flying down the streets of Covington as if we owned the place. I couldn't stop laughing as we sped along, bouncing into the air at every frozen rut and drift we hit. As we flew around the corners, the hood swung wide tossing us high over the curbs and leveling anything in our path. Garbage cans didn't stand a chance as they were either flattened or sent flying. Street signs, on the other hand, could be dangerous.

That first ride only lasted about ten minutes, but that was all it took to convince me that I had just experienced one of the most thrilling events of my entire young life. I stayed around all afternoon hoping to ride several more times, but there were quite a few kids waiting to join in the fun that day so I only got to ride once more. That didn't deter me though. I had every intention of coming back first thing the next morning and being the first in line.

When I got home that evening, I couldn't stop talking about it. I bubbled with enthusiasm as I described the thrill I felt from all the turns, the bounces, the hits, and the near misses I had experienced riding the hood that day. I filled Mom in on every detail, and when I was finished, I was pretty shocked to find that she didn't share my enthusiasm in the least. In fact, she made several disparaging points, which I did my best to argue against. Problem was, in the end what she said made sense. I'd never been one to ruin other people's property and those were not my garbage cans we were knocking about, nor were they my road signs. That really wasn't the kind of kid I was, and I knew it. When Dad got home I got even more of it when he pointed out the dangers of it all by saying there was always the chance we'd be swung into the path of an oncoming auto or that we could even slide under the wheels of the car that was pulling us. Then there was the possibility of hitting a telephone pole or a street sign that wouldn't give. And, although neither Mom nor Dad forbade me from going back the next day and climbing right back onto that hood, to my great disappointment I decided that they were right in everything they said. The best snow discovery I'd ever experienced lasted exactly one day. For the other kids it didn't last much longer either. Within days, the Covington police department put hood riding out of business once and for all.

There was a little stand of water called Hunter's pond that also figured into my winters for many years. Hunter's pond was located behind the houses at the corner of Stringtown Road and Spring Street and was a Covington landmark for many years. Until a heavy storm broke its containment wall and caused it to drain, it was Covington's unofficial wintertime skating rink. At least it was when I was a kid.

I wasn't much good on ice skates, probably because I never had a pair that actually fit. My ankles just wouldn't stay up, so I skated with my feet turned either in or out, just trying to hold myself up with half the ice touching my blades and the other half touching the sides of my skates. But it didn't matter; I still had a great time playing hockey with my friends during my high school years and for a couple of more years after I went to college. I remember how disappointed I was when I came home for Christmas break my first year at Purdue to find that Hunter's hadn't yet frozen over.

Sometimes we'd build a fire next to the pond and skate late at night, but mostly we just played hockey during the day when we could see, using sticks from the woods and a rock or a can for a puck. The last time I skated there was during my sophomore year of college when I came home one winter weekend and decided it would be fun to play some hockey. It didn't happen. All my old friends were either at college themselves or busy with something else. So I put on my skates, took a couple of awkward turns around the deserted pond and went home. I never visited Hunter's pond again.

Car hopping, hood riding, and ice skating were all great fun, but they were all teenage activities. What I think made me love winters to begin with started when I was only seven years old, the year Santa laid a sled beneath our Christmas tree. Oh was it a beauty, and just my size. It was only a three-footer, so when I jumped on belly-first my whole upper body was on the sled with my knees bent up so that my feet were in the air and not dragging the ground. It was made of wood with metal runners and had Radio Flyer splashed in red written over the wooden slats. I thought it was the best Christmas gift Santa could ever have brought.

I had heard of Douglass hill before I ever got a sled. I had also heard that it was the place you could go sledding if you were brave enough. I had no idea why it was called Douglass hill, that was what the kids called it, but realized some time later that the family whose yard so many kids in town cut through to get there and who actually owned the hill was named Douglass. I didn't know them, but I do remember seeing a lady looking out the window from the nice brick home that sat a little ways from the top of the hill, and feeling that they must like kids a lot because there would easily be a hundred of us behind their house on any given snowy day.

The first time I took on Douglass hill I was eight years old; old enough to walk from Pearl Street to what is now Douglass Manor, which is just an extension of Seventh Street. There was a piece of rope attached to the front of my little sled, so on the seven-block journey I could either pull the sled behind me or pick it up, run as fast as I could, plop it down, then jump on belly-first and slide for ten or fifteen feet before having to repeat the process all over again. As I got closer to Douglass hill, I would run into other kids who were also headed there and it became a race to see who could get there first. As the years passed, I came to realize that the trip itself was often as exciting as the hill.

I'll never forget the first time I looked down from the top of Douglass hill and now frighteningly dangerous it seemed. Not only was it long and steep, but there were a number of trees toward the bottom, all of which had to be navigated around or suffer the consequences. There was also a creek about a hundred feet past where the hill bottomed out, and if you had the momentum, you could actually coast all the way to the creek. More than once I saw kids get soaking wet because the creek hadn't frozen completely and they hadn't stopped themselves in time.

Kids came whooping and hollering from every corner of town, lugging all kinds of sliding contraptions. Like me, the majority had sleds, but others had such things as scoop shovels, garbage can lids, or even pieces of scrap plywood. Those riding anything but a sled, which at least had a limited amount of steering, had to lean their bodies from side to side in an effort to avoid hitting kids walking back up the hill, or worse yet, a tree. Their only other alternative was to fall off or, as we called it, "bail out." It usually worked, but I recall one kid hitting a tree square in the middle because he hadn't bailed out of his scoop shovel in time.

For those of us with sleds, there were several ways we could attack the hill. You could sit up straight and put your feet on the two wooden wings used to steer. In this position, you had a good view of where you were going and could usually avoid hitting the kids in front of you who were either headed down or climbing back up. Plus, you could also steer away from the trees. The second popular position was to lay belly-down on your sled and put your hands on the steering wings. This didn't give you as good a view as in the sitting position and any collisions that occurred were always head-first. You could also use this position to stack a sled, which was two or three kids lying one on top of the other. Seldom did the top kid on a stacked sled make it to the bottom without falling off, but then falling off and having wrecks was half the fun.

Kids situated themselves on their sleds and non-sled contraptions about every way you could think of, on their knees, sideways, standing up (but not for long), and on each other's shoulders. But, there was one position that was popular with sleds that you couldn't do with anything but sleds. It was called forming a train. To do it, you lined up several sleds in a row, one behind the other. Everyone got on their own sled belly-down and grabbed hold of their steering wings, then hooked their feet into the two little spaces on the front of the sled behind them. This made all the sleds connected like a train as long as everyone kept their feet in the holes of the sled behind them. When everyone was set, two or three kids from the sidelines gave the train a boost and over the hill it went. For an eight year old, observing a sled train for the first time was amazing.

Kids got broken bones at Douglass hill. I saw it happen to one kid, a broken leg or ankle. Just plain bad luck is what it was. He was headed up when another kid was headed down and he didn't jump out of the way in time. Happened all the time, but this time I guess the bone didn't give. It was the talk of the hill for days, but it didn't stop anyone from coming back.

When I was ten years old, I thought for sure I had broken my own leg. It happened on a particularly cold day after I'd been sledding for a couple of hours. I was numb from the cold, couldn't really feel my hands, ears, legs, or feet, in other words, a normal winter day. Three of us decided to form a train and I ended up in the middle. Everything started off fine, nice line of three sleds headed straight down the hill and gaining speed. One problem with trains, or one of the really fun things about them depending on what happened, is that the train could get out of line, sometimes way out of line. It could be even more fun if it got so out of line that the last sled was whipped back and forth, what we called cracking the whip. Well this time I didn't see it coming until the last second and then it was too late. As we neared one of the larger trees at the bottom of the hill the lead sled went to the right of the tree, but the back sled had gotten whipped around so that he was running sideways. Not only was he running sideways, but he was going to pass the tree on the left. Of course that left me to take the tree smack in the middle, which is exactly what happened.

To my horror, my left leg caught the full brunt of the collision. Thankfully, it wasn't my head, and thankfully also, I was nearly numb with cold. But still, ohhhhh honey did it ever hurt and definitely brought tears to my eyes. But at ten years old, I was too old to cry in front of all the kids, even if it was as much pain as I'd ever felt in my life. The fact was, if you were going to sled Douglass hill you had to take a few lumps now and then. You didn't complain and you didn't cry. So I sat there in the snow for several minutes unable to move. The kids I'd come down the hill with scrambled back up without a thought that I'd been hurt. They hadn't even realized what had happened. That was fine with me because I was too embarrassed to tell them that I might have broken my leg.

I'm not sure how long I sat there, but eventually I decided it wasn't broken after all, so I got up and headed home. I told Mom I hit a tree and she asked if I was all right. I said, "Yeah, fine," and that was that. My entire thigh was black and blue for a week, but I never let on and I never stopped going back to Douglass hill. That was, however, my final train.

# Chapter 2

# *Downtown Square*

## The Courthouse

Of course, Covington's downtown square would never have been the square without its central attraction, its reason to be, its heart—the courthouse. Being the county seat of Fountain County, Covington's present courthouse was built in 1936, the fifth such building since the first one was erected in 1827, and other than the obvious years of weathering, it looks today much like it did during my childhood.

I was in awe of the courthouse; I guess most kids were. With its marble floors and staircases, marbled columns, its heavy brass-clad doors and mural-covered walls, to me it was vast, mysterious, and oh so beautiful. The fact that every step I took while running up and down the stairs created an echo simply added to its mystery. There wasn't another building in the county, much less the town, that compared to it. And the best thing about it was that my Aunt Mary worked there. So, on those days when she had me in for a visit, I was pretty excited. For not only was I going to get to go to lunch with her at the Courthouse Café, but Aunt Mary always gave me a dime or so to spend at the concession stand that was located on the main floor lobby.

Having money for a candy bar or a pop was always exciting, so my eyes lit up whenever Aunt Mary started digging in her purse. And it wasn't just the treat that I looked forward to when I went down to that concession stand; it was the man behind the counter.

Robert Dale Auter ran that concession stand for as long as I knew him. I suppose he might have been in his thirties when I was old enough to start visiting my Aunt Mary, and I'd never met a nicer or friendlier shopkeeper in my young life. But what I found most interesting, of course, was his handicap. Robert Dale was blind. Robert Dale was totally blind, wore dark glasses, and when he left his concession stand he tapped his way along with a white-handled cane. And I ask you, what could be more interesting to a seven-year-old boy than to buy your special treat from a man who could not see?

To me it was like magic that he had no sight, yet knew where each and every candy bar was located in his glass case. And if I asked him for an Orange Nehi, there was only the slightest hesitation as he reached into an upright cooler, ran his hands along the bottles, stopped and pulled out exactly what I'd ordered. When it came to paying him I never handed him anything but the right coins, but I did watch as he made change for others. With coins, it was no problem, but with bills he had to ask the customer what denomination it was. I never saw him miss giving anyone the right change back. I often wondered if people ever cheated him. Back then, probably not, but something makes me think it wouldn't work today.

I would spend long minutes down at that concession stand just to visit with Robert Dale and watch him work. He was the first blind person I ever knew and I often pestered him with questions. He showed me how he read Braille, how he knew the candy bars and coins by their size and weight, and how he used his cane to feel his way along. I also came to realize that what he couldn't see was often compensated for by what he could hear. As I grew older, and my visits to Aunt Mary diminished and eventually ceased, I made stops into the courthouse just to say hello to Robert Dale. What was amazing was that after the first or second time I dropped in on him when I was a kid, he knew who I was by my voice. Even after my voice changed and I left Covington to go off to college, whenever I came home and stopped by the Courthouse, I never had to tell him who I was. "Hey Robert Dale, how's it going," I'd say to him. "Bobby Dean, is that you?" he'd answer me with his big smile. "Where have you been?"

## Burrin's Drug Store

Covington had several stores that sold what were commonly known as sundries, things such as over-the-counter medicines, cosmetics, hair and body products, and other drug-store-type merchandise. But there was only one business in town that I ever thought of as a real drug store because all the way in the back it actually had a pharmacy. That was Burrin's. It occupied the building on the east side of the square just south of The Fountain Trust Company, and it was owned and operated by a pharmacist named Joe Burrin. Joe was a friendly sort, tall, slender and sprouting a pencil thin salt and pepper mustache. He had a wife and two children, one a daughter named Karen who was my age and my classmate through all twelve years of school. Karen was also a fellow member of the Methodist Church junior choir. I liked Karen, but we were never what I'd call good friends. For years the Burrins lived in a home that I always found very attractive. It sat on the corner of Seventh and Pearl and it's where they lived until they bought an even nicer brick home three blocks east and up the hill on the corner of Tenth and Pearl.

I loved walking into Burrin's drug store and taking that first breath. It had an exotic and pleasant aroma that I'm sure was an odd mixture of the fragrances wafting up from the soda fountain, the candy rack, perfume samples, cosmetics, hot nuts spinning around on a Lazy Susan, various sundries, and all those drugs back behind the prescription counter. To me that odor was intriguing, and who knows, maybe that's one of the things that led me to become a pharmacist in my adulthood.

Burrin's was usually a beehive of activity, although I imagine if Doctor Suzuki and Doctor Hoffman hadn't been dispensing their own medicine to most of their patients, Joe Burrin would have had more pharmacy business than he could handle. As it was, it was probably the candy, card, film, sundry, and fountain business that kept the place going. Of course, Joe didn't run the store by himself, in fact you were seldom waited on by Joe. His staff consisted of Harold Hegg, who I remember most because his friendly and outgoing attitude made every customer in the store feel warm and welcome, a fellow named Jack Spinning, Jack's aunt Lura Spinning, and Lometa Tuggle, among others. Those were the regulars during most of my childhood, until sometime during my high school years when Joe hired another pharmacist to help him out. His name was Phil Young and it was with Phil that I often discussed Purdue, Phil's alma mater, about Purdue's School of Pharmacy.

During my childhood, however, it was the soda fountain that made Burrin's so memorable. The soda fountain was situated along the south wall, which was to the right when you walked in, and consisted of a sit-down counter fronted by six red-vinyl cushioned bar stools with chrome footrests. Along the same wall, a little past the fountain, were three small round tables with two ice-cream-parlor chairs at each, giving you the choice of sitting at a table or up at the counter. Hanging from the ceiling throughout the store were several fans with their blades always in motion, summer and winter. As I see it through my mind's eye today, the setting was so quaint it could have been a scene right out of a Courier and Ives painting.

Also typical for the day, Burrin's soda fountain could whip you up any number of treats in a large variety of flavors. They had ice cream in dishes or cones, sundaes, sodas, parfaits, milk shakes, malts, root beer floats, and fountain drinks that could actually be built from scratch. A Green River was one of my favorite fountain drinks as was a cherry phosphate. With a Green River, Harold would squirt lime flavoring into an ice-filled glass then fill it up with a pull from the carbonated water dispenser. A stir with a long handled spoon and it was ready to go. For a cherry phosphate, he'd go through the same process except with cherry flavoring, and then at the end, Harold would add a small squirt of phosphoric acid from the phosphate bottle. The addition of phosphoric acid made it a phosphate, enhanced its flavor, and prolonged the "fizz". You could have phosphates in any flavor for an extra nickel. I tried a Green River phosphate once, but decided it was too tart and was probably something like biting into a raw lime, so I stuck with the traditional Green Rivers.

Burrin's was the only place I've ever seen a real ice cream soda made, and I'm sure you'd have a hard time finding anyplace today that still makes them. I didn't know what to expect the first time I ordered a soda, but having seen someone else lovingly fawn over one, I was anxious to try it. Watching Harold or Jack make one was a treat in itself. They started with a tall flared molded glass that was used exclusively for sodas. Into this went two scoops of vanilla ice cream out of the ice cream freezer, followed by several squirts of flavoring from a row of highly polished stainless steel syrup dispensers. Depending on the flavor, some flavors were pumped on while others were dollopped on with a dipper. My favorite was a cherry soda and the flavoring had to be added with a dipper because it contained small chunks of cherries. Then the real fun in the making came when they placed the soda glass under the seltzer dispenser. For regular fountain drinks like Green Rivers, they pulled the seltzer water lever toward them and a regular soft stream of seltzer (carbonated) water flowed out. But for a soda, they pushed the same lever forward and a small, but powerful, little stream of seltzer was forced down the inside of the soda glass and into the ice cream and flavoring mixture. This caused the whole thing to bubble up wildly, filling the top of the glass with a plethora of iridescent bubbles. The soda was then topped off with a squirt of whipped cream, a maraschino cherry, a long spoon, and a straw—and voilá—the best treat that you could ever imagine was ready to be devoured.

The only other treat that I considered being anywhere near as good as Burrin's soda was their root beer float, which by the way, cost a dime less. Trouble was, until I was old enough for a paper route, when I was around 11 years old, I couldn't afford either of them very often. In fact, until I began earning some of my own money, I seldom went into Burrin's at all.

A quarter-a-week allowance for doing a few chores around the house didn't buy too many quarter or thirty-five cent treats, so until I had a paper route, I normally settled for a Green River or a Vanilla Coke, which, at only a dime, were a little more in my price range.

One day this discrepancy between what I wanted as a treat and what I could afford became a little too tempting. As a result, I committed an act of thievery that, even to this day, I've never quite lived down. And at such a young age too. I knew it wasn't right, but it didn't seem all that wrong either. Besides, it wasn't much, only 20 cents. And on top of that, looking back now for an excuse, it may well have happened because I was a victim of circumstance. Could I lay some of the blame on my mother? In the court of law I believe there are special considerations sometimes afforded lawbreakers for what are called mitigating circumstances. Could that be the case for me? Well, maybe, and here's why. I found at a very early age that the quickest way to my mother's heart was through a clean plate. As a mail carrier, Dad made an average living, but with a family of seven to feed, our table was usually loaded down with bowlfuls of what you might call the cheaper staples, often fried-up in grease, full of starch, and served with heaping portions of sugar, butter, and salt. It was carbohydrate and fat heaven, and I made my mother very proud by eating every morsel that was placed in front of me, then asking for seconds. Wasn't anything my mother loved more than to see her children with clean plates at the end of a meal.

Because of that, you might be able to see that I could at least lay some of the blame for what I did that day on her. You might also see why I might have developed a voracious sweet tooth. Oh yes, candy, cakes, cookies, pies, sweet rolls, ice cream, pop, they were all at the top of my favorite things in the whole world list. Problem was, my mother didn't spend much money on ready-made sweets because they were not in the budget. She made up for it by doing plenty of baking. I distinctly remember the first time I walked into the kitchen and asked Mom if I could have a nickel so I could run down to Meharry's and buy a candy bar. She just looked at me like I'd fallen on my head. I got the picture and I never asked for anything so crazy again. Instead, I learned to make my own spending money.

My first paper route, a 12-customer route that ran me all over town, gave me a profit of about a dollar a week. And where did most of that dollar end up? Well, between the time I'd done my collecting on Saturday morning and arrived home in the early afternoon, most of that dollar had been divvied up amongst Burrin's, Ellmore's bakery, and Meharry's grocery store. Then I had to suffer through a full week of sweets withdrawal until collection day rolled around again.

The point is, I liked to eat, especially sweet things, and there was seldom enough money to keep my sweet tooth habit satisfied, which brings me back to my story of temptation.

Our family attended the Covington Methodist Church where on special occasions, four or five times a year, the junior choir got to perform. Now I dearly loved the junior choir. Not only did I like to sing, but I liked hanging out and cutting up with the other kids who were choir members, most of whom were my school classmates. It was directed by a couple of very nice ladies named Martha Wallace and Margaret White who were fun, kind, and amazingly patient. And for a group of mostly seven to ten year old kids, I thought we sounded pretty good singing those child-friendly hymns in our squeaky two-part harmony. About three or four weeks before we were scheduled to perform, we'd start practicing every Thursday afternoon for about an hour after school. It was during one of these Thursday practices that my bold crime was committed.

Practice took place in the sanctuary choir loft, which was located above and behind the pulpit. Directly in front of the pulpit sat a table with a brass cross, a candle on both sides of the cross, and two collection plates. These same plates were passed each Sunday morning during service. On this particular Thursday night at the beginning of practice, as I was ascending the stairs into the choir loft, one of the collection plates caught my eye because lying in it was some loose change. Wow, I thought to myself, I'd never noticed that before. Practice seemed to take forever that night because for the entire rehearsal I was formulating a plan for an after-practice treat. I thought I knew how much money was in my pocket, but I checked again to be sure. Nothing had changed as I pulled out a lonesome dime. That meant I was fifteen cents short of a root beer float.

I was nervous about it, but not enough so to divert my plan. As it turned out, it was all too easy. At the end of practice, I simply lagged behind as everyone left the choir loft. When I reached the table holding the collection plate, I looked around quickly to see that no one was watching, then reached over and snagged two dimes up from the plate and slipped them into my pocket. Another quick glance verified that no one had seen me. Slick as a whistle, I'd pulled it off without a hitch.

In the end, I was bothered more by the extra five cents I'd stolen than anything else and then began to wonder if the whole thing had been a set-up. Had this been God's test that I had failed so miserably? Had I sold my soul for a root beer float and a nickel in change? A little guilt did settle over me, and even though I noticed later that there was often loose change in the collection plate, I was never tempted to steal it again. On that day, however, I'll have to say I consumed what may have been the best Burrin's root beer float of my entire life.

It wasn't until I was a senior in high school that I took advantage of Burrin's little round tables because until then I had no one to share a table with. That all changed in the summer of 1960 when I started going with the first girl I ever dated, the very same girl I married six years later and have been married to ever since, Alinda. I can remember ordering several of those wonderful root beer floats and asking for two spoons and two straws. As we shared them, I sometimes spent the entire time looking across that small round table into her big brown eyes. More than once she asked me what I was looking at and my answer was always the same, "You."

One other thing that stands out in my mind about Burrin's took place when I must have been five or six years old, at least too young to walk home from downtown at night, which I was doing by the time I was eight. Dad had driven me to the Lyric Theater for a movie that I was going to see by myself, and he told me to go to Burrin's afterwards and ask to use the phone to call home. Then he would pick me up. It was the first time I'd ever had to call home from anywhere and maybe the first time I'd ever made a phone call at all. Mom had written the number down and stuck it in my pocket. After the movie, when I asked to use the phone at Burrin's, they asked why and I told them I needed to call home. They informed me that they didn't normally let anyone use the phone for personal calls, that it was a business phone, but they'd let me this time, but not to ask again. I was a bit embarrassed by it all and was thankful when they finally sat the phone on the pharmacy counter for me to use. I picked up the receiver and waited for the operator to ask, "Number please?" I remember feeling quite proud of myself when I remembered the number without looking at the note and told her 211. She said, "Thank you, I'll connect," in a nasally tone that all operators seemed to have on those old phones. After a couple of rings, Mom answered.

## Lyric Theater

In those days before television, going to the movies was one of America's favorite forms of entertainment. Most every town, big or small, had their own movie theater, and Covington's was named the Lyric. Sitting on the east side of the square between Burrin's drug store and the Grab-It-Here grocery, the word LYRIC in large white capital letters was prominent on both sides of its triangular-shaped marquee. After dark, that marquee glowed with an incandescent splendor of neon and blinking lights, lighting up at least half of the east side of the square. Owned and operated by a rather short and rotund man named Dutch Merryman and his wife Phynus, the Lyric provided Covington's kids and adults alike with the day's most popular movies, usually a number of months after they'd made it to the big cities.

During most of my growing-up years, the Lyric showed the feature movie twice a night, at 7:00 and again at 9:00 and sometimes they also scheduled an afternoon matinee on Saturday and Sunday, especially if the movie was popular.

The Friday night, Saturday matinee, or the first show on Saturday night were the showings I most often attended along with a hundred or so other kids. An adult wouldn't normally get caught dead taking in a movie during any of those times. What with Milk Duds, Jujyfruits, and Sugar Babies flying through the air unabated, these showings were as likely as not to be a complete madhouse.

Dutch would be up and down the aisles the whole movie long tapping kids with his flashlight either on their heads, trying to get them to shut up, or on the tips of their shoes, to get their feet off the seat in front of them. I got bopped only once as I remember, but some of the more rambunctious kids got it on a regular basis. And Dutch had this procedure down to a science. A kid got bopped once and once only. He knew it would be his first and last warning. Next time it was out the door. And if there was a bit of pain when you got bopped, well you have to remember that in those days such terms as "child abuse" had never been heard of, at least not in Covington. I'm pretty sure if I had ever heard that term when I was growing up I would have envisioned a child abusing his parents, sassing them or throwing a hissy fit. After all, parents were masters of their surroundings and children might be punished good and proper, but they were never "abused".

Resting your feet on the back of the seat in front of you or talking too loudly were only bopping offenses; getting caught throwing something through the air was an immediately kicked-out-of-the-theater offense. However, I only knew one kid who was banished forever, and it was because he threw an entire Holloway Slo-Poke sucker through the movie screen. It was on a Saturday night when the theater was completely full of kids, and it took Dutch some weeks to figure out who did it. As I recall, in the end someone squealed. That Slo-Poke ripped a large hole in the upper right hand portion of Dutch's new wide state-of-the-art Cinemascope-friendly screen. Even after it was repaired, you could still detect that patch up there in the corner of the screen for every movie shown during the Lyric's remaining years.

I don't recall going to the movies at all until I was probably five years old, and even then, from five to seven, I didn't go often because I had to be driven downtown by Mom or Dad. By the age of seven, however, I was allowed to walk from home to the movies by myself as long as there was daylight, and when I turned eight I was walking back and forth day or night. When I first started going to movies, a child's ticket for anyone who hadn't yet turned twelve years old was 15 cents. An adult ticket was 25 cents. Per my mother's instructions, I was still asking for a child's ticket after my twelfth birthday. However, sometime between my twelfth and thirteenth birthday I convinced Mom that Phynus was giving me dirty looks every time I asked for a child's ticket. After much pleading Mom begrudgingly gave in and gave me permission to spend the extra dime. By the time I left for college, adult tickets had gone up to 35 cents.

As much as kids made fun of him, Dutch was really a nice guy, and so was Phynus. He did all he could to keep the noise to a small din and kids in their seats. Sometimes it worked and sometimes it didn't. Oftentimes Dutch also had to run the projectors, which were located upstairs in the projection booth, in addition to his ushering duties. Once in a great while, he also took tickets and ran the concession stand. In the days of huge movie reels that had to be wrestled onto antiquated projectors, then pampered through each showing, it was all he could do to maintain any control of the kids at all. Of course, anytime the film broke, producing a blank screen bathed in bright light, or the film got caught in the projector and you could watch the visual affects of melting film right up there on the screen, it was audience bedlam until Dutch had it up and running again. And if the picture ever became blurred, an instantaneous ear-splitting roar of "FOCUS DUTCH! FOCUS!" was screamed up toward the projection booth by every kid in the house.

Even though Phynus was Dutch's wife, I never saw her helping when Dutch came downtown to sweep out the theater every morning. Phynus's job was to take tickets and from what I could see, that was her job every day, every night, and every minute the theater was open. I never saw Phynus anywhere else in the theater, and I seldom saw the ticket booth without Phynus sitting in it. When you left the theater in the middle of a movie, you reported to Phynus that you'd be right back, then you reported back to her on your return. And kids had to report in and out to Phynus quite often because the Lyric had no restrooms.

I recall the first time the urge hit me to use the bathroom during the middle of a movie. As luck would have it, the movie was *Abbott and Costello Meet Frankenstein*, a film that had me so involved I didn't want to leave it for any reason. So I held it as long as I could before deciding I couldn't hold it any longer, then I ran out of the movie, into the lobby, and up to the ticket counter where I asked Phynus where the bathroom was. She said there was none in the theater, but that I could go across the street to the Courthouse where there were public restrooms, or if I only needed to do number one I could go down the alley next to the Grab-It-Here.

I was worried about having to pay again when I came back in, but she assured me it wouldn't be a problem, just to wave as I re-entered. The alley was closer, but I didn't like that idea. For one thing, it would be embarrassing to run into any other kids down there, and secondly, on this particular night anyway, there was Frankenstein to worry about. So over to the courthouse I ran. It was only about a 30-second trip, but to my dismay and a little bit of leakage, when I arrived I found the restroom locked.

Time was now of the essence because I was on the verge of wetting my pants, a humiliation no kid would ever want to face, so away I flew back across the street not caring now who or what might be down that alley. I didn't even hesitate as I ran from the sidewalk into the alley a few feet, stopped, then with sweet relief peed against the brick wall of the Grab-it-Here. Up until that time in my life, it may have been the most satisfying pee I'd ever taken, and when I was finally finished, I quickly zipped up and a few seconds later was waving myself back into the Lyric. The whole thing probably took less than two minutes total, and after that I decided there was no reason to ever try to use the Courthouse restroom again.

Over the years I often ran into lots of other boys taking a leak in that alley, but there was plenty of room so we all just found our own space. I knew it wasn't really the right place to be going to the bathroom, so it was always just slightly embarrassing. And when you were down there, it was an unspoken rule that you never recognized anyone you saw, never said hello, goodbye, or how you doing. I don't know what girls did when they had to go because I only saw a girl down that alley one time. I was really embarrassed by it, so I went back to the sidewalk and waited until she left to do my business.

One of the things I liked about going to the movies were those little films they called "short subjects" that were shown before the main feature, along with the coming attractions. These shorts varied from night to night and week to week. Usually they consisted of one or two cartoons like a Looney Tunes or a Disney, followed by a *Three Stooges*, or *Joe McDoakes-Behind the Eight Ball*, or some other little comedy sketch. These all took up about fifteen or twenty minutes of time before the feature started.

From time to time Dutch would entice kids with shorts that were called serials. These were a series of continuing stories designed so that the end of each episode left every kid in the house hanging on the edge of his seat and hungry for the next. Of course, that next one wasn't going to be shown for another week at the cost of another movie ticket. Some of the best serials brought kids back week after week no matter what the feature movies were. One full serial would typically run for eight to twelve weeks from beginning to end, so Dutch had something of a captive audience during that two or three month period.

I couldn't afford to go to the movies once a week, so I never saw a full serial from start to finish, but I relished watching the ones I did see. *Superman* was one of my favorites, although I never wanted to emulate him in my play life as I did Roy Rogers and Gene Autry. All the science fiction serials like *Flash Gordon* and *Rocket Man*, plus the cowboy serials were high on my list too. Kids loved these things even though they were far from what you would call well-made. They were all B-grade material for sure and all loaded with lots of shoot-em-up action. I expect it was the violence that was portrayed in most all these serials, whether from six-shooters or ray guns, that was most captivating to many of us.

I'm convinced that Dutch finally got back at all us noisy kids the year he introduced a new series of shorts. Sitting through one of these little jewels was, without a doubt, the longest eight minutes a kid ever lived. They were called travelogues, and were short movies of what someone must have considered beautiful places. Not only was the depicted scenery excruciatingly boring, but they were narrated by a man whose lulling soft voice could put you to sleep in an instant. They were nothing short of absolute torture to any kid I ever knew and to this day I can still hear the words at the end of each travelogue as the narrator closed with something like, "And as the beautiful sun sets over this enchanting land of blah-blah-blah, we bid farewell to our hosts of blah-blah-blah and blah-blah-blah-blah-blah until we meet again."

Before I graduated from high school, the Lyric had stopped showing serials. I suppose it was because television had been around for a few years and the idea of a show that continued week-in and week-out was becoming old stuff. *The Fugitive* running from the law every week in search of the one-armed man was a bit classier than the Lyric's lame run of serials. But still, those serials gave Covington kids a lot to look forward to for many years. I was sorry to see them go.

There was only one movie that I ever saw at the Lyric that left me so frightened I was afraid to leave the theater that night. The name of the movie was *Invaders from Mars,* which was released in 1953, so I must have been ten years old when I saw it. In the movie, people were being sucked into the ground where invading Martians were waiting for them in tunnels down below. The Martians then implanted something in the Earthlings heads, just behind their ears, so that the Martians could control the Earthlings. I don't remember how the movie ended, but watching those people being sucked into the ground like they'd just stepped into quicksand, which, by the way, was the absolute scariest substance on the planet as had been demonstrated many times over in the Jungle Jim movies, had me shaking. When the movie ended I slowly made my way into the Lyric's lobby, then simply stood there watching other kids leave the theater. I wasn't about to step my foot out onto that sidewalk until I was fairly certain the Martians, who I also felt pretty sure were there, weren't going to suck me into the ground. Finally, I got up the nerve to leave, but I walked home that night with great speed and trepidation.

Some memories of the Lyric are affectionately intertwined with memories of other more important events in my life than simply going to a movie. Two of these occurred during the years when Dr. Suzuki was still delivering babies in a family's home, or at least in our home. The main purpose of delivering at home, of course, was to save several hundred dollars in hospital bills, a strong Dickinson incentive. Mom must have met whatever requirements Dr. Suzuki had for this service because my youngest brother, Charlie, and my two sisters, Mary Ann and Nancy, were delivered in this fashion. Nancy, the youngest, just got in under the gun, because Dr. Suzuki announced that she would be his last home delivery. As far as I know, she was.

I don't recall the circumstances of my brother Charlie's birth; I must have gone to sleep before any of the commotion because I had no idea my brother Charlie had even been born, let alone right there in our living room. I just know I went to bed one night and the next morning I had a new baby brother.

I was nine years old when my sister Mary Ann was born, and for her delivery I was given specific instructions. Take my brother John with me and walk down to the movie. After the movie, we were to walk home, enter through the back door, and go straight to bed. I don't know if Mary Ann was born before or after the movie, but the next morning when I went into Mom and Dad's bedroom, I found my new baby sister asleep, wrapped up in a blanket in her little bassinet.

For my own selfish reasons I guess it was my youngest sister Nancy's birth that was most satisfying of all. I had asked Mom earlier in the day if I could go to the movie that night. I don't remember what was playing, but it was something I really wanted to see. Naturally, we didn't always get what we wanted, no matter how badly we wanted it, and on this occasion Mom said no. I had learned early on in my life not to ask for too many things that cost money and made myself quite happy with what I had, so even though I might have been a little disappointed, I certainly wasn't disheartened.

Then, as the six of us were sitting around the kitchen table that evening eating supper, something miraculous happened. There was a bit of a commotion, and I heard Mom tell Dad that her water broke. I had no idea what that meant until Dad informed me that Mom would be having a baby that night. I looked at Mom expectantly and she smiled at me and said she guessed I'd be seeing that movie after all. Quite honestly, I should have been happy over the fact that the next morning I would be the big brother to a new brother or sister. But in truth, I was pretty much ecstatic because I was going to get to see that movie after all. So again, it was take John to the movie, walk home, in the back door, go to bed. I think Charlie and Mary Ann might have spent that night upstairs in my grandmother's apartment. Anyway, next morning I peeked in the same bassinet in the same corner of Mom and Dad's bedroom where I had found Mary Ann two years earlier and, sure enough, there was my new baby sister. Mom was awake and looking at me.

"What is it?" I asked.

"A girl," Mom said. "Just like Doc Suzuki predicted. Her name's Nancy Ruth."

"Oh, wow," I said. Then I ate a bowl of cereal and went to school.

When I was fourteen and had already been earning my own money as a paperboy for about three years, I took what I considered my first "real job". I had heard that Dutch was looking for someone to run the concession stand at the Lyric. Dutch wanted to move Jim Keller, a boy in the class ahead of me, from the concession stand to the projection room, so the job was going to be available. I was thrilled when I asked Dutch for the job and he hired me. To be earning a huge salary of 60 cents an hour and all the popcorn I could eat made me feel rich. I did that concession job for a couple of years, and looking back now, I'm not sure that particular job was in my best interest. You see, I was a fat kid, and all the free popcorn you can eat was a bad idea. On top of that, there was Coca-Cola, and Snickers, and Mounds, and Milky Ways, and Hershey Bars, and Mild Duds, and any number of other wonderful high-calorie treats, all of which I loved and all of which ate up the majority of every dollar Dutch paid me. By the time I quit that job, I was probably two inches taller, but also sixty pounds heavier, not the most healthy of proportions.

I felt a real sense of responsibility when Dutch gave me my own key to the concession room, and I was usually there and working even before he and Phynus arrived. The job consisted of working on Friday nights, Saturday nights, and Saturday matinees during the school year and a couple more nights a week during the summer. For the evening shows I came in about 6 p.m. to start popping the popcorn then closed up about half-an-hour into the movie's second showing.

Popcorn was the big money maker in the concession business, so my number-one duty was to never let it run out. The minute I walked through the door, I flipped on the popcorn machine, letting the kettle get hot, then I added a glob of orange solidified popcorn oil from a 5-gallon bucket that sat under the hot-pan. When it got hot I added a scoop of unpopped corn. It was one of those all-enclosed popcorn machines where the popcorn overflowed out the top of the kettle as it pushed the lid up. After it finished popping, I turned the kettle on its pivot to dump the remaining popcorn down onto the stainless steel hot-pan then repeated the process for the next kettle. By the time the first kettle of popcorn was ready to dump, I had straightened out and restocked the candy and soda pop and had gotten my money box set up next to the customer window. As the popcorn began filling the hot-pan space under the kettle, I scooped it into white paper bags and stacked them on top of the hot-pan, leaning them against the window of the popcorn machine. In order to get enough of these made so that I didn't run out at the first rush, I had to stack them two rows wide and two bags high. The problem was that these bags did not want to stand one on top of the other. They tended to tip over, resulting in popcorn either spilling inside the machine, which was okay even though I still had to re-bag it, or it fell outside the machine and all over the floor, which for obvious reasons was not okay.

In the days before buckets of popcorn, most movie theaters used boxes, boxes that would have stacked nice and neat, no tipping, no spilling. I mentioned this to Dutch more than once and his pat answer was always, "Two cents will buy one box or a dozen bags, so what do you think?"

One summer night about a year after I started the job, I came to work in what was most likely a sour mood. I'm not sure of that, but I say it because it wouldn't have been the first time I came to work when I didn't really want to be there. As is the bane of many a working kid, I often had to miss something fun that my friends were doing, something like roller skating at the park, or playing cards at one of their homes, or doing just about anything except working. So I might well have been feeling sorry for myself that night when I walked through the door. And to my disgust and eventual embarrassment, on this particular night the popcorn bags were going to have it in for me.

As it happened, about 15 minutes before the lobby was to open, a time when I should have had everything ready to go, two bags of popcorn, the two in front and on top, actually had the nerve to fall off the stack. Not only did they fall off, but they fell out the popcorn machine door and onto the floor, scattering popcorn all over the place. That made me more than a little aggravated, it made me angry, but anger didn't get it cleaned up so I quickly swept it up. I then rearranged the bags so that they seemed a bit more stable, even though I knew well enough that stability was impossible. I then filled two replacement bags and set them back in the fallen popcorn's place.

They could have stayed there. They should have stayed there. They could have been two nice, quiet, friendly, buttery and salted, unmoving replacement bags of popcorn ready to make some movie-going kid a nice happy treat. But that's not what happened. Oh no. As I turned to put the broom back where it belonged I heard the awful, terrible, nerve-shattering sound of two bags of popcorn hitting the floor—again!

Throughout my entire life, I can remember every time that I lost my temper so badly that I actually flew into what I would call a rage. I can count those times on the fingers of one hand. And on this particular night, when I was 14 years old and working in the concession stand of the Lyric theater, I experienced what the first finger on that hand represents—my very first red faced, spitting mad, curse filled, arms flailing, dumb blind rage. And all those bags of popcorn stacked up there nice and neat and ready to feed the hungry crowd that would arrive in only a few minutes didn't stand a chance. I tore into them like Godzilla had torn into Tokyo only weeks earlier, all 150 pounds of me. Reaching back to the last bags, I ripped them all forward in one swift and angry motion, tearing at them with my fingers, crushing the popcorn with my arms and hands and sending the entire mess hard to the floor with all the strength I could muster.

And then, like some strange metamorphosis, as quickly as the rage began, it lifted and was replaced by something much more appropriate—FEAR! Fear, because as I surveyed the mess around me, I realized what a big mistake I'd made. Just as I had experienced my first all-out rage, I was now terrified that I might soon experience my first firing. It was nearly time for the lobby to open, but more frighteningly, it was time for Dutch to arrive. What I knew for sure was that I couldn't, under any circumstances, let Dutch see what I had done, so with speed I didn't even know I had, I swept everything up and dumped it into a large grocery bag. Then I hid the grocery bag so I could take it with me when I left that night, lest Dutch see it when he emptied the trash the next day. Thankfully, in the end, everything worked out all right. Dutch didn't even pop his head in when he arrived, so I survived to fight another round. However, from that night on, until I left the Lyric for a job at the new IGA, I treated those popcorn bags with great care. In retrospect, I doubt that Dutch would have fired me that night, but the embarrassment I might have faced would have been a real killer.

Cowboy movies were always big with me. Roy Rogers and Gene Autry provided me my alter egos when I was playing cowboys and Indians with the kids in the neighborhood. When I was eight or nine, I saw a movie featuring a good-looking cowboy named Rex Allen. On the way out of the movie that night, the Lyric was handing out free 8x10 autographed glossies of Rex wearing his signature Stetson and a cowboy shirt with an embroidered lasso on its collar. I took my photo home and spent the next day studying it before I finally broke down and cried, knowing I'd never be a cowboy or that good looking.

Dutch once brought in a real western movie star to put on a live performance. The actor's name was Smiley Burnette, and he played Gene Autry's plump comical sidekick in many of Gene's movies. Smiley performed his act up on a little stage that protruded maybe four or five feet in front of the Lyric's screen. As far as I know, it was the only live performance ever presented at the Lyric, at least in the 1950's. I found Frog's (Smiley Burnette's screen nickname) act entertaining, but what I remember most was that when it was over and I left the theater, I was so surprised, and truly disappointed, to find a travel trailer with the name "Smiley Burnette" painted on its side. It was hitched up to a fancy Cadillac and parked right there on Washington Street. I don't know what I was expecting, but to realize that Gene's famous sidekick hadn't ridden in on a horse, in fact had no horse around anywhere, was a shocker. That was the night I guess I grew up a bit, because from that night forward playing cowboys and Indians was never quite the same.

The draw of the Lyric began to fade as television became the number one form of entertainment, and by the time I graduated from high school, I was catching most of my movies in Danville, which offered three theaters and a couple of drive-ins. I did discover, however, during my senior year in high school that the back row of the Lyric was one of the few places in Covington you could neck, so my newfound sweetheart, Alinda, and I did occasionally put it to good use.

After my senior year, I doubt that I saw another half dozen movies there. I don't know when the Lyric finally closed. It may have been in the 1970's, but I was long gone from Covington when it did. I know that I had many great memories from that theater and really was sorry to hear that it had closed.

## Grocery Stores

When I was a kid, there were at least six stores around town that sold grocery items. They ranged all the way from the full-line grocery stores, carrying everything from thumbtacks to t-bone steaks, to the mom-and-pop neighborhood stores, where we might only go for a loaf of bread or bottle of milk or a special cut of meat.

Kroger was definitely the number one store in town and was located on the SE corner of Third and Liberty, making it the busiest corner on the town square. I call it the number one store because it was the largest, the best stocked, and the store where most of Covington did their grocery shopping. On any given Saturday, you might have to park a full block away. The entrance consisted of a set of double doors that were separated by a handrail, which small kids loved to reach up and swing from. This entrance didn't face either Liberty or Third, but was located in the corner of the store so that it faced into that corner of the square.

When you entered Kroger, you were met by dark wooden floors, narrow aisles, and the aroma of fresh ground coffee beans intermingled with the smell of oiled sawdust used to sweep the floors at night. You were also met with lots of friendly hellos because Covington had that small-town atmosphere, where everyone seemed to know everyone else whether you wanted them to or not.

The narrow aisles ran north and south, and on busy days customers were so thick you could barely get your cart down them. The meat counter, dairy cases, and freezers were located in the back of the store, and there were four checkout lanes up front. On most Saturdays you would likely have to wait in the checkout line a good ten or fifteen minutes. At the meat counter customers waited three and four deep as Mr. James and his contingent of butchers bantered with the customers, took their meat orders, then either pulled the selection from the case or turned to cut it from the hanging stock nearby. The meat was then thrown on the scale, weighed, wrapped up in white butcher paper, tied up with string, and priced with a black grease pencil. There was no use in being in a hurry at the meat counter, so it was the perfect place for customers to visit with their neighbors. It was a tossup as to whether more gossip got passed at the Kroger meat counter or around the town's barbershops and beauty parlors.

I have fond memories of the Kroger store for a number of reasons, one of which was that I worked there for a year or so when I was 16 years old. Prior to that I worked at the new IGA, which opened in 1959, the year I turned 16. At the IGA I was a stock/sack/errand boy and worked there for a month prior to its opening, then for another couple of months afterwards before I quit and went to work for Kroger. I left the IGA because something happened about a week before it opened that just didn't sit right with me, and subsequently caused me to have a problem working for the owner, Don Clark. I'm sure to him the incident was small and innocent, but I was just learning to deal with adults in the work world, so to me it was a big deal.

It happened on a day when some IGA bigwigs had come to inspect the store prior to the big opening. They went from aisle to aisle and shelf to shelf with Don Clark in tow, giving him advice and pointing out this and that. When they finally arrived in the aisle where I was working, they stopped in front of the Kellog's Corn Flakes. One of the men reached up to the top box and pulled it down, telling Don that a short woman wouldn't be able to reach these and they shouldn't have been stacked so high. Don immediately turned to me and told me I'd stacked these shelves too high and warned me not to do it again.

Looking back now I suppose it could have been an innocent mistake on his part. After all, everything was quite hectic. Or maybe he was just trying to make a good impression on those IGA honchos. In his place I might have done the same. But being a wet-behind-the-ears kid, I was dumbstruck by it. Not because he had told me what to do, or even that he had said it with a nasty scowl, which was definitely uncalled for, especially under the circumstances. No, it was because he had as much as accused me of stacking the boxes wrong in the first place, something I hadn't done. And I suppose I could have even forgiven him that had I not seen Don himself place that entire caseful of Kellog's Corn Flakes on the shelf the day before, stacking them right up to and including the box on top that the man had just pulled down. I never cared much for Don Clark after that and quit a few weeks later. Soon after, Vernon Bilsland over at Kroger hired me. I liked Vern and I liked Kroger.

If I wanted any spending money, Kroger was a good place to work. I suppose I worked an average of 10 to 15 hours a week during the school year and maybe 20 a week during the summer. I did all the things a 16-year-old boy can do in a grocery store. Sweeping, bagging, carrying out, cleaning produce, stocking shelves, and unloading the trucks were all part of my job.

I thought Vern was a great guy to work for, even though he had a reputation of yelling at his employees and using some colorful language. But I seldom saw his temper and actually felt it only once. That was the morning after the first time I had put the produce cart in the walk-in refrigerator overnight. The next morning when the cart was pulled back out, all the bananas were black. Vern asked me in his rather high pitched but piercing voice what the hell I thought I was doing, putting the bananas in the refrigerator. I told him no one had told me any different. His reply was, "Well I don't suppose anyone told you not to shit your pants yesterday either, but I'll bet you didn't shit'em did you?" He always had a special way of making his point. I never put the bananas in the refrigerator again.

Vern liked to tell jokes whether they were funny or not, especially if they were at the expense of Paul Mills, manager of his competition, the Grab-It-Here, or Freddie Jenks, one of Paul's employees. A couple that I remember went like this. "I heard Mrs. Fenters was in the Grab-It the other day comparing the toilet paper that was on sale to a brand that wasn't on sale. She asked Paul what the difference was. Paul studied the two packages for a second then turned to Mrs. Fenters and said in that slow gentle drawl of his, 'Well, I reckon on the whole (hole) they're all about the same.'" Vern then roared with laughter as he told it to everyone who'd listen, employee and customer alike. Of course, I thought it was hilarious.

Another time Vern came up to me and asked me if I'd heard that Freddy Jenks had been fired. I said I hadn't and he told me it was true, that Freddy had been caught putting get-well cards inside of Kotex boxes over at the Grab-It. Vern thought the joke was great fun, but I didn't find much humor in it. Vern was that way.

One day he called me aside and told me I was at the age where I needed to start wearing deodorant. I was quite embarrassed by this revelation and couldn't say anything but okay. Not only was I embarrassed, but at first I was more than a little perturbed at him for making the remark. After thinking about it though, and after smelling the armpit of my shirt, I knew he was right. I was actually grateful that he'd brought it to my attention. My parents hadn't broached the subject with me, and I guess how I smelled simply hadn't crossed my mind. I did reluctantly talk to Mom about it that night, although I never mentioned the fact that it was Vern who pointed out the problem. Mom helped me find a deodorant and the problem was, if not solved, at least covered up. Even then, the idea of taking a bath and changing clothes more often than every other day, and sometimes every three days if I could get by with it, never crossed my mind.

One of the best things that happened in that Kroger store happened one Saturday morning during the summer of 1960. It was one of those serendipitous moments that happen only a few times in an entire lifetime, and this one would change my life forever. I was stocking bags of flour that morning, down low near the bottom shelves in the second aisle. I was on my knees jabbing the flour bags with my price-stamper when I looked up to place the bags on the shelf. It was then that I saw her coming down the aisle, pushing the shopping cart along-side her mother. They both stopped and we exchanged "hellos" and "how are you's", then her mother, Frances Dickson, took the cart and moved on. Her daughter, Alinda, didn't. I could hardly believe it when I saw that she was in no hurry to catch up to her mom, and instead, stayed and talked with me. Not only could I not believe it, I was ecstatic. I had hoped for a moment like this to come along all my life and now here it was, just as I might have imagined it.

It wasn't the very first time I'd ever spoken to her, but it was the first time we'd ever said much more than a "hello" to each other. For one thing, Alinda was two years younger than me, so I was going into my senior year of high school while she was only going into her sophomore year. That meant we'd never had any classes in common, and seldom saw each other at school. She was just that really cute girl that I saw around sometimes. The other place I saw her was at the city park during the summer where we both liked to go skating. I'd seen her there quite often. I think we'd even skated together a time or two, probably during one of those special skates where you skated with one partner for a few minutes, then the whistle blew and you moved up to the next partner.

So we talked about skating and probably swimming too, and after about five minutes it was becoming obvious to me that she was actually enjoying our conversation. I couldn't believe it. Now when I say I couldn't believe it, I assure you I really couldn't. To me, Alinda was one of the prettiest girls in the entire school, and

I had thought more than once about how great it would be to go out with her. However, I never let that thought linger for long because I knew I had no chance of ever dating anyone with her beauty. In fact, other than my prom date for the junior/senior prom my junior year, a date that was more or less leftovers getting together so we could go to prom, I'd never had a real date with anyone in my life. So to think that one of the girls of my dreams would actually be standing there talking to me about something we both had in common was in itself a miracle. Not only were we talking about these things, but the conversation sounded to me like we were actually proposing something like a date. A date with Alinda Dickson? My dream girl? Well, maybe not. I couldn't be sure if that's what she had in mind or not. I still had my doubts. In the end what we arranged was that we'd probably be at the skating rink that night and maybe we'd see each other there. As life would have it, we did meet at the skating rink that night, the first of thousands of dates and 50 years together, and still counting.

The Grab-It-Here was the second busiest grocery store in town, and it too was located on the square, on the east side just north of the alley. It was managed by the tall, lanky, and very friendly gentleman named Paul Mills, the brunt of Vern Bilsland's worst jokes. The Grab-It was much smaller than Kroger and since Mom never really shopped there, I seldom entered the store. However, it was easy to see that people poured in and out of there on any given Friday night or Saturday, so I guess it did okay. And even though I seldom saw Paul in the store, for a couple of years Paul's son, John Mills, was one of my best friends, so I spent a lot of time in Paul and Mary Jean's home, a couple of the nicest people I ever knew.

Sullivan's was the third and last grocery store located downtown. It sat on the NE corner of Fourth and Washington and was owned and operated by a man named Mac Sullivan. I was never in Sullivan's when there were more than three or four other customers shopping, so I don't know how it stayed open, even before the IGA came to town. But it was open and doing business long before I was born and during all of my youth, so he must have been doing something right. One of my best friends, Jim Bodine, worked for Sullivan from time to time, and whenever I went in to visit him, the place was pretty much deserted, except for Jim of course, who was usually reading a comic book. One day I walked in while Jim was practicing his quick draw with an imaginary six-shooter. I snuck up on him and when I finally startled him, quick as a wink, he turned, drew, and put an imaginary bullet straight through my heart. I never let Jim live that one down.

Besides the three grocery stores around the square, there was a smattering of them elsewhere in town. An old fellow named Ora Day had a store out on the southeast corner of Eleventh Street and Liberty. It was a dilapidated wooden building and had just a few grocery items, a few drug sundries, and a hodgepodge of odds and ends. It seems there may have been a gas pump out front at one time, but I don't think it was in operation when I was in high school. I'd never been in the store more than half a dozen times, but the last time I was there, I did something that, even to this day, I wish I hadn't.

Ora always looked old to me. He looked old when I was in grade school, and he looked old when I was in high school. Not only that, I always thought he looked to be in poor health, which by the time I walked into his store for the last time, it was obvious to me that he was. He looked gaunt as a coyote, with white hair, trembling fingers, glasses so thick they made his eyes look owl-like, and he was walking with a shuffle.

I'd been in several months earlier, the first time I'd bought anything in that store in years, and was amazed as I had watched Ora total up my purchase. First, after slowly examining the candy bar and a small package of cheese crackers to ascertain their prices, he entered them into an antiquated adding machine. Then he grabbed a long, three-celled flashlight that he kept under the counter and shined it on the receipt paper while bending down, so that his head was within inches of the receipt. He then grabbed a large magnifying glass lying next to the adding machine and held it up to one eye while squinting his other eye closed. After a second or two of concentration, Ora finally looked up to me and said, "Fifteen cents." I hate to say it now, but to a teenager who had so little compassion for a feeble old man, I thought it was downright comical.

Sometime in the next year word had gotten around school that kids could pretty much shoplift anything they wanted from Ora Day's without fear of being caught. I became personally aware of it one day when three of the guys I ran around with talked me into paying Ora a visit after school. We walked in and spread out, not that there was a need for much of a plan since Ora could barely see you anyway. One of my friends reached up to a wall shelf and pulled down a couple of Zippo cigarette lighters from the lighter display. Then he slipped them into his pocket without Ora having a clue. While this was going on, another friend walked over to the candy rack and slid a couple of Milky Ways into his pocket, then looked at me and smiled. Jim Bodine was with us, but I don't think Jim ended up swiping anything.

As for myself, I didn't feel good about what was going on, not that I was a prude, but other than stealing a few cents from a church collection plate, an experience I've described elsewhere, I'd never stolen anything in my life. I wasn't a thief, at least not much of one. Watching my friends steal those dollar lighters and the candy bars actually bothered me, so I just wasn't about to pick up something and put it in my pocket without paying for it. On the other hand, I didn't want to be called "chicken-shit" by my buddies either. So I thought about it and soon came up with my own little scheme.

I discovered after some experimentation that not only could I hold one package of Twinkies in my hand, but if I arranged them perfectly I was able to hold two packages, one behind the other in the same hand. Aha! I'd just come up with a brilliant plan that didn't involve stealing at all. It would be an honest purchase and I would pay for it like any other customer. So up to the counter I went with my two packs of Twinkies. And now came the moment of truth as my friends looked on.

Ora stood behind the counter as I lifted my hand not a foot from his eyes and showed him what I wanted to purchase. "How much!" I asked Ora as nonchalantly as I could. Ora squinted and studied my hand for what seem like an eternity, then finally looked up into my face with his rheumy old owl-like eyes and said, "That'll be ten cents." The price of one pack-age. A wicked smile crossed my face as I laid my dime on the counter, turned down his offer to bag my purchase, thanked him heartily, and walked out. And wow, just like that I had outsmarted one old man and shown everyone that I was still one of the guys.

As I said, I wasn't proud of what I did that day, even though at the time I hadn't considered it out-and-out stealing. After all, I had showed him what I wanted to purchase and paid him what he asked. But I knew it wasn't right either, and as time went on I even considered going back in and dropping a dime on Ora's counter. But I never did. In fact I never stepped foot into Ora Day's store ever again. It wasn't long after that day that Ora closed his store, and of course, I wasn't surprised. I don't know when Ora died, but when I heard that he had, I hoped that in the end my pseudo-theft of a pack of Twinkies hadn't made any real difference in the sad old man's life. Ora's building is no longer there, having been replaced many years ago by what is now a small restaurant.

There was a decent-size store on Liberty, between Eighth and Ninth Street, that specialized in fresh meat. It was named, owned, and operated by Jim Hendrickson, and I wish that I could describe it to you, but I wasn't in that store more than once or twice. What I think I remember is that it had quite a few groceries, but a large meat case and all of a meat market's paraphernalia—scales, butcher paper, string, cutting block, cleavers, saws and knives—occupied its prime up-front space. I know that many people in town swore by Hendrickson's fresh meat and wouldn't buy it anywhere else, but I heard my mother say more than once that Hendrickson's was overpriced, so she always bought her meat from Kroger. Going into any store that was "overpriced" was more or less a sin in the Dickinson household, so I stayed out.

Even though there were four or five of these smaller stores scattered around town, the only one that my family ever used was Meharry's. We used it often because it was only two blocks from home and because they ran a tab for us. Running a tab was extremely convenient for two reasons, we kids could make the purchases without having to handle any money, and Mom could pick up whatever she needed between paychecks, when money was running short. Of course, we didn't make our major purchases there, Kroger was for that, but it was where we'd pick up a loaf of bread, a quart of milk, a can of beans, or some other small item Mom either ran out of or had overlooked on her weekly trip to Kroger.

As often as not, Mom would be in the middle of making supper when I'd hear her voice calling out the back door, "Bobby Dean! Bobby Dean!"

Mom could yell pretty loudly, so I was normally within earshot. I'd reply, "Over here Mom."

"I need you to run down to Meharry's and pick up a box of orange Jell-O for supper," she'd yell back to me and, for that matter, anyone else in the neighborhood who had a mind to listen.

I usually felt inconvenienced when this happened. When I heard her calling my name I knew I was going to have to stop playing war, or cowboys and Indians, or rolling in leaves, or digging a hideout in the ground, or having a snowball fight, or throwing walnuts, or building a race car, or shooting my BB gun, or splashing in a mud puddle, or putting on a Little Rascal's show in one of our neighborhood's numerous sheds, or any of about a thousand other things that I loved doing. Still, I didn't argue, at least not often, because going to Meharry's sometimes had its own rewards. Like the adventure of the trip and what I might discover on my way there, or after having arrived, eyeing all that colorful candy that Meharry's had displayed behind the counter, even if I didn't have money to buy any of it. And if it was a really good day, Mom would give me a penny to spend and then I'd have to decide whether to buy wax lips, Chum Gum, or Lik-M-Aid.

So off I'd go, past the alley and up to the corner where the Babbs lived and where there was a big red rock sitting right on the corner. That rock still sits there today. I usually couldn't resist climbing on the rock and jumping off before crossing Seventh Street and hurrying past the full length of the grade school before turning right and crossing Pearl. It was only two and a half blocks from home, but it seemed like quite a trip for a little boy. Of course, as the years passed the trip became shorter and shorter, especially after I started riding a bicycle. By the time I was in junior high the adventure of it all had disappeared, and if I didn't have any of my own money jingling around in my pocket that I wanted to spend on a treat, it became just another trip to Meharry's. By then, however, I had a couple of brothers old enough to run the errands, and more and more often it was their names Mom yelled out the back door.

Sometime during my last couple of years of high school, a butcher named Ed Selby bought Meharry's and tried to pump up the business by offering fresh meat. During the fall of my senior year, I was in the store visiting with Ed and his wife when he asked me if I'd like to come to work for him. I told him I was pretty happy at Kroger with one exception, that there were some school activities I wanted to attend, especially since this was my senior year, but I'd have a tough time working them in around my Kroger schedule. Ed said that wouldn't be a problem, that he'd let me work my own schedule, then offered to increase what Kroger was paying me. I wondered to myself whether the little store could actually make enough money to pay an employee. I didn't want to come back to Vern Bilsland a month later begging for my job back. But after thinking it over a couple of days, I took Ed up on it.

Ed was good at his word, and I worked for him until I graduated from high school. In the job I learned a couple of useful things, like how to handle the cash register and how to order from a wholesaler. I also learned the fine art of just how much lean and how much suet to send through the meat grinder to make hamburger. I came to realize it often depended on just how much of each you had lying around.

I liked Ed, but from time to time I had to turn down Ed's invitations to share a highball with him. Ed did like his highballs, and I think it's because of them that he occasionally found himself "under the weather." During these times, I actually had to act as the butcher and cut fresh meat, a job I knew nothing about, but did my best to fumble my way through. One day I came to work to find Ed perturbed. He said that Mrs. Livengood had tried to cook the liver I sliced for her the day before, but it was so tough no one could eat it. He had to refund her money and was holding me responsible for cutting the liver against the grain. He mentioned taking it out of my paycheck. I told him I had no idea there was a right and a wrong way to cut liver and that if he wanted it cut right then he should have been here to cut it himself. This little exchange made neither of us happy, but the next day he offered me a highball to "bury the hatchet." Once more, I turned him down, but peace was made and come payday I got my full pay.

At Selby's I also learned to work around one of the grumpiest people I had ever met in my young life. I'm talking about Ed's wife, whose first name slips me right now. The woman had a permanent scowl chiseled across her face. It was years later before I ran across another of those rare folks who had a complaint or an unhappy tale to tell about anything and everything. Mention the beautiful weather, a great trip, a nice person, or even a sweet baby and Mrs. Selby soon set you straight. In the eight months I worked there, I don't think I saw that woman smile more than a handful of times. She was downright depressing, so I learned to tune her out. I didn't ask questions, but I did wonder to myself what could make a person so unhappy. It crossed my mind that maybe Ed's highballs had something to do with it.

By the time I graduated from high school in 1961, the IGA was beginning to solidify its foothold on Covington's grocery business. When it came to town in 1959, my mother said it wouldn't last. She wasn't going to shop there for any number of reasons, but mostly because they were selling pre-packaged meat. She had no doubt that the only reason the IGA pre-packaged its meat was so the fat and gristle could be easily hidden on the backside of the package where it couldn't be seen. I believed her of course. After all, if your mom swears by it then it must be true. And I knew that at least half of Covington believed the same thing. They'd never had to buy meat that they couldn't inspect from all sides, and it just didn't seem right.

But the IGA soon began to take its toll. It was big, clean, well lit, well stocked, and looked much more cheerful than the old stores we were all used to. In time the town began to realize that the meat wasn't as bad as they had convinced themselves it would be (although Mom never did fully accept it). Within a very few years, the other stores closed one by one, and the memory of their glory days were soon forgotten. Today half of those grocery store buildings are gone, replaced at this writing by a laundromat, a restaurant, and a bank. In the half that are still standing, Hendrickson's building is now a pizza parlor, the Grab-It-Here an antique store, and Meharry's/Selby's, that later became Edward's, a private residence.

## Barbershops

Mom being the queen of thrift, I think it was difficult for her to let go of the fifty cents it cost for a haircut at Albea's barbershop, especially when it was so easy to put it off just one more week, one more day. That's why I got pretty scruffy looking before I was handed two quarters and sent off for a haircut.

I wasn't particularly fond of haircuts anyway. I felt they were a waste of time and fit into the same category as taking a bath, shampooing, brushing my teeth, washing my hands, and putting on clean clothes. But as years passed, I discovered that entering

Albea's barbershop was so much more than getting a haircut. Until I was in high school, and began to spend a little more time in front of a mirror, I learned that these trips to the barbershop were actually more of an adventure in small-town life than a grooming experience. It was in the barbershop that I learned the gospel truth on what was happening around town. When I came out of there I knew who had been Covington's good Samaritans that week for helping Mrs. Miller stoke her furnace because Mr. Miller was still in the hospital, or who took Mr. Overpeck to Doctor Hoffman for his appointment, or who'd been thrown in jail for breaking into the pool hall, or what the coaches should have done to win the ballgame on Friday night. And if Judge Fenters was getting his hair cut that day, there would be no doubt as to how badly we had been robbed by the referees.

By the time Effray or Louie was dusting the hair off my face with a powdered brush, I knew what good-for-nothing was dating the Methodist Church secretary, where the fire was that sent the volunteer fire department out of town with their whistles blaring in the middle of the night, waking up half the "damn" town, what the mayor had in mind for the potholes and the low water pressure, and who I should vote for in the city election, never mind that I couldn't vote for another 10 years. Truly, the place was a plethora of swear-to-God-you-can-bet-your-life-on-it information. Being of a tender age, and knowing that the barbers and their customers knew exactly what they were talking about, I believed every word of it.

I don't know why I started out at Albea's since there were a number of other barbers in town, but I guess it was the most prominent shop on the square. Also, it was located halfway between Third and Fourth Streets on the north side of the square, so it was the closest once I reached the downtown. I don't recall my dad going there, so that wasn't the reason.

Long and narrow, Albea's had one of those rotating barber's poles right next to the front door that was easily visible from the street and also from where you sat in the barber chairs. Many times as my hair was being cut, that pole mesmerized me as I followed its red and white stripes up the pole until they disappeared into its top.

The shop was manned by several barbers with names like Effray Harden, Louie Henderson, and an older, white-haired barber named Ed Albea who owned the shop. While I was still quite young, Ed, who looked to be quite a bit older than the other barbers, either retired or died, but he had a son, Jack, who took over his chair. A few years later Effray left to open his own shop, and later still Louie retired. A year or two before I graduated from high school, a nice young fellow named Dale Clawson inherited one of the barber chairs while he was still attending Indiana State. After graduating he became one of Covington's friendliest school teachers and at the same time continued to cut hair part-time at Albea's.

Saturday was the barbershop's big day, and on any given Saturday I would walk in to find the three barber chairs full and not a spot left on the long black-leather cushioned bench where the customers waited their turn. After discovering the one great reward the barbershop had to offer besides a haircut, I never minded the wait. You see, I loved comic books. But at 10 cents each I couldn't afford to buy them, meaning there were hardly ever any at home. Albea's to the rescue. As interesting as the gossip was, it usually became secondary to the many well-read comic books that were scattered in among the *Popular Mechanics* and *Sports Afields*. By the time it was my turn for a haircut, I had already devoured as many of them as possible and more than once had wished I could have sat there and read a little longer. I thought one of the luckiest moments of my young life was the day Louie Henderson noticed that the shop's comic books were pretty ragged and in short supply, so he gave me a dollar and asked me to run down to Paxton's and buy ten of them. I'd say it was probably the best time I'd ever had spending someone else's dollar bill. If there was a heaven on earth, I thought I'd found it that day. I realize now that those barbershop comic books were the first reading I ever really did for pleasure.

The three barber chairs were lined up along the length of the east side of the shop, and there were three large square mirrors hung on the wall behind them. On the west wall, three round mirrors hung. Because of this arrangement, when you looked into either the square or the round mirror, you saw your own reflection on the opposite wall reflecting back and forth across the room. These infinite reflections created an image of me getting my haircut over and over and over again, with each returning image growing smaller and smaller, until finally, I saw myself disappear into the center of the mirror. Along with the disappearing stripes on the barber pole, I found these two phenomena quite intriguing and spent most of my haircut time trying to figure out just how they worked.

On a shelf behind the barbers and just under the mirrors sat their tools of the trade. There were electric clippers, scissors, combs, a jar of liquid that they kept the combs in, and a floppy, long-haired brush they sprinkled with talc then used to brush the loose hairs off your ears, neck, and forehead. They also had a fine assortment of sweet-smelling hair tonics, one of which would be sprinkled on your hair and worked into your scalp after every haircut. It was usually the green Jeris tonic that went on my head, and I thought it smelled a bit like lime, but that may have just been my imagination.

The place was a constant buzz of people, clippers, and the ever-playing radio while the barbers snipped, combed, and

brushed without missing a stroke, taking time between customers to sweep up the hair that had fallen all around them.
To me it became a ritual as much as a haircut and one that I
grew to look forward to. Thanks to Dale Clawson, who is now
retired from teaching, it's still operating today, although I don't
suppose anyone has called it Albea's in years and the price for a
haircut is no longer 50 cents.

Of course, Albea's wasn't the only barbershop in town.
There were several others, but only one other on the square.
It was called Smitty's and was owned and operated by a fellow named Hayden Smith. I could have gone to Smitty's just
as easily; it was only a block further over on the west side
of the square. But to tell you the truth, I was a little hesitant to even walk past. I was a town boy, and Smitty's clientele
seemed to me to be more countrified, more rural, backwoodsy,
maybe even hickish in my young mind. Looking back now,
I don't know how a poor boy from what many would call a
one-horse-town could feel the least bit superior to another
group of poor folks from the same one-horse-town simply
because they were getting their hair cuts from a different
barber. But I did. In my own little world, I felt like there
was a difference.

One of the things I didn't like about Smitty's was that you
always heard the twang of 1940's country and western music
coming from the place. You couldn't walk down the west side
of the square on a summer day without hearing the sound of
steel guitars, Eddie Arnold, and Hank Williams wafting out
from Smitty's radio and assaulting your ears. To me it was little
more than a cacophony of yodel and twang about heartache,
whiskey, and lost love. We never played country and western at
home, so it was foreign to me. I didn't like it, and I didn't feel
totally comfortable around anyone who did.

I sort of gathered that they never talked about the same kinds of things at Smitty's that we did at Albea's either. The discussion and rendering of decisions pertaining to Covington sports was the exclusive right of Albea's, of that I felt certain. However, I'd heard that if you ever had a question about hunting, fishing, or coon dogs, then you should ask Smitty, he was the expert. My problem was that I had no interest in any of those things.

Most kids came out of Albea's sporting crew cuts or flattops, whereas many of Smitty's teenage customers walked out with something long and wavy, like duck-tails, more commonly known by the kids as DA's which stood for ducks-asses. All shiny and black with some kind of hair oil, DA's were a full head of hair swept back along the sides that required a great deal of primping and combing by all who sported them. Guys with DA's wore their collars up, had a pack of cigarettes rolled up in their shirt sleeves, and when they weren't combing their hair, which they did often, they carried their comb sticking half way out of their back pocket. I don't know if these guys had a name for the likes of me and my crowd, but we had a name for them. They were greasers. I didn't have much use for greasers. I only went into Smitty's one time and that was to deliver a sale flyer that I'd been paid to distribute around town. Just walking in there made me uncomfortable and I never went in again.

There were a few other barbershops around town too. They came and went over the years, but other than the time I went to a family of barbers named Gondzur, who had moved here from France, I always went to Albea's. The Gondzur's shop was generally known as Frenchie's and was operated by the father, mother, and son. To this day, the son still operates the shop on the corner of Ninth and Liberty. The one time I went there, at my Aunt Mary's insistence, I left with what I thought was a lopsided cut. It was my first and last visit to Frenchie's.

## Paxton's

Besides the hardware and barbershop, there was one other establishment on the north side where I spent a good deal of time. We called it Paxton's drugstore, but I'm not sure why we used the term "drugstore". All they sold were sundries, tobacco, and newspapers along with their soda fountain concoctions. Maybe it picked up the name because it had a whole section of shelving devoted to over-the-counter medications. But unlike Burrin's, it was not a pharmacy.

Paxton's was located in a building next to Norma's dress shop. I'm not sure when it opened, but I didn't discover its beauty until about the time I was entering high school. With two pinball machines, the only ones in town as far as I know, and a jukebox chock full of the newest genre of music, rock-n-roll, Paxton's became a very popular teenage hangout. Paul and Alta Paxton were both funny, happy people and always had a joke to tell. They also laughed the hardest at their own jokes. They hadn't spent a lot on décor, as the place consisted of mostly empty space. There were a few booths along one wall, a couple of small tables in the middle, some sundry counters spread here and there and a soda fountain counter behind which you could usually find Paul and Alta. In the back of the store were the pinball machines and jukebox.

The pinballs constantly rang, whistled, whirred, and buzzed while Elvis, Jerry Lee, and Fats Domino wailed from the jukebox. Paul had no rules against playing cards or smoking and wouldn't even say anything if you spent half a day in there without buying so much as a soda pop. So over a period of a couple of years, I spent a goodly number of Saturday afternoons hanging out there. It's where I learned to play euchre and pretty much where I became addicted to cigarettes. My friends liked hanging out there too, so it was a fun place to be. Few adults ever came into Paxton's, but you always had to be on the lookout. One word to the football coach that you were down at Paxton's smoking could bring a quick end to your season. As soon as an adult walked in, you sort of scrunched down and snatched the cigarette hanging from your lips into your cupped hand. All in all, I'd say Paxton's wasn't a good influence on a young Covington boy, but at the time, I'll have to admit, it made me feel pretty darn cool about myself.

Paul and Alta had a son named Jay who was in my class. Jay wasn't one of my closest friends, but he was a football teammate and a guy I liked because he was about as funny as his parents. The two of us had a knack for making each other laugh and we did that a lot. The problem was, Jay also had a knack for making me angry. Strangely enough, during our senior football season Jay brought out the extremes in both of those emotions when he made me laugh as hard as I'd ever laughed in my life, then turned around a few games later and made me fighting mad.

One night before a home game, the two of us were already dressed in our uniforms and pads and were waiting in the gym for the bus to take us to the football field. For some reason I mentioned a cartoon that I'd seen on television the previous day, and Jay said he'd seen the same one. The animated cartoon had to do with a man who'd entered a talent contest as a one-man band, made unbelievable music pretending to play half a dozen instruments at the same time, and ended up panting and soaked through in sweat. Only then did he turn around by mistake to reveal a record player strapped to his back that had actually been playing the music. Realizing he'd been caught, the man then turned red with embarrassment and said with a mischievous smile while still trying to catch his breath, "I cheated!" That was it. It was stupid. But the image of the guy in that cartoon struck the two of us as being so funny that we both started laughing and couldn't stop. Tears ran down our faces as we rolled around on the gym floor saying, "I cheated," over and over and trying to catch our own breath. It was the hardest and longest I'd ever laughed in my life, and I wish that Jay were still with us so that I could thank him for that great memory.

That was the laughter part, and now to the anger. Jay and Ken Tuggle, another classmate of mine, were the starting ball carriers for our football team my senior year. They both did a good job of running the football, but I, and I was definitely not alone in my thinking, had the distinct feeling that Jay often carried on more than he needed to after he was tackled. Numerous times Jay lay there too long and complained too loudly. We may have been harsh, and I suppose we could have been wrong, but to put it bluntly we all thought that Jay faked it most of the time.

That was probably the real reason I became so angry with him that night. The play in question came at a critical point in an all-important game, and I laid the blame for the outcome of that game squarely on Jay's shoulders. Perrysville had us down 13 to 6 in one of the last games of the season. It was the 4th quarter and we were driving the football down the field. I was pumped up. We all were. I knew we were going to score, and at the very least, with time running out, we were going to tie the game. It had been a rough game. We were playing at Perrysville on a field that had seen little rain the entire season, where there was no grass whatsoever, and the dust rising up on each play was blinding.

Perrysville had a good team that year. They didn't have much of a running game, but their quarterback, Phil Richardson, had a good arm, and even though we easily broke through their line and chased him around all night long, he could scramble. They also had a couple of tall receivers, one of them or maybe both of them named Dunham, who could catch the ball. To that point in the season, Perrysville had won all their games and we had lost only one. A win for us would put both teams in a tie for the conference championship. As a senior playing one of my last games, I wanted this game badly.

With just a few minutes left in the game we were 7 points behind and had moved the ball from our own 20 to Perrysville's 30 yard line. As usual, Jay and Ken were our running backs and on this play Jay got the call from our quarterback, Tom Hoagland. It was a quick opener up the middle. I made my block and saw Jay break free. When I broke off my block, I quickly looked up field to see how far the play had gotten us. I saw Jay several yards beyond me now laying on the ground curled up into the fetal position holding his stomach. That didn't bother me. I didn't really think it bothered Jay either; it was just Jay being Jay. Then I noticed the terrible part. Jay wasn't lying on the ball—a Perrysville player was.

Jay had fumbled and I knew what it meant. I knew we were going to walk off the field that night as losers. I was devastated. And I was really, really angry. At that point, if Jay hadn't been taken out of the game, I have no doubt I would have slugged him, my own teammate right there on the field. Looking back now, I confess I may have been unfair about the whole thing, and probably was, but the fact is, after that night, Jay and I didn't share many laughs together.

Paxton's stayed open for a while after I graduated from high school. I don't know how many years it was in business altogether, but it seems to me that Faust and Frey eventually bought the building and used the space to further expand their business.

## Street Carnival

There was one special summer activity that topped all others. For in my mind, nothing could even begin to compare to Covington's annual American Legion street carnival. I loved the three months of summer vacation, loved the freedom, the weather, and all the activities that were possible when you didn't have to spend all those hours in school every day. And although it came in early summer, and there would be many more summer activities to follow, the carnival was definitely summer's crowning jewel. Each year around mid-June, about three weeks after school let out, colorful little posters went up around town announcing the coming of the Drago Brothers carnival, sponsored by Covington's Fulton Banta Post 291 of The American Legion. Of course, I didn't know who the Drago Brothers were, but as the years went by, I began to think of them as a part of Covington, like Faust and Frey or the Lyric. I also thought of them as very lucky brothers to own something so wonderful, especially since they were the best carnival in the whole world, a thought I had conceived even though I'd never even been to another carnival. Tacked up to the telephone poles all over town and hung in many business windows, the posters were the first indication that the best week of summer would soon be upon me. I couldn't wait.

The carnival always started on Monday and ran through Saturday night. The big trucks carrying the rides and all the concessions began pulling into town on Sunday morning, and by Sunday night they filled two sides of the town square. That same week the city closed the public swimming pool, and all the kids in town were told by their parents to keep their bicycles locked up or hidden. I'd never known a kid to have his bike stolen by the "carnies", but we were all assured it would happen if they weren't locked away. On the other hand, since most of the carnies camped down at the city park, I didn't have a hard time believing that they might very well take their baths at the city pool, and that was why it was closed for the week.

The carnival was set up on the north and east sides of the square which were blocked off, meaning that during the week there was no parking in front of the businesses on Washington or Fourth Streets. Every year I could hear downtown merchants groaning and moaning about that fact. Dutch Merryman would tell anyone who'd listen that he might just as well close down the theater during carnival week because it killed his business. To my knowledge, he never took his own advice. I never understood all the fuss though, I mean how lucky could anyone be to have this magnificent event sitting right outside your business for a whole week?

With Monday night being opening night, Monday day was set-up day, and from the time I was eight years old until I was in high school, I went downtown every one of those Monday mornings looking for work. It always paid off. It only took a few minutes of asking around before one of the game concessionaires broke down and hired me to help him set up his tent and paraphernalia. It usually didn't take more than a couple of hours to finish the all-too-easy jobs I was given, which consisted of such things as putting some pre-fitted wooden framework together to hold the canvas top, or filling the duck-pond with water to float the ducks, or propping up the dishware at the dish toss so that if nickels landed on them they would most likely bounce off. If it stayed on, the dish was yours. At our house, you could always tell when the carnival had been to town because, invariably, we had new additions to the dish cupboard. That also meant there was never a complete set of matching dishes in our home, a fact that didn't seem to matter to Mom. She always acted like she was thrilled when one of us kids brought one of those oddball plates or saucers home. She'd make like it was exactly what she'd been looking for as she put it right there in the cupboard with all the others. Same with cups and drinking glasses, we seldom had two alike.

One year I had to blow up balloons for the dart throw, and yet another I had to hang stuffed animals at the duck pond. When I had finished my job each year, the guys who'd hired me would reach into their pockets and hand me two or three wadded up dollar bills and maybe a couple of free ride tickets, then tell me what great help I was and not to spend it all in one place.

I was pretty proud of myself, not only had I made some spending money for the week, but I felt like I was really a part of the carnival. Yes indeed, wasn't a year went by that I didn't dream of being a carny man. "Wouldn't be a bad life at all," I expressed to Mom once. And of course, she had to pass it along to Dad, who mostly laughed, but still ended up having a short talk with me. It would be a pretty tough life, he pointed out, always on the road, no home, always looking to steal something, always dirty, and poor, and living like a Gypsy. Well I didn't know anything about Gypsies, and I didn't necessarily think he was right about any of it. The carnies I'd help set up for each year all seemed pretty nice. And to an eight-year-old boy, being a carny man sounded adventurous, and maybe even a little romantic. Still, I knew what Dad wanted to hear so I told him I guessed I wouldn't be me a carny man after all. And of course, the day the carnival left town every year was the same day any thoughts of being a carny man left me too, at least until it rolled into town again the next year.

By Monday night those two blocks were alive with loud activity as the carnival rides, game concessions, food vendors, civic group raffle tables, local bake sales, and crowds of town folks began milling about the streets elbow to elbow. Huge electrical lines, like giant black snakes, lay across the streets, all of them plugged into a huge generator truck that was parked in the Washington Street alley between Norma's dress shop and Crain's plumbing. The cables were so thick you had to watch your step or you'd easily trip over them.

Of the rides and the concession stands, I'm not sure what I enjoyed the most. I loved them all. The Ferris Wheel was one of my favorite rides, and it always sat on Washington Street just east of the Fourth Street intersection. The Tilt-A-Whirl, a ride I got so vomiting sick on the last time I rode it that I never ever rode it again, was always on Fourth Street just north of the Washington intersection. Sullivan's grocery was the corner store that separated the Ferris Wheel and Tilt-A-Whirl. The Octopus, which I hate to say also made me nauseous the last time I rode it, sat at the other end of Fourth, in front of the Ben Franklin store, and the Merry-Go-Round sat at the other end of Washington, in front of the Friendly Tavern. These four rides seldom changed in appearance and never changed where they were set up. In addition, depending on the year, there were various combinations of the Bullet, Swings, the Scrambler, and any number of kiddie rides. The fun house sat right across from where I was working at the Lyric, so for a couple of summers I was entertained by watching everyone who came out of the funhouse get a blast of air that was shot up at them from a hole in the floor. Some of the girls were especially shocked as they tried to push their skirts back down to re-cover their underwear, then ran off the platform completely mortified.

The game concessions were scattered among the rides along both streets. This was where you could perform some feat of skill, or in the case of the duck pond, simply pick up a duck and win a prize, usually a stuffed toy. The game concessions were a very big hit in those days and probably took in as much money as the rides. And although I hardly ever had the money to play, I could spend hours watching others play them. There was definitely no lack of players, or suckers as the carnies must have thought of them. Among themselves, I often heard the carnies referring to their customers as "locals", but if they were talking to the customers directly, especially if they were egging them on to play their game, then most of the time they called the locals "Sport".

The locals would sometimes line up five deep to try their luck, and why not? You have to remember that there were no video or computer games back then. If you wanted to play a midway game you couldn't do it virtually, you actually had to go to the midway. For some, these games became a yearly ritual, and conquering them a mark of their manhood. Young men and boys were the main participants, of course. These games were a challenge to their male ego, supported fully by the influence of their flowing testosterone.

The carnival barkers were good at snagging you in. As you walked by their concession, they would show no mercy in challenging your manhood by asking you to show your friends, and especially your girlfriend, what a big, strong guy you were. "Hey Sport, come on in, win that sweetheart of yours a big ole teddy bear! Big strong guy like you, one toss ought to do it. Come on Sport, don't be shy, don't let her down, only 50 cents, Sport." And just like that, you were digging in your pocket. After such a challenge, what else could you do but hand the guy 50 cents for two tosses at three stacked milk bottles. Looked easy. Besides that, you wanted to give it a try anyway; he didn't really have to talk you into it.

The problem was that after you had spent two or three bucks and still hadn't won a teddy bear for your sweetheart, even the toughest of guys began to realize that these were not ordinary milk bottles. Oh no, unbeknownst to the players, these bottles had heavy lead bottoms, and no matter how many times they where smacked with a baseball by the strongest of he-men, unless you hit them just perfectly, near their bottom, those three stacked bottles would not fall off that old wooden Coca-Cola case. Still the suckers came back time and again.

Cotton candy and snow cone machines fascinated me and were also at the top of my list of favorite carnival treats. I loved watching the pink or blue cotton candy form in the pan while the carny man with a white hat expertly wrapped it around a paper funnel. If you took your time, you could make a cotton candy last a good half-hour.

It was the sound of the ice being crushed that I really liked at the snow cone machine. At ten cents for a snow cone and a quarter for cotton candy, I had to figure my money carefully in order to buy a couple of each of these during the week. And even though there's nothing I would have liked better than to sample the Coney dogs, hamburgers, barbeques, french fries, and all the other great stuff being served up by the food vendors, none of them were in the ball park of my meager budget. One year, however, I did break down and buy a deep-fried-fish sandwich. The smell coming out of that stand was so overwhelmingly good, I just had to have one. It was the one and only sandwich I ever purchased at the carnival, and it was really either great-tasting cod or it was the sweat dripping into the batter from the carny man frying it up that gave it that good

ole carnival flavor. Either way, I thought it was the best sandwich I'd ever tasted.

I never had more than a dollar in my pocket on any given
carnival night, at least not until I had a paper route, so I spent
the majority of those nights meandering from one end of the
carnival to the other, taking everything in. That was almost
as much fun as riding or gaming, because not only were there
other kids there whom I could run around with, but there were
lots of people I didn't know, oftentimes very weird people, and
I liked watching them. The carnival back then, as it still does
today, tended to attract more than its share of what I thought
of as greasers, crazies, hippies, and other oddball groups from
both Covington and the surrounding area.

This was the 1950's, when motorcycles represented terror on
the streets, so guys who dressed in Harley leathers were not only
rare, but were pretty scary to me. Their girlfriends weren't much
better either, although there was something titillating about
seeing them in their tight t-shirts and leather pants. There were
guys with Mohawks, long hair, long beards, and shaved bald,
all signs of real weirdness to me, and watching them strut up
and down the midway was a bit like watching a free freak show.
Also, I don't suppose there was a year that went by that I didn't
witness at least one rough-and-tumble fistfight.

One attraction that I really liked was The American Legion
betting wheel. It was a beautiful big wheel made of blue
and white colored glass, wood, mirrors, and shiny metal that
gleamed under the glare of the overhead lights. The pegs surrounding the outside edge of the wheel were bright silver and,
when the wheel was turned, a flexible wooden flapper snapped
from one peg to the next until it finally came to rest between
two of the pegs, pointing to the representation of two dice that
were painted on the face of the wheel.

The American Legion sponsored and operated this concession in an open-sided tent where the betting was done by placing your money on the top of one of the three 1x12 boards, each about four feet high, that formed the framework for the tent. In the middle of the tent stood the wheel mounted on its own holder. The numbers 1 through 6 were painted on each of the 1x12's and you placed your bet on the numbers you wanted. The two dice the flapper pointed to at the end of the spin were winners, and each paid one for one. If the wheel landed on a 2 and a 4, then the Legion matched whatever was bet on those two numbers. If two 5's came up, and you had put your money on the 5, then you were paid double your money.

Besides sponsoring the carnival itself, the wheel was a Legion fundraiser and they had few qualms about who placed their money on the board. If you were tall enough to reach up and place your money on a number, you were old enough to bet. And bet I did, but usually not until the end of the night. I'd learned my lesson on that one. I waited until I was down to twenty cents left in my pocket, then away I went, placed a dime on a couple of numbers and prayed for a win. Sometimes it actually worked, and when I was back up to fifty cents in my hand, I usually walked away and spent it.

However, as I grew older and began to earn some of my own money, I got a bit braver. I also set my mind to devising a surefire betting scheme. What I came up with was quite simple really, and I could hardly wait to try it out. The next night after plopping my dime on number 6, a number I'd been pretty lucky with, I anxiously waited for the wheel to stop. When it landed on a 2 and a 5, I didn't hesitate to double my bet—the scheme. When I didn't win again, I doubled again by throwing 40 cents on the number, knowing that the odds were very close to being in my favor. I was beginning to feel some serious disappointment when neither the 40-cent nor the 80-cent bets hit either. So, after a great deal of thought and some amount of consternation, I begrudgingly pulled out $1.60 and carefully placed it on number six. As the Legionnaire reached up to spin the wheel, I made a quick decision and slid my money from the 6 to the 2, a number that had come up 3 out of the 4 previous spins. Crossing my fingers and holding my breath, I prayed for that wheel to stop on the 2. I wanted it to stop on the 2. I wished with all my heart that it would stop on that number 2. It stopped on a double 6.

In theory, I knew my scheme of doubling my bet every time I lost would have worked. The problem was I didn't have unlimited funds and the maximum bet you could place was five dollars. My scheme lasted all of five spins and I was done. I don't think I ever went back to the wheel again and I've never been much of a gambler since.

I was always excited about the nightly raffle. Many of the merchants in town donated prizes for a raffle drawing that was held at 10 p.m. each night. Every evening they started with an empty raffle barrel and by drawing time it was probably a quarter full of tickets. Most years the tickets were free and some years they sold for a quarter apiece or five for a dollar. Since Mom and Dad hardly ever went down to the carnival, something I never quite understood at that time, Mom would often hand me fifty cents and tell me to buy a couple. You had to be an adult to sign up for the free raffles, so in the years when they were free, Mom made a special effort to get downtown every night for no other reason than to sign up. The good thing about it was that you had to be present to win, and by 10 o'clock at night there were few adults still around. Luckily for the Dickinson family, their raffle prize hero, me, was at the carnival every night from opening to closing, so I was always there for the drawing. We often won, sometimes more than once a night. The prizes weren't big, a half-gallon of Wright's ice cream from Burrin's drug store, a loaf of bread from Kroger, five gallons of gas from Bus Allison's gas station, things like that. But I always felt good about bringing those gift certificates home to Mom. It made me feel like I was giving that little extra to help out the family. Besides that, it gave me one more good reason not to miss a night at the carnival.

As I grew older, entered high school, and formed other interests in my life, the street carnival began to lose some of its appeal. During my last couple of years of high school, even though the carnival was still going strong, I don't suppose I got down there more than once or twice during what used to be the best week of summer.

I'm not sure when it ended. I noticed some years later that Covington switched the carnival from the Drago Brothers carnival to some other brothers, and maybe that was the beginning of the end. Or maybe The American Legion decided it wasn't worth it, or the downtown merchants rose up against it, or the 4th of July committee was formed and decided it would be more suitable to hold it at the city park. All I know is that there was something very magical about those days when I spent every night of the week down on Covington's square enjoying the sights and sounds of that wonderful street carnival.

## Halloween Parade

In the fall of the year, Covington held its annual Halloween costume contest. That was always an exciting event, one that I anticipated the entire month of October. A whole slew of kids participated and quite a few adults came to watch. It started off with the costumed contestants making a short march from the

Methodist Church to a makeshift hay-wagon stage that was set up on Fourth Street in front of the courthouse.

For me, it was as much fun seeing the costumes the other kids wore as it was dressing up myself. For some reason, I usually ended up as a hobo, or bum as I always referred to them, along with half-a-dozen other hobos. I would cut off a pair of my Dad's old pants and use one of his old button-up shirts, put some rips in them, dirty my face with a little coal dust, lay a small piece of black construction paper on the front of a couple of my teeth so they looked like they were missing, fill a handkerchief with paper and tie it to the end of a stick to carry over my shoulder. Just like that, I was a bum. Almost all the costumes were homemade. After all, at a dollar a costume from Ben Franklin, who could afford a store bought? Robots made out of foil-wrapped cardboard boxes were the craze for a couple of years, and of course, there was never a lack of witches, devils, ghosts, and clowns.

They divided the kids into three or four costume categories, the winner of each category winning a couple of dollars. To my great disappointment, I never won. Bums were in the same category as clowns and it was usually the clowns who took the prize. One reason was that one of the kids, I think it was either Tony or Jerry Shuman, had a clown's head made out of papier-mâché and ended up taking the prize for that category a couple of years running. I was pretty jealous of that big head. By the third year, thankfully, it had seen its better days and was beginning to cave in. It seems to me that after the contest that night it ended up on the courthouse lawn being used as a kick ball.

For a while, they also had a greased-pole climbing contest for older kids. A pole, wooden I think, about half the diameter of a telephone pole, was liberally coated in some kind of grease and erected in the courthouse lawn. Then a ten-dollar bill was placed on top. I don't know how they determined who was going first, but the kid who shimmied up that pole first and grabbed the sawbuck got to keep it. It was usually one of the rougher kids in school, one you didn't want mad at you and one who didn't mind getting himself covered with grease. As tempting as a ten-dollar bill was, I knew I could never shimmy up that pole, so I never even tried.

After the costume contest and greased-pole climbing, everyone, kids and adults alike, were invited to help themselves to the free ham and bean and cornbread dinner sponsored by the Lion's Club. Long wooden tables, folding chairs, and huge pots of ham and beans were set up on the courthouse lawn, and it always turned out to be a great meal and a fun night for the entire town.

## More Downtown

On the north side of the square, in a large three-story building, was Covington's one and only hardware store. It had been a hardware store for many decades and was run, and I guess owned, by Guy Faust and his son-in-law Charlie Frey, thus the name proudly displayed in giant letters on the side of the building, Faust and Frey Hardware. This was a store right out of the 1800's. The walls were lined with wooden shelving, much of which was filled with sliding-box drawers that held the store's myriad of screws, nails, nuts, washers, and bolts. A long wooden ladder hung from a metal track high above the shelving, which could be slid along the track to reach the hardware that was out of reach. There was a scale to weigh nails, which were sold by the pound, and your purchases were rung up on huge cash registers that were as ancient as the store.

Over the years, they added new inventory, added more space, and provided new services. But the original store was never really changed, and I doubt that anything was ever thrown out. So, if you wanted almost anything in the line of hardware that had been produced in the last hundred years, Faust and Frey probably had it. The only question was, where in the store could you possibly find it? In the end, you often had to ask Charlie or one of Charlie's older sons, Jerry or Dick, where to look. One of them seemed to know exactly where to find everything you needed, and if they didn't have it, they tried to order it for you. Going into Faust and Frey was an adventure, and I always thought of it as a "happy" place to shop. It was, without a doubt, one of the friendliest stores in town. It was a Covington institution.

Guy Faust also had a brother named Mont Faust, a dentist who occupied one of the downtown second or third floor businesses. His office window announced his name in bold letters—Dr. Faust, DDS. I always wondered if he bought his tooth-pulling pliers from his hardware kin. There were many other businesses in those upstairs offices overlooking the square. They were occupied by doctors, dentists, lawyers, insurance companies, and other assorted business people. They all had their names painted on the street-front windows so you could read them from the sidewalk. Some of these upstairs businesses were one story up and some were two, but it didn't matter; in both cases the stairways leading up to them were dark and uninviting to a kid my age. I didn't climb those stairs very often, and the few times I did, I felt the same about the offices as I did the stairwells. They were dark, dingy, and full of old musty odors. I avoided those businesses whenever I could.

No town would be complete without a lumberyard, and ours was owned and run by a man named Lyle Hegg. Lyle was also the town mayor during much of my youth. Hegg's Lumber Company sat just north of the square, right behind Faust and

Frey. I have little impression of the lumberyard, although I know I was in there a few times, probably looking to sell them something, maybe a newspaper subscription or some garden seeds. Dad probably bought most of his lumber there for his many home-building projects, but I don't recall ever going in with him.

About halfway between Faust and Frey and Albea's was the building that housed the post office. It was here that my father started working when I was about seven years old. After the war Dad got a job with the city of Covington, where he worked for the streets, water, and electric department. But after a few years he was able to get a job with the U.S. Postal Service and that's where he stayed for the next 30 years. Dad took me in with him a few times and let me send the letters through the cancellation machine. That was also where I had to pick up the Journal and Courier newspapers when I first started my paperboy stint.

That post office was old and ramshackle, so in 1956 a new one was built on Liberty Street across from The American Legion. The day the new post office opened was a big doing for Covington. The U.S. Postmaster General, Arthur Summerfield, came to town to honor the event and Covington's own U.S. Congresswoman, Cecil Harden, gave a speech. Those were the days when a penny postcard really did cost a penny and a letter went for three cents. As for the old post office building, Faust and Frey used it to expand.

There were four or five car dealers in town, depending on the year, and they were located either on the square or within a block of it. At one point at least four of them were up and running simultaneously. Names like Miller, Allen, Starkey, Harden, Dicks, Clayson, and Warrick owned and operated these dealerships at various times, selling among others Fords,

Chevrolets, Oldsmobiles, and Pontiacs for under $1000 each. I never really dealt with any of them because I never had a car of my own. When I was old enough to drive, Dad let me borrow his car, which was usually a Dodge purchased from a dealer in Danville. It was also usually dirty from the gravel roads on Dad's rural route and certainly not the least bit sexy. Because of this, I seldom asked. We didn't have a second car until I was in high school and it was an ugly blue and white used station wagon. It wasn't even close to "cool", so again, I seldom asked.

Besides the barbershop and hardware store, there were several other businesses on the north side of the square, but since I had no need for legal services or the offerings of a tavern, I never had the pleasure of dealing with, or even entering, Wallace and Wallace law firm or the Friendly Tavern. I could almost say the same for Norma's women's shop, except that I did go in maybe three or four times. It was owned by a woman named Norma Waite, but it was her husband, a really nice and very thin man by the name of Skinny, who I remember most. That was because I thought the name "Skinny Waite" was so cool, and seemed to fit his physique perfectly. I don't know why I ever went into Norma's at all; maybe it was with Mom, or later on to accompany Alinda. I never bought anything there. Mom didn't buy her clothes there because she claimed the selection was limited and the prices were high. Being a small store in a small town, I imagine Mom had a point.

In the middle of the west side of the square was a large brick building with an arched roofline that housed what everyone called the "food locker". I suppose it had a business name, but I don't recall what it was. However, "food locker" did aptly describe the services it provided. In the 1940's few people had a home freezer. In fact, a good number of homes still had iceboxes rather than electric refrigerators, so John Hayden's ice company had to deliver ice to their homes to keep them cool. People who could afford it, and desired more freezer space, could rent one of the freezer compartments at the food locker for their own use. I have no idea how much one of those freezer compartments rented for, but my parents didn't use the food locker and I suppose cost may have had something to do with it.

I seldom walked past the food locker, mostly because there was nothing that interested me on the west side of the square. There was Smitty's barbershop, the Green Lantern tavern, a gas station, and it seems to me there was another tavern over there. Besides that, the area around the food locker often had a pungent odor that irritated my nose. I found out when I was older that it was the smell of ammonia escaping from the cooling system. So the one and only time I ever went into the food locker was with my friend, Bob Dicks, and his family. And to me, what I saw on that day was pretty amazing. The room itself was big and plain and filled with several rows of long freezer compartments of various shapes and sizes. Each compartment had a metal door with a latch and each latch had a padlock attached to it. Other than the freezers, the only other things in the room were huge white asbestos insulated pipes running all around the inside of the building, crisscrossing the ceiling and running up and down the walls. These carried the ammonia that at that time was used as the refrigerant. At least once that I remember, and I think maybe several times, they had to evacuate the area around the food locker because of ammonia leaks.

On the day I went in with the Dicks family, we walked up to one of the metal doors and Bob's father, Larry, pulled a key from his pocket and unlocked the padlock. Then he flipped the latch and swung the door open for all to see. Two things made my eyes grow wide. First of all, an icy fog of air belched forth and fell onto me, sending a small shiver down my spine. It was summertime during those years when air conditioning was rare indeed, and the feel of that cold air against my hot skin was unforgettable. Reluctantly, I backed off a couple of steps to let Bob's mother, Ruth, get into the compartment, but not before I glimpsed its magical contents—the second wonder. In that freezer compartment I saw giant containers of frozen strawberries, blueberries, and peaches, gallon buckets of chocolate and vanilla ice cream, and little bags of assorted frozen vegetables. And that was just on one side. Against the other lay stacks of white butcher-paper-wrapped roasts, steaks and pork chops, along with two or three fryer chickens, and what was either a large roasting chicken or a turkey. Needless to say, for me, in those days when about the only thing that would fit in our little refrigerator freezer at home was ice cubes, it was a sight to behold. Even in my wildest childhood dreams, I had not imagined that anyone could have such a wonderful selection of delicious food right there at their fingertips. As impressed as I was, I never had the opportunity to return again.

While I was still in high school, the food locker began to lose its usefulness as everyone got newer and better refrigeration right in their own homes. Not long after that, it closed its doors, going the way of all the other businesses on the west side of the square. Today the IGA parking lot occupies the entire west side.

There were a number of businesses around the square that I only went into from time to time out of necessity. One of those was Covington's little newspaper office. Since the mid 1800's Covington had always had a weekly newspaper that was named either "The Covington Friend" or "The Covington Republican," depending on the time frame. For some of those years both papers were up and running simultaneously, reflecting the differences in political leanings of the publishers. Deaths, births, weddings, meetings, local sports, who had visited whom, what church was having a potluck, and almost anything you wanted to know about the happenings around Covington were all there. During my youth it was "The Covington Friend" and it was owned and operated by a friendly, mustached, short, and balding man named Tony LePage.

I only went in occasionally, and at my parent's request, to place an ad for something my parents wanted to sell or maybe to renew our subscription, which was something like two dollars a year. I also remember dropping off some announcements, probably a family reunion or my grandmother's birthday or some other family occasion. The paper would gladly print for free most anything you brought in.

Located on the south side of the square, I liked the newspaper office. In a way, it was similar to walking into Burrin's drug store because it had a distinct aroma, one of printer's ink and newspaper stock. I liked the smell. Then there was the springy little bell attached to the door that dingle-dinged when you walked in, and I liked the sound. After entering, you walked up to a chest-high wooden counter on your left to conduct your business. Its top looked ancient, with lots of scarring and deep etching from what must have been a century of use. I was not a neat child, but even to me I thought the place was always in a clutter, as if a small tornado had just passed through. On the other side of the counter sat a huge desk that was always stacked high with, for lack of a better description, stuff, none of which seemed to be in any order. The lighting was poor, making for a dark atmosphere, and you could often hear the printing press beating out a noisy steady rhythm from the next room.

The "Friend" really was a friend to Covington's citizens and, for over a hundred years, provided the town with a mirror into itself. But that wasn't enough to save it. No matter how noble its purpose, in the 60's and 70's society began to change, the town began to change. Businesses started to close and advertising revenues dried up. Sadly, after serving the town for over a century, Covington's weekly newspaper became the victim of "progress".

Dick Shelby's furniture store was in the same block, along with the Courthouse Café and the dry cleaners. Roy and Louise Hunter's restaurant was down on the corner, but I don't think it was there for long because I only remember going in one time. Neither did I make many trips into Shelby's or the dry cleaners. The only thing that impressed me about Shelby's was that it had a huge hand-operated elevator in which furniture could be moved between the upper and lower floors. I rode it with my mother once when I was very young and remember being a little frightened by it.

The Courthouse Café, on the other hand, I visited whenever I got the chance, which isn't to say was nearly as often as I would have liked. It was owned and operated by a family named Warrick and, as far as I was concerned, they served up the best macaroni salad in the world. Not that I had anything to compare it to. Mom never made it, so it was the only macaroni salad I'd ever tasted. Still, I'm pretty sure it was the best in the world. Whenever Aunt Mary invited me to the courthouse, where she worked in the county highway department, she let me play on the typewriter, stamp her stamp pads, go down to Robert Dale's for a treat, and at noon she'd take me to lunch. Fittingly so, we always went to the Courthouse Café. For me it was a hamburger, macaroni salad, and a Coke. Years later, on the Saturdays when I had to work an eight-hour shift at Kroger I'd spring for the $1.50 and treat myself to their Saturday lunch special, which usually consisted of a hamburger steak, green beans, and macaroni salad.

I didn't get to many restaurants growing up; they just weren't in our budget. So they weren't important to me. After all, Mom always cooked up a good meal and made certain I never suffered for even one second from the pangs of hunger. However, the few times I did go to the Courthouse Café I always found it to be a real treat and something I truly appreciated. Since then the Courthouse Café has gone through numerous owners and closings, but is still in operation today. However, I doubt that homemade macaroni salad can be found on the menu.

I may have spent more time on the east side of the square than any other. Burrin's Drug Store and The Lyric Theater were both on that side and as I've already said, I spent many hours in both of them. Other businesses located on that side and in operation during my entire youth were The Fountain Trust Company, the Ben Franklin Variety Store, and Elliot's Jewelry. There were some businesses that were there for only a portion of those years. They included Wisdom's Dime Store, the Western Auto, which was something of a hardware/auto supply, and Ellmore's bakery, of which I still recall the wonderful smell of those freshly baked sweet rolls.

Elliot's Jewelry was owned and operated by Bill Elliot. Mr. Elliot's store was next to the Lyric and not much larger than an oversized closet. I had little use for Mr. Elliot's services and wasn't in there more than a few times, but whenever I did go in he was bent over his small workbench examining a watch. Looking through his jeweler's magnifying glass, which he always wore on his head, he would carefully manipulate the watch parts with a pair of tweezers that were held in the hand of his normal arm. I don't know what was wrong with Mr. Elliot's other arm but it was deformed and somewhat shorter that the other.

Today of course, we would say that Mr. Elliot was "disabled". But in those days, Mr. Elliot had a "crippled" arm. I saw Mr. Elliot out and about more often than I ever saw him in his jewelry store and I always thought that trying to repair a watch with only one good arm would have been a real challenge. However, his disability didn't affect his friendliness. Even though I was always a bit shy towards him because of his arm, he was the one businessman in town I could always depend upon to greet me with a smile and a hello whenever we passed on the square.

I didn't spend much time in The Fountain Trust either, which was at that time Covington's only bank. With its double-stone columns rising high above the sidewalk, I thought it was Covington's answer to New York City. I liked its interior of gray marble that exuded a feeling of coolness, even on a hot summer day, and the large empty space of the lobby that echoed at the slightest sound.

The only thing I really knew about the bank was that my parents had always banked there, as had my grandparents ever since they moved to Covington in 1905. It was owned, at least as far as I knew, by Luke White and his wife Margaret who lived just a couple of blocks from our home. Margaret was one of my junior choir directors at the Methodist church. Their daughter, Mary Pat, was not only a classmate of mine, but was the smartest one of us all. My dad's first cousin, John Myers, was an officer in the bank for several years and was later elected to the U.S. House of Representatives, serving 15 terms. Other than that, The Fountain Trust Company was just a place where I opened a savings account after I got my first paper route and tried to make some small deposits every few weeks. It never amounted to much because I needed most of my meager earnings for root beer floats and movies.

Wisdom's and Ben Franklin were variety stores that were similar in nature, but Wisdom's was much smaller and was only there for a few years. They were both what were called five-and-dimes, which I thought was pretty stupid because what I wanted almost always cost more than a dime. Not being one who yearned for things I couldn't afford, I normally didn't spend a lot of time in either store, and when I did, it was mostly to look around.

Ben Franklin was owned by Mr. Brooks, a tall gray-haired man, who for some reason always intimidated me and who was nearly always nearby. The store was divided into two sections separated by a ramped doorway. One section, the smaller of the two, was carpeted and filled with sewing and knitting supplies. Yarn, thread, cloth, patterns, and all the paraphernalia that was required to make a garment could be found in this carpeted and more feminine room. Needless to say, I did my best to avoid this part of the store.

The other larger room had a tiled floor and was stocked with a variety of all kinds of wonderful things. Office and school supplies, toys, kites, candy, clothes, holiday decorations, kitchen things, picture frames, dishes, knick-knacks, and on and on went the choices, most of which were neatly displayed on wooden shelving or waist-high tables. With Mr. Brooks always lurking nearby, and a black-haired clerk named Pearl staring at you with a permanent scowl, the store was not child-friendly, one of the reasons I didn't spend much time in there. They made me feel like if I wasn't going to buy anything, then I'd probably better not touch. On the other hand, the most memorable downtown purchase I ever made was from that Ben Franklin store, and it occurred after I was earning a little of my own money and had a few dollars to do some Christmas shopping.

Ever since I'd gotten a paper route I'd budgeted a dollar or two each for both Mom's and Dad's Christmas gifts and the same for Mother's and Father's Day. I loved my parents and felt a great sense of satisfaction when I was finally able to afford to buy them these gifts. I took my giving seriously, but being a typical boy who needed to be doing more important things with his time than shopping, I doubt that I ever spent more than an hour altogether in Ben Franklin, Burrin's, and Wisdom's deciding just how to spend those two dollars on my parents at Christmastime.

One December day I walked into Ben Franklin, where up and down the aisles I went trying to find the perfect gifts. The necktie that I'd given Dad the year before had been worn to church only once, so I skipped right past the tie department. I could always get Mom a box of chocolate covered cherries, but I knew it would have no lasting value. I'd done that before and she'd shared it with all of us. With seven people in the family, it had lasted all of about 30 seconds. I preferred to get her something more useful, something like the spatula I'd given her a couple of years before, a gift of lasting quality, one I could watch her use every time she made burgers or pancakes and made sure to remind her occasionally as to where it came from.

Having made it through most of the store that day without any luck, I finally came to the Christmas decorations. And there I saw it, a single open box sitting on the floor propped up against one of the table legs. I knew instantly that it was the most perfect Christmas gift I could have ever imagined. About two feet tall, with fat red cheeks and a stubby white beard, Santa's jolly plastic face looked straight at me in all of its glowing glory. I immediately bent down and found the price tag, $5.95. That was more than I would normally spend, but it only took a second to decide that the price didn't matter. I had to have it. The Dickinsons had never had an outdoor Christmas decoration. This would be a first. This would be a triumph. The simple thought of it gave me a thrill.

Since there was only one of the Santas in stock, I asked Pearl if she'd keep it behind the counter while I went home and robbed my little stash for more money. It may have been the only time I ever saw Pearl smile. I didn't buy Mom and Dad their separate gifts that year as the Santa was a gift to everyone. And I didn't wait until Christmas day to give it to them either. I couldn't. My anticipation of their reaction to such a fine gift was almost overwhelming, so I gave it to them that night. And I'll have to say, they didn't disappoint. They made over it quite sufficiently, which of course made me feel about 10-feet tall. The next day Dad took it outside along with the ladder, hammer, nail, and an extension cord and hung my Santa conspicuously above the stoop for all to see. Then we all stood on the sidewalk and examined it until it was agreed that it was one of the nicest decorations in town.

Dad put that Santa up each Christmas for the next 20 years, maybe longer. I have no idea when it finally hit the trash, but for the few remaining years I lived at home, it was 601 Pearl Street's single outdoor Christmas beacon to the world.

The only thing I recall buying from Wisdom's variety store was a bottle of very cheap perfume that I gave to Mom one Christmas. It was called Evening in Paris and I thought it was about the sweetest smell I'd ever encountered. At 99 cents, it must have been the perfect gift, because Mom made over it like it was Channel #5. She even put some behind her ears that Christmas morning so I could smell it. For some reason I never smelled it on her again. I ran across the very same perfume several years later, told Alinda the Christmas story and asked her to take a whiff. She nearly gagged. By then it was selling for $1.49, so I guess some people don't appreciate quality.

I don't recall ever purchasing anything from the Western Auto, although I did like a lot of the things they had to sell, so I did my share of looking. They had some wonderful boy toys, things like bicycles, Radio Flyer wagons and sleds, and Red Ryder BB guns. I would love to have had the money to buy any one of those items, but they were all way beyond my means. That's not to say my parents didn't buy anything there. About that, I'm not sure, because in the course of my childhood I did receive each and every one of those items, and always as Christmas gifts. Some of them may have come from Western Auto, but I have a feeling that most of them came from Sears and Roebuck or Montgomery Ward, always referred to as Monkey Wards around our house. Both of those stores were located over in Danville.

Some other businesses located on the square or within a block were Philpott Shoes, Grubb Implement, Parrish Tire and Battery, Edwards Radio Repair, Hegg's Funeral Home, and the Sprague Hotel. In addition, there were some gas stations, also called service and/or filling stations back then. Two of these were Sweet's Standard Station; it later became Buss Allison's, and one belonging to Oral Hale. There were a couple of pool halls and another one or two taverns. There was the City Building on Washington Street that housed the city of Covington offices and The American Legion building over on Liberty Street. Rex Keller had an upstairs law office and Charlie Massey had an abstract office. There were also from two to three dentists located on the square depending on the year. The most prominent of these were E. J. Martin, and for a while his brother Rudolph. Another was the aforementioned Doc Faust.

Of these men, Rudolph Martin was the first and only Covington dentist I ever went to. It was in those days before fluoride had been discovered to prevent tooth decay and quite honestly, Mom and Dad were extremely lax in making me brush my teeth. So at the tender age of eight I had developed a cavity, maybe several, and had to make my first terrifying trip to the dentist.

It was Dad who got the dirty job of telling me about that first visit, which thinking back now, was quite odd. Mom would have normally handled a communication of this nature with us kids, so it's my guess that Mom didn't want to face the reaction she figured I'd probably have. There must have been a great deal of trepidation from Dad too, because he wasn't the least bit direct about it. I knew right away that something was amiss when he began the conversation by asking if I wanted to go to the movie the next night. Dad never asked if I wanted to go to the movie—ever. I asked him, or more precisely, I asked Mom if I could go to a movie. It was never the other way around. So, I wasn't sure what was up. However, I never missed a chance to go to the movies, so I said, "Yes." But, as I suspected, that wasn't the end of it. He then went on to say that before going to the movie there was something I needed to do in the afternoon.

Hmmm, stranger and stranger I thought to myself when I asked him what it was I needed to do. I'll always remember his next three words and the tone in which he said them. Almost apologetically, he said, "It's a surprise."

A surprise? Being asked if I wanted to go the movie had been a surprise. What could possibly top that? Of course, I immediately asked, "What kind of surprise?" And he replied, "Just a surprise, wait and see."

I'd heard Mom and Dad discussing the dentist a few days earlier. I hadn't been included in the conversation and more or less absented myself at the mere utterance of the word "dentist." I knew what dentists did to you and pain was not something I wanted to think about. So the instant Dad said, "just a surprise, wait and see", it hit me. They'd finally done it. They were going to take me to the dreaded dentist. At that moment my chin started trembling. I didn't cry often. By the time I was in first grade I'd been told many times that big boys and men didn't cry. It was a sissy thing to do, so tears only came at the most devastating of news or with the most serious of pain.

"The dentist," I finally blurted out, trying to hold back the tears welling up in my eyes. I was hoping Dad would jump right in and deny it, but he didn't. "Please Dad, I don't want to go to the dentist," I begged over and over through sobs and slobber. And I'll have to give Dad credit, he tried the best he could to comfort me, to tell me that everything would be all right, and besides, I'd be going to the movie later that night.

In the end Dad never wavered, and after a few minutes of begging and complete terror, I accepted the fact that I would be going for my first dentist visit. As it turned out, the next day Rudolph Martin didn't do much more than look in my mouth. I think he told Mom and Dad that I didn't need any treatment at that time but to bring me back on such and such a date. That was the first and last time I ever went to Rudolph Martin. By the time I got to the dentist again, Mom was taking one of my siblings to Dr. Neely in Veedersburg, so that's where I started going. However, that was years after that first appointment with Rudolph Martin, and by the time Dr. Neely saw me, I had more cavities in my mouth than teeth. Needless to say, as wonderful as my parents were, when it came to dental hygiene, even they agreed later in life that they might have failed me.

Philpott's and Sprague's were Covington's shoe stores. For some reason, Mom preferred Philpott's, so that's where she usually took me after the only pair of shoes I ever had at any one time got so many holes in them, or the soles were flapping so badly, that they would no longer keep out the rocks and snow. I don't remember ever outgrowing a pair of shoes, I wore them out, although it was quite possible that some of the ripped seams may have been the result of my ever-expanding feet. Besides selling new shoes, Philpott's could also have shoes repaired for you, but they had to send them to Danville. If there was a chance that a sole or heel could be replaced in order to add a few months of wear, that was always Mom's first choice. It was cheaper by far. If they were finally too far gone for a repair, then I was up for a new pair and Mr. or Mrs. Philpott started pulling out boxes. As for myself, there was no problem in getting a good fit. I was easy to please. On the other hand, my youngest sister Nancy always recalls how the first thing Mom would say whenever the two of them walked into Philpott's was, "She'll need a wide, she has a FAT foot." Nancy says it embarrasses her to think about it even to this day.

I think at some point Philpott's moved from one downtown building to another, but both locations were old and dimly lit. Like so many of those downtown businesses, my olfactory memories are the strongest and Philpott's was no exception. I loved walking into their store and catching the first smell of new leather. As much as I disliked shopping for shoes, that was always one reason to come back. By the time I was in junior high, Philpott's had closed down, but a cobbler named Ooley had moved into town and set up shop on the square. Mom was thankful for Mr. Ooley and used his repair services often. I couldn't have cared less about Mr. Ooley or his cobbler shop except for the fact that when he moved to town so did his family, and his family included his daughter Beth. I never got to know Beth very well, I was way too shy with girls for that, but

Beth was in my grade, she was friendly to me and everyone else, and I thought she was one of the cutest girls I'd ever laid eyes on. She was a great addition to our class.

Leon Edwards had a radio repair shop next to the City Building in the block running east of the square on Washington Street. This was the same block where a pool hall, Hegg's Funeral Home, and the Methodist Church were located. Leon was a slight man with a mustache and a very friendly smile. Whenever I saw him, whether on the street or in his shop, he'd say, "Hi Bobby Dean," then asked how my parents were. That was one reason I remember Leon so clearly. The other reason was that, like Bill Elliot, Leon was another of the downtown business people with a handicap.

I'd never seen anyone with Leon's handicap, nor have I since. His two feet turned in toward each other at nearly 90-degree angles. When he walked, he had to put one foot over the other. But walk he did, and since all of his repair work was done by hand, I didn't see that he was slowed down at all. Later on, Leon's Radio Repair became Leon's Radio and TV Repair.

Leon's wife, Mildred, had a beauty shop in their home on Railroad Street and that's where Mom always got her hair done. The one thing I recall about Mildred's shop is that I avoided going in there whenever possible. After smelling that hair permanent setting solution just once, I told Mom I wasn't ever going in there again.

There were two funeral homes in town. The one named Bodine and Shelby was larger, and definitely had more funerals. It was located on Third Street, where by the way, it is now named Shelby's and is still decking out Covington's deceased for their final journeys. The other was Hegg's Funeral Home, which was owned and operated by a mortician named Bob

Hegg. Hegg's was located directly across Washington Street from the Methodist Church.

I attended only one funeral at Hegg's, and that came many years after I graduated from high school. By that time, it had changed names from Hegg's to DeVerter's. The funeral I attended was for my Grandma Dickinson, but that's not what I think of when I think about Hegg's. The two things that do come to mind are Santa Claus and a book of extremely gory pictures.

There was, and still is, a stoop on the front of Hegg's, covered by a small flat roof. Every Christmas season the Heggs stood a nearly life-size Santa Claus, pack slung over his back and all, up on that roof. To a kid, he looked just like he was ready to head down the nearest chimney. They even had a spotlight shining on him at night, which made it even more realistic. Anytime I saw Santa up there on Hegg's roof, I knew the big day itself was swiftly approaching, and it just added to the excitement of the season. I guess Santa must have come with the building, because even after the funeral home closed and other businesses moved in, Santa's place on that roof remained a Christmas tradition for many more years. I did notice several years ago, after what must have been at least 40 years of service, that Santa was beginning to look ragged around the edges, and a few years after that he simply failed to appear. He was nice while he lasted, and I'll admit that I felt a bit of loss when he was gone.

One day during my sophomore year in high school, Bill Huffman told me he'd gotten word that one of the high school girls who we knew was babysitting the Hegg children. The Heggs lived in the same building as the funeral home and word was that she had run across a book containing pictures that would make you puke. Of course that's all it took for Bill and me to make a beeline to Hegg's, apparently, after a dozen or so other kids had already been there. When we got there, she made us promise not to tell anyone about it or she would probably be in trouble. We promised not to say a word, even though I doubted there was a kid in town who hadn't already heard about it.

As if it were a treasured relic, she carefully extracted the book from its place on the bookshelf and, holding it in her own hands with us looking over her shoulder, she began to flip through the pages. She already had the page numbers memorized and knew where the best pictures were. As it turned out there were only three or four pictures that had any real puke potential, but that was enough. In the days before the internet or even before the graphic violence of movies or television, which came along years later, looking at a colored photo of a real gunshot wound to the head was a shocker, and definitely worth seeing even if it did make me feel a bit queasy.

There were pictures of gunshot wounds, human deformities, and all manner of disgusting diseases of the skin. All were gross to some degree, and also impressionable. That night, lying in bed, it was all I could do to go to sleep with pictures of gunshot and leprosy victims swimming around in my head. I heard later that the Heggs found out about the kids paying a visit to their home while they were away, and to my great disappointment, a second look at that book was not going to be possible. And just as well I suppose, because even to this day I can still see a couple of those morbid pictures in my mind.

When I got old enough to drive, and had to put gas in Dad's car, I usually stopped at Bus Allison's gas station at the corner of Fifth and Liberty. As you pulled up to the gas pumps, you had to run over a black hose that was stretched across the drive, which in turn rang a bell inside the gas station. In a few moments, Bus or one of his helpers would come out from the bay area wiping their hands on a greasy rag that normally hung from their back pockets. They asked if you wanted regular or ethyl and how much you wanted. You always answered in dollar amounts, like $3.00 worth, or if money was no object, you told them to fill it up. I don't ever recall telling them to give me more than a dollar's worth, which was about three gallons. While the gas was pumping, they'd ask if you needed your oil or air checked, then they cleaned your windshield without asking. It was all part of the free service. After they were finished, you paid them in cash, no credit cards back then.

I liked going into the grease-bay area whenever Dad had to have the car serviced. Seeing that hydraulic lift raise that big old car high above my head was worth the trip. They did tire repairs in there too, and in later years, I'd bring my bike down to fill the tires with air and a couple of times had them repair a flat for fifty cents.

Next to Allison's was The American Legion building. My guess is it's one of the older buildings in town, and other than some newer tuck-pointing and painting, it doesn't look much different today than it did sixty years ago, although it's no longer the Legion. Today it's a bank. We occasionally held Boy Scout meetings there, in the upstairs area where there was a pool table. But the best time I remember was the night they honored the Hoosier Boy's State recipients from Covington, of which I was one. I don't know if they still have such a thing as Boy's State, but in the summer before my junior year in high school, The Legion sponsored two boys from Covington, Bob Dicks and me. When we got back, we were honored at a banquet held at The American Legion.

I'm not sure if the meal was only in our honor or if there was other American Legion business going on, but I felt a sense of pride when, after eating a delicious meal, they announced my name and I got up to tell everyone what I had done at Boy's State. Bob's dad, Larry Dicks, was my Scout Master and was also a friend of my father's. Just as Bob and I were classmates, so had my dad and Larry been when they were in school. And just as Bob and I played football together, Larry and Dad played side by side on the 1932-1933 basketball team. I'm not positive of it, but I'm pretty sure it was Larry's influence that got the two of us selected to Hoosier Boy's State.

A three-story building named Sprague's Hotel occupied the corner across Liberty Street from Ben Franklin, and it had a department store at street level. Apparently, in the 1950's there was little use for a hotel in Covington, and by the time I left Covington it was turned into an apartment building. I don't recall going into that department store more the once or twice while it was in business. In fact, for much of my childhood, I was a little confused by Sprague's department store. When I was quite young, Sprague's was on the corner across the street, in the building that eventually became Brooks's Ben Franklin. Then, without my knowledge, it moved to the hotel building where it was still called Sprague's department store. The switch thoroughly confused me. First, a Mr. Sprague was usually present at the store on the north side of Liberty, and they called it Sprague's. Then one day, months later, I walked into the same building, into the same store, and a Mr. Brooks was there, and they called it Brooks's. I knew that people were still talking about going to Sprague's department store, even after there was a Brooks's Ben Franklin. I think all the confusion came with the fact that I didn't know Sprague's department store had moved across the street and was still in business in a new location. I seldom paid any attention to that side of Liberty, so it took me a long time to get it straight in my head, and now I've probably confused even you, dear readers.

While Sprague's was still in the future Ben Franklin building, it had a snack bar along one of its walls, and I recall having a treat in there once before the store moved and the snack bar closed. Until I was about nine years old, at which time the Rowes moved out of town to a place in the country, Dick Rowe lived a block and a half north of us on Sixth Street. Dick was one of my best neighborhood pals. Shortly after they moved, I made arrangements to go to the movie with Dick one Saturday night when he and his family came to town. That was the night of the week when everyone in half the county came to Covington to do their shopping. I had brought money for the movie that night, but that was all, so after the movie there was some discussion between Dick's parents as to whether they could afford to take all of us for a treat. In the end, I guess they decided they could, because we all ended up at the snack bar in Sprague's Department Store where Dick and I were treated to ice-cream sundaes. I still remember all the hubbub of the crowd around the square that Saturday night, the excitement of watching a movie with a friend who had moved away, and the pleasure of an ice-cream sundae. That was the only time I ever recall sitting in that snack bar, and it was also one of the last times I was with Dick Rowe. We had little opportunity to get together after he moved.

A couple of doors east of Sullivan's grocery, you entered Deek's Pool Hall by walking half a floor up on iron-grate steps. Except for the big lamps hanging over the pool tables and the card table, Deek's was not exactly a beacon of light, and other than the well-worn pool tables and one big card table, it was just a lot of empty space. I didn't spend much time in Deek's, mostly because I wasn't much of a pool enthusiast, and secondly, I was way too young to sit down at the continuously-running game of gin with a bunch of feisty old men. I always pictured myself a decent card player. Cards were one of my parent's favorite pastimes, as they had been for my mother's parents, Grandma and Grandpa Stanton. But given the chance, these old boys would have chewed me up, spit me out, and sent me home without a shirt on my back. Deek's wouldn't have won the Good Housekeeping seal of approval either, as it was the only place I'd ever seen a spittoon that was any more than a decoration. Deek's had two of them, one on either side of the card table. You'd never guess they were made of brass because I never saw them when they weren't completely covered in poorly aimed tobacco juice.

# Chapter 3

# *Grade School*

I didn't consider it lucky at the time, but when it came to all twelve of my Covington school years, I had at least one advantage over most every kid in school. I lived only one block away. I lived one block west of the grade school and one block east of the high school. That meant that on those cold winter days when other kids had to walk from one end of town or the other, I had only a hop-skip-and-a-jump to a classroom that was usually overheated and spitting steam from the radiators. Not only was it convenient, it allowed me to walk home for lunch each day, saving my mother the chore of either packing a lunch or the unthinkable of giving me lunch money.

As it must have been for many of my classmates, and I imagine for most kids who attended Covington's schools, the years I spent in school provided me with many pleasant memories and maybe a few minor worries. Grade school in Covington during those years consisted of first through fifth grades. I don't know if kindergarten had yet reached our little community. If it did, I didn't go. It seems to me that I once saw a picture of my brother John's class, who was four years behind me, which had been cut out of the local newspaper, with a caption stating it was a picture of Covington's first kindergarten class. I know that when kindergarten did start it met in the basement of the public library for a few years.

Neither had I attended any kind of preschool. At that time a preschool in our community would have been as foreign as seeing a person of color walk down one of our sidewalks. In Covington, neither existed. On top of that, my parents didn't read to me. Sing, yes, and often. But read? It never happened. So when I started in the first grade everything was new to me. I didn't know an A from a Z and couldn't count to 10.

I loved those first five years of grade school, which met in the old elementary school building, a structure that was razed nearly forty years ago to build a new one. The new building, which is still in use today, was built just north of the old building on the grounds of an empty field that may still echo "Red Rover, Red Rover" from a few thousand kids' voices from long ago. The building I attended sat on the north side of Pearl Street between Seventh and Eighth in the center of the block, where the playground is located today. There were two first and second grade classes on the first floor, two third and fourth grade classes on the second floor, and two fifth grade classes in the basement. Presently, the only sign of what existed back then is the basketball court, which is still in the same exact location it was then. In fact, I've examined them, and it looks to me like the four baskets are still supported by the very same goal posts that were there sixty years ago. Could that be?

I don't recall the exact date of my first day of school, but we didn't start until after Labor Day. This was in the fall of 1949. On that day I walked the one block from my house to the grade school, where I found myself in the classroom of Miss Hester Kay, a kind and gentle teacher who made everyone feel welcome. Thus began my education built around those basic 3 R's—"readin", "ritin", and "rithmatic". It's not so easy to say just how much I learned that year. A review of my grade cards from those grade school years indicates that I got all but maybe a couple of S's, which meant I did satisfactory work. So I guess I was an average student, and I don't think I ever caused Miss Kay a bit of trouble. I didn't struggle with any of the subjects, and didn't necessarily dislike any of them except for writing. I hated writing. Not that it matters anymore, but I never did conquer the simple task of writing nice even letters between two straight lines. Maybe it was a deficiency on the right side of my brain, very little artistic ability. My letters leaned, drooped, zigged, zagged, and closed in on themselves.

About halfway through the year, Miss Kay divided the class into two reading groups. One was called the blue birds and the other the red birds. I was in the red birds group, and in the beginning thought that was nice. I liked red birds. I didn't realize until a few weeks later that my reading group was made up of the slower readers, a fact that I was a little disappointed in. But I did observe soon enough that when the blue bird kids read aloud to the class, they didn't have to hem, haw, and stumble around nearly as much as I did. So begrudgingly, I accepted the idea that along with writing, reading was another of my weak points.

Beyond the learning process, there were a couple of interesting, but simple things during my first grade year that brought me a real sense of happiness, much as they still do today whenever I recall them. And as trivial as they were, I wouldn't be surprised if both of them didn't help to shape my outlook on the world around me for the rest of my life.

One of them was a little paper booklet that came out each month that contained pictures and stories about whatever season we were in. It was mostly a coloring book, but it also had a few short stories, and sometimes Miss Kay would read one of the stories to us. I loved coloring those pictures of Santa, the Pilgrims, Easter eggs, and the leaves of fall. I looked forward to those booklets every month and treasured them each until the next one came along.

The other things that so impressed me were very similar in nature to the booklet. They were the cardboard character cutouts that Miss Kay hung in the windows each season. I can't tell why these things had such a positive effect on me, but as I thumbed through those booklets or looked out those windows with the colored cutouts, good feelings pervaded me, and I felt that my young life was just about as nice as anything could be.

A funny thing about those booklets, I nearly missed out on them. It wasn't required that we have them. They were sort of extra-curricular and had to be purchased. Some kids got them, and some kids didn't. The first time they were handed out, I didn't get one. From where I sat, I could see the kids around me studying the picture on the front page. It was a picture of a boy and girl flying a kite. After that I saw them slowly flipping through the pages, and my heart began to sink. Not only was I deflated, but I was jealous, and wondered how I'd been left out.

Miss Kay was kind enough to explain why some kids got a booklet while others didn't. In the back of my mind I vaguely remembered that we had been informed that the cost of these booklets was not part of the school-year fees, and that Mom and

Dad would have had to pay something extra for me to participate. In my case, for some reason, that fee had not been paid. It could be that I never carried the message home, or maybe my parents read the message and decided the fee wasn't worth it, or that it just wasn't in the budget. In any case there I was, sadly watching most of the kids holding on to their dear little booklets, and wishing with all my heart that I could hold one too.

When I got home that day, I told Mom about the booklets and how I wished I'd been given one. After that, I'm not sure what happened. Probably Mom gave me the required money to take to school. I don't remember. But when the next booklet came out a month later, I was thrilled when Miss Kay handed me my very own copy. Those cutouts and booklets were, and still are, what I consider among my first great treasures on the road of life.

## Grade School Carnival

It was just a few weeks after school started that first year that I was introduced to one of the most endearing events of my grade school life. It became an annual event that I greatly anticipated, always attended, and then participated in for the last four of my grade school years.

It was a simple affair really, and took place on only one night during each of those five years. It was called the grade school carnival. I expect they are long forgotten by many of my peers, but for me, the grade school carnival was absolutely magical and ended up taking a coveted place in my memories right alongside Christmas, Halloween, Easter, and of course the annual street carnival. It was put on in the fall of the year, in October or possibly early November, just as the leaves were falling, carpeting the tree-lined streets of Covington in beautiful yellows, golds, and reds.

In those days there was little reason to worry about the safety of a child walking the streets of Covington, day or night, so just a few weeks after I entered the first grade, and knew my way to and from school, my mother handed me a quarter and sent me off to the grade school carnival. In 1949, with little discretionary spending money in most people's pockets and no television to keep us in constant contact with the outside world, people just weren't as sophisticated as they are today. Most of us worked, lived, played and socialized in our own little enclave of familiarity, seldom venturing into the vast world beyond. And so, at the tender age of six, even though it was only a block away and I had been walking it to school each day, to me the school seemed a fair distance from home and certainly not in my neighborhood. So walking there in the dark was a little scary. But Mom encouraged me, said there'd be nothing to worry about, then explained to me about money, getting change back, and spending it on just the right things so it would last the night. She convinced me. I put a quarter in my pocket and headed off on my first great adventure just a block up the street.

The events of that autumn night left an indelible impression on me, because to this day I can remember vividly the sights, sounds, and smells that filled that old schoolhouse over sixty years ago. Upon arriving, I entered the west entrance and slowly climbed the first flight of stairs. This brought me to the main floor where I stopped, stood, and took in my surroundings. On this floor, there were four classrooms, one of which was mine. This floor I was familiar with. I'd never been on the top floor, and I'd only been to the basement a few times because that's where the restrooms were. But I was familiar with this floor. The whole place was crowded with laughing, talking, noisy people, more people than I'd ever seen in one place before.

I felt excited by what I was seeing, but at the same time a little frightened. It was all new to me.

The apprehension of those first moments didn't last long, as I spied something I'd never been close enough to examine before, a real live turkey. It was cooped up in a cage and sitting on a table behind men wearing soldier-type hats that said Lions Club on them. I was held spellbound as I watched this huge bird trying to wiggle around that small cage while making that gobble-gobble sound that turkeys make. I must have studied that turkey for five minutes before moving on, but later I returned and gave him a good look once again. Today of course, who in their right mind would spend a quarter or five-for-a-dollar on chances to win a live turkey? But on that night, sitting on the same table as the gobbling turkey was a homemade turnable drum made out of wood and chicken wire about half-full of raffle tickets. Every time a chance went in, a kid who was the son of one of the Lion's Club members, would tumble the drum round and round, mixing the tickets up. Watching the kid spin the drum was a treat in itself, and I wished right then and there that maybe someday I could be the drum tumbler, although as the years passed more interesting things came along, so that wish never did come true. Later in the evening the kid would tumble the drum around one last time, and a name would be pulled out to win what would most likely be someone's main course on Thanksgiving day.

Right next to the turkey raffle was the live hog raffle, sponsored by another of Covington's civic groups or The American Legion or the VFW. On their table sat another one of those homemade raffle drums filling up with raffle tickets. But the hog itself wasn't there. I knew where it was, it was right outside the south door of the school penned up in the back of an old farm truck that was parked out there. I'd seen the truck and heard the oinking and squealing even before I'd stepped into the schoolyard that night, and when I saw that truck with slotted wooden sides, I felt like I just had to inspect it before going into the school. As I had gotten close, I saw that there were some big kids up beside the truck oinking back at the pig and poking sticks through the wooden slats to tease him. Those kids were older and kind of scared me, so I didn't go all the way up to the truck before I hurried around to the other door to enter the school. What puzzled me was, although I was pretty sure what would happen to that turkey, because I'd seen my Dad chop the head off a live chicken once, and then Mom cleaned and cooked it, but I just couldn't figure out what anyone would do with a live pig.

As impressive as the turkey and hog raffles were to me that night, and considering all the rest of the hubbub that was going on around me, I'd have to say that it was actually the soda pop concession that ended up taking the prize as the most memorable sight of my very first-ever grade school carnival. Why was I so impressed with it? Well, it probably had to do with that fact that I loved the taste of soda pop combined with the fact that the sweet, tasty drink was all but non-existent at our house. To describe soda pop as memorable might seem weird to you, but take my word for it, to me, on that night, I was very impressed.

There were these two enormous metal tubs (I later learned they were horse watering troughs brought in from someone's farm) and both were chock full of more soda pop than I could have ever dreamed existed all in one place at any one time. I stood watching in wonder as men with metal ice grabbers picked up huge blocks of ice from another large newspaper-covered tub and moved them over to the tubs of soda pop. Then, with ice picks in hand, they commenced to chop chop chop at these blocks, sending chunks and chips of ice everywhere, but mostly covering the beautifully colored bottles below them. While this was going on, other people were dipping their hands down into that icy water searching for tasty bottles of RC, or Dr Pepper, or green bottles of 7UP, or brightly colored bottles of orange and grape Nehi, or Dad's root beer, or red bottles of cream soda.

Giant blocks of ice, men with picks stabbing at them, so much pop all in one place, and people dipping in up to their elbows in search of their favorite drink was all absolutely amazing to a boy who'd never seen anything like it in his life.

I don't know how long I stayed there that night; it seemed like a long time. But a first grader's sense of time and space doesn't translate into anything resembling reality, so it probably wasn't more than an hour. I spent ten cents of my quarter on a bottle of pop, I don't recall what flavor, and another nickel on the fun house. I knew there was a little ice cream stand set up in the entryway, for I had seen it when I came in, and I painstakingly hoarded my last dime for another one of my favorite treats in the world, and one that I seldom had the chance to hold in my little six-year-old hands.

There were a couple of fourth or fifth grade kids manning the ice cream stand, neither of which I knew. The little homemade sign scotch-taped to the front of the table said 5¢ per scoop. I wanted chocolate, but they said vanilla was the only flavor they had left, so I told them I'd take two scoops. Looking back a few minutes later, I recalled that the boy making my cone had plopped both scoops loosely onto the top of the cone and hadn't taken time to tamp them down. At the time I didn't really give it any thought, since I'd seldom ever seen an ice cream cone made anyway, so I gave the kid my dime and happily walked out the school door to go home.

Sadly, I didn't even make it to the street. Because as I put the cone to my mouth for my very first bite, the ice cream, both scoops (*OH NO!*) toppled from the top of my cone and onto the sidewalk with a gentle splat. I looked down in a state of disbelief. In that first second all I could do was stare at it. There it lay squarely in front of me, my two scoops of vanilla ice cream still connected one to the other. In my hand, I held an empty cone. My first thought was that I could just simply pick it up and put it back in the cone, but it was only a split second thought and I quickly realized I couldn't do that, the ice cream would be filthy. I also knew I couldn't go back in and buy another; I had spent the last of my money.

I was heartbroken. When would I ever have the opportunity to hold another double-dip ice cream cone in my hand? My next reaction was one of anger, because thinking back I knew that the boy hadn't made it properly in the first place. It hadn't been my fault that it fell out; it had been his. I wanted to go back and tell him what he'd done, but he was much older and a whole lot bigger than me, so I decided against it. Now, having considered all my alternatives and realizing that the ice cream cone was forever gone, I felt completely shattered. In the end, I did the one thing left to do. I cried all the way home.

I was still sobbing when I arrived home and related my ice cream tale to Mom. Many years later as we were reminiscing about that night, Mom commented that, "Oh yes," she remembered it very well. She said when I came home that night and told her my sad story, she nearly cried. Then she did cry when she related the story to my Dad later that night. She said she felt guilty for not taking me that night herself, even though she did have good reason with my two-year-old brother at home and Dad working. This was when Dad was still working for the city and sometimes had to work at night. I was surprised to know that Mom and I both remembered that night so well all those years later.

For the next four years I couldn't wait for the school carnival to roll around once again. And the best part was, beginning in the second grade I was now old enough to become a real participant in all that was going on. As the years went by, I helped with the spook house, the fishpond, and the cakewalk. For two years I was also in, of all things, the minstrel show.

You have to remember these were the late 40's and early 50's, and at least 10 years away from the civil rights movement of the 1960's. The term racism was not common. In fact, I'm not sure it was even a word back then. Certainly, it wasn't a word that would have ever been heard around Covington. And I don't suppose anyone living in Covington thought that a minstrel show might be offensive. After all, Covington had no black citizens, referred to at that time as Negroes, or something worse, although I seldom heard that term used. So at least for the years when I was in grade school, white kids dressed up in blackface and put on a minstrel show as part of the grade school carnival.

My first year in the minstrel, when I was in the fourth grade, I played the part of Mr. Interlocutor, the white man in the shiny top hat who sat in the middle of all the black faces and prompted them to tell jokes, or play a piece on their instruments, or to sing a song, or dance. I don't recall who most of the other minstrels were, but one of my classmates, Paul Hershberger, who might have been named Rastus in the show, was probably the dancer. I think it was Karen Burrin, as Liza Jane, who played the clarinet.

As Mr. Interlocutor I would say something like, "Rastus, I hear you learned a new dance this week. Maybe you could show the folks how it goes while Liza Jane plays that there licorice stick of hers." At this, Rastus would say, "Yessa' Missta Intalockata, I gonna show you my new dance right now." Then Paul would get up and do his dance while Karen played her clarinet. The show only lasted 15 or 20 minutes, but it was a hit every year. We put the show on in Mrs. Mars's third grade room twice during the evening and it was always standing room only. Our parents were so proud of us. The next year I played Ham Bone, a raggedy black man who told a couple of jokes, then bent over and shook his head back and forth in laughter while slapping himself on his knees. It went sort of like this.

Mr. Interlocutor would look toward me and say, "Ham Bone, have you heard any funny jokes lately?"

I'd answer, "Yessa' I sure have. Did you hear what the big chimney said to the little chimney?"

"Why no I didn't Ham Bone, what did the big chimney say to the little chimney?"

"He said, 'Ain't you a little too young to smoke!'"

I don't remember the other joke; I imagine it was just as silly. But for a fifth grader in a fairly innocent world, it was pretty funny. And of course seeing the smiles and laughs from my family and friends was the big payoff. My mom and dad absolutely beamed.

Of course, I didn't let my participation in these events keep me from enjoying all the other things going on around me. Loving sweets, I particularly liked walking the cakewalk. Many of the mothers baked and donated cakes, and I don't think there was a year that went by when someone in my family didn't win one. One year Dad and I each won one. Dad picked the cake Mom had made and brought it home as his prize, telling her later he had no idea it was the cake she'd baked, but said it sure was the best-looking cake there.

For at least a couple of years they had boxing matches, boys actually putting on boxing gloves and facing off against each other in a makeshift-boxing ring in the school basement. I couldn't believe that I actually had classmates willing to get up in the middle of a boxing ring and pummel each other to the cheers of mostly adult onlookers. But they did it, and you knew these weren't the kids you wanted to mess with on the playground. Jim Cadman was the kid in my class who seemed to have no fear and who took on all challengers. For some reason I never got to know Jim very well. Maybe it was because I avoided him whenever possible.

The spook house was more fun to work than it was to go through because once in a while you could actually scare a little kid by hiding along the curtained trail and grabbing them as they passed by. Otherwise, there was virtually nothing spooky about it.

Then there was the fishpond, which I really liked to help with because the prize was always under my control. For a nickel, a kid got a "fishing pole" with line attached and the fishing line was draped over a rope that was stretched about five feet off the floor and had a blanket hanging down from it. Behind the blanket, I could choose a prize of my choice and attach it to the line. Then I gave the line a tug, and the kids pulled up their "catch". The fun of it for me began when I peeked from behind the blanket to see who was "fishing". If it was someone I liked, they ended up with the choicest items, a plastic spider, a snake, a Chinese finger torture. If they weren't one of my pals, they got something like a comb, or if it was a girl, maybe a plastic-bead necklace or a ring. If it was someone I really didn't like, they definitely ended up with something to read.

For at least two years, there were wonderful turkey dinners served in the grade school cafeteria, and it seems to me that they were on the same night as the school carnival. If it wasn't that particular night, it had to have been close to that time because I'm sure it was in the fall, but not yet the cold of winter.

On the east side of the grade school, the fire escape ran up the side of the building from the ground to the second floor. If I climbed those metal stairs, I could lie on the top landing and look down into the cafeteria. On this particular night, for one dollar, many of Covington's citizens invested in the most delicious smelling turkey dinner I could ever imagine. It was prepared by the school cooks, who it seemed to me were world-class chefs. Turkey, mashed potatoes and gravy, stuffing, green beans, cranberries, hot rolls, and an aroma that made my mouth absolutely water is what brought me to that fire escape that year and again the next year. As much as I loved food and eating, spying on those folks as they went through that cafeteria line, filled their plates to overflowing, then topping it off with a piece of pumpkin pie was a sight to behold. Not only was it a visual delight, but the smell was out of this world. Of course, I would have given anything to be able to go through that line too, but I never did. I knew if I asked if we could go what the answer would be, so I didn't even mention it to Mom. In retrospect, I suppose the watching, the smelling, the dreaming itself was what impressed me, and just maybe those things were far better than the meal could have ever been.

I don't know when the grade school carnival was abandoned. After the fifth grade, when I made the move from the grade school building to the high school building, I didn't attend it again. I suppose I outgrew it about the same time it began to outlast its popularity. A new entertainment medium called television was beginning to replace a myriad of social events in the community, and I imagine that was the signal that the grade school carnival would soon be coming to an end.

## Miss Smith to Mr. Porter

In the summer between first and second grade, I ran into some older kids who were talking about school. They informed me that no matter what, I didn't want Miss Smith for my second grade teacher. "She's a mean old bag," one of them told me. "Yeah, and she likes to paddle kids too," said another. I believed them. So when I walked into school that first day of my second grade year, 1950, I was pretty shaken to find my name on Miss Smith's roster. I didn't want spanked. I didn't want a mean old bag for a teacher.

As it turned out, I need not have worried. In my opinion, Miss Smith was a great teacher and that was probably because she didn't let her kids get away with anything. On the other hand, even though I never had a minute's trouble with her, there were others, some of my more boisterous classmates, who probably did find her to be a "mean old bag". I'm also pretty sure a couple of them ended up feeling the "board of education."

We were introduced to the audio/visual room in the first grade, but Miss Smith seemed to rely on it much more than Miss Kay did. In the days before TV, these little movies were quite a thrill for all of us, and it was the highlight of our day any time they were a part of our curriculum. The audio/visual room was located in the school's basement, right around the corner from the boys' restroom. In this A/V room I learned that little invisible things called white corpuscles, which were white and carried long dangerous looking spears, could march though the blood stream and fight off regiments of nasty germs, which of course were black and also carried spears. It was a very simple animation depicting how our bodies fight infection, and of course, the white corpuscles won. I can still see that battle of good over evil taking place up there on that small white screen, while seated on those cold metal folding chairs, in a little dark room, where the audio always had to compete with the constant clickety-clicking of the noisy projector.

Speaking of the A/V room, which as I said was right next the boy's restroom, I'm reminded of a conversation that took place during my second-grade year in that very restroom. One day I was standing at the urinal when the kid at the next urinal said to me, "Hey, did you hear that Al Jolson died?"

I'd heard the name Al Jolson, I suppose everyone had. But all I knew about him was that he was a well-known singer. That may have been the first time I'd ever heard that a celebrity had died. For some reason I didn't want Al Jolson to be dead. I guess I thought of him as some kind of national treasure, and it made me sad that he was dead. Like any good gossip though, that evening I couldn't wait to tell Mom and Dad that I'd heard Al Jolson had died. Their response was, "Yes, they'd heard it too," so they guessed it must be true. I asked them a couple of questions about Al Jolson, and they filled me in on just who he was. Mom even sang a few bars of his song "Mammy". I don't suppose I could tell you more than a few conversations I ever had in grade school, but for some strange reason that short little second-grade conversation in the boy's restroom while taking a pee stuck with me.

My third grade teacher was every bit as good as Miss Kay and Miss Smith had been. Her name was Mrs. Marr, and I felt truly fortunate to have her. As with Miss Smith for the second grade, I had heard that you definitely didn't want Mrs. Starnes for the third grade. Since I'd learned a lesson about listening to such warnings, I hadn't given that too much thought until the first day of class when I was somewhat relieved to find my name on Mrs. Marr's door. As the year went by I heard complaints from some of my friends who were in Mrs. Starnes's room that she was not very nice, and it seemed to me that I saw more than a few students from that class standing punishment in the hallway. Hearing and observing these things, I became even more appreciative that Mrs. Marr was my teacher.

One of my most outstanding third grade memories took place just before Christmas vacation began. Our teachers passed out to all of us mimeographed sheets of paper, smelling fresh of mimeograph fluid and containing the words of several Christmas songs. Then all the students in school were herded out of their rooms and into the common areas where the hallways and stairwells were soon completely packed with kids. Mrs. Crook, our music teacher, then led everyone through several Christmas songs a cappella. I thought it was marvelous, maybe the best music I'd ever heard. To me, all the kids' voices bounding around in those hallways were sweeter than Bing Crosby singing *White Christmas* on the radio, only a hundred times better. Those Christmas sings only took place during my third and fourth grade years, maybe that's as long as Mrs. Crook was there, I don't know, but being an enthusiastic participant and hearing those Christmas carols reverberating throughout that old school house gave me such a wonderful feeling that my mind still returns to those hallways most every Christmas season.

Mrs. Luke, a woman who had come out of retirement to fill an unfilled teaching position, was my fourth grade teacher. Mrs. Luke was a small, older woman with white hair, a wrinkled face, and a very quiet voice. She was nice most of the time, but was the only teacher I ever had who smacked the back of your hand with a ruler if you were causing trouble. I guess I was good, or maybe I never got caught, so I never experienced the pain or the embarrassment. Others weren't so lucky.

As far as I was concerned, Mrs. Luke was every bit as competent as my first three teachers. Oh, I didn't think she made school very interesting. She never showed the enthusiasm my other teachers had shown. She was meek and soft-spoken, and I actually thought she was generally boring. Nevertheless, the year passed and I learned what I was taught. It was at the end of that year that I heard adults talking, including my parents, about how ineffective her teaching had been, and in their opinion she never should have been called out of retirement. What brought this talk on I don't know. What does a nine-year-old know about a teacher's abilities anyway? From all the talk, I came to think of that fourth grade year as something of a loss, even though I spent no time worrying about it. That was Mrs. Luke's first and last year out of retirement.

The one positive that did come from Mrs. Luke's class was that in the spring of that year our class won the best attendance contest. As a reward, after recess one afternoon, we were given the remainder of the day off to celebrate on the playground. Our class was out there all by itself, a weird feeling not to have the playground full of kids, and we were provided refreshments. A table was set up in the schoolyard right outside the cafeteria door, and on it was a large bowl to hold orange juice. The orange juice was poured from large cans into the bowl, and then water was added to it. That might not sound like much of a treat today. So simple, what's the big deal? Well, unbelievably, that was one of the best treats I'd experienced. I hadn't tasted anything like it. I'd never had orange juice from concentrate before; I think it might have been something new at the time. I'd probably never had any kind of orange juice at all more than half a dozen times in my whole life. But here it was, sweet and cold, and in a bowl with a ladle, with no limit on how much you could have. I know I drank at least a quart of orange juice that afternoon and would have drunk more if that bowl hadn't run dry.

At the end of my fourth grade year, Mr. Johnson, the school principal, who by the way was our neighbor living catty-corner across Pearl Street, asked me if I wanted to be a patrol boy the next year. I replied that I'd already been thinking about it and was going to ask him if I could be one. He said we must have been thinking alike, then began to rummage around in his desk drawer until he found a patrol boy pin that said "Lieutenant" on it. He handed it to me. Lieutenant! Wow, was I ever impressed with myself.

He also told me that another boy had been given the "Captain" pin. I figured that made me second in command until a couple of months into the fifth grade when I asked Mr. Johnson about posting patrol boys at the doors to open them for the kids on rainy days. He just looked at me like that was a silly question and said, "That's up to you, you're the Lieutenant aren't you?" I was a little surprised he put it that way. Hadn't he remembered that he had a Captain? Yet, I hadn't seen the boy with the Captain's pin doing much of the patrol boy duties and wondered if he even knew he was the Captain. To be honest, I was a little unhappy about that and wanted to tell Mr. Johnson that he ought to get the Captain pin back and give it to me. But I didn't say anything, and simply settled for the fact that, even though my pin said "Lieutenant", I was the real "boss" of the patrol boys.

I was issued a yellow rain slicker with hood attached and a patrol boy belt to wear across my chest. I'd never had a raincoat before, and wearing that rain slicker on a rainy day was very pleasing to me. Not only did it make me stand out as one of the patrol boys, but it made me feel snug and cozy, so much so that I began to love walking to school on rainy days. That may be one reason I like taking walks in the rain to this day, without the yellow slicker of course.

The patrol boys' jobs were to man the four corners of the school block when kids were either coming to or leaving school. We told the students when they could cross the street and when they had to wait. I took my job seriously and seldom missed a morning or an afternoon. One of the privileges of being a patrol boy was getting out of class about five minutes ahead of the other kids so you could be at your post by the time school let out. It wasn't much, but I felt it was a worthwhile reward.

That patrol boy year was my fifth and final year in the grade school building. Both of the fifth grade classes were in the basement, along with the audio/visual room and the restrooms. There was also an enclosed-ramp hallway leading from the basement to the cafeteria, which was in a newer separate building. During my first grade year, there was no separate cafeteria; the lunchroom was in the basement of the school. I barely remember it because I don't recall ever eating there. Throughout most of my school years, living just a block from both schools, I went home for lunch. Mom would have lunch ready for me, sometimes eating with me and sometimes not, depending on the schedules of my younger siblings. Often times I would eat lunch while Mom ironed clothes and listened to her radio soap-opera called, "Our Gal Sunday." All 1 remember about that show was its ending, when the announcer said in a soft voice, "So listen in again tomorrow to find out what happens...." At this point the announcer would always pause and change the tone and rhythm of his voice to emphasize the words, "...to our gal Sunday."

As I got older, I did get to the cafeteria occasionally, at least often enough to appreciate my favorite lunch of chili served with peanut butter sandwiches. To this day, I have to eat peanut butter on crackers with my chili. I never ate a meal at the cafeteria that I didn't like. On the other hand, I hardly ever ate a meal anywhere that I didn't like. That's why I was such a fat kid from about the fourth grade on, at least until my junior year in high school when I finally began to grow up more than out. To me the cafeteria itself was a happy place to eat. We sat at long tables with bench seats surrounded by walls painted in large, colorful, school-themed murals that I'm pretty sure were painted by some talented high school students.

Whether I ate at home or at school, if I hurried through lunch I could be back out on the playground for 20 minutes of playtime before the bell rang. That was the longest stretch of time each day that I could be on the playground, since we only got 15-minute recesses in the morning and afternoon. It was usually during this long lunchtime break that we headed out to the grassy field just north of the school, the land where part of the new school sits today. It was the only area of the playground that was all empty space, and it was just right for Red Rover, or baseball, or football, or tag. I didn't play baseball, but I liked Red Rover and football, so that's what I did.

In Red Rover, two teams formed lines about 50-feet apart with the members of each team locking arms to form a solid wall of bodies. There was no choosing sides, you just eyeballed the groups so that the numbers were close to even, and kids could join or leave as they pleased. Someone from one team would then yell over to the other team, "Red Rover, Red Rover send Bobby Dean (or whoever) over," at which time I would run as fast as my little legs would carry me and try to crash through the locked arms of the other team. If you broke through, then you got to take a member of that team back to your team. It was then your turn to issue the challenge to the opposite team by again yelling, "Red Rover, Red Rover send so-and-so over." If you didn't break through the line, then you had to join the new team. Supposedly, the team with the most players at the end of a period of time, usually when the recess bell rang, was the winner. However, I never paid much attention to that. To me the whole point of the game was breaking through the other team's line or holding someone from breaking through my line. Both suited me just fine.

I liked Red Rover for the rough and tumble aspects of it. I suppose that's why I liked football too. We didn't get to play football very often, but when we did, I was always in the thick of it. Except for the fact that I liked playing the rougher games, I was a pretty gentle kid. That is, I tried not to give anyone much trouble, and in return, I didn't expect them to give me any. In all my school years, I can only recall actually getting physical with someone one time.

Like any schoolyard, there were always a few bullies around, and it was just my good fortune to have had run-ins with only one of them. He really wasn't much of a bully, at least to me, but he had a way of picking at me just enough that I tried to avoid him. He was a year behind me, but was probably six inches taller. I say he was a bully because I knew that he caused other kids problems too, and I knew that quite a few of my classmates didn't like him. Today I can't even tell you what it was that he used to do to me. Maybe he shoved me a few times for no reason. He might have tripped me a time or two, I don't know. He never really harmed me in any way, but over several months' time, his picking at me started to make me angry. One day I guess I'd had enough, and when he bumped into me, I knocked him flat to the ground, jumped on him, and raised my fist to slug him in the face. Then I looked at him. Although he was holding his arms up to protect himself, I could still see his face. What I saw was that he was shocked. It was in that instant that I knew he had no idea why I'd knocked him down. He had no idea that he was a bully and that half the schoolyard was afraid of him. He was just being who he was. It was enough to keep me from actually hitting him when I had the chance, and I was glad I didn't. I guess we came to an understanding that day because he never bothered me again. And as the years have gone by, even to this day, when we see each other we speak as old friends.

I had my first male teacher when I was in the fifth grade, and I thought he was a super teacher. But as much as I liked him, there was a problem that bothered me for some time. The first semester was half over before I decided whether he was one of the good guys or one of the bad guys, and here's why. His name was Mr. Porter. That's all, just Mr. Porter. The first names of my teachers had never been important. Actually, some of them hadn't even registered. They were Miss Kay, Miss Smith, Mrs. Marr, Mrs. Luke and Mr. Porter. So it came as a shock to me a few weeks into my fifth year when I heard one of the other teachers call Mr. Porter by a name that was synonymous with pure evil. "Comrade"! That's what the teacher had called him. "Comrade"! Right to his face. And he had responded as if it was the most natural thing in the world.

It didn't exactly upset me, but it did set my mind to wondering. It just didn't seem right that he was being called Comrade. In those days, there was a complex of nations, namely the USSR, China, and North Korea who all rallied around a doctrine of communism. They also threatened, almost daily, to wipe America from the face of the earth. This struggle between east and west was generally known as the "cold war", and television fed America a heavy dose of this worldwide drama through their evening newscasts. On top of that, there was one TV show in particular that made the struggle personal, and was the harbinger of spy shows to follow, shows like "I Spy" and "Mission Impossible". It was a weekly show called "I Lead

Three Lives" and was touted as the true story of a real FBI spy named Herbert Philbrick who had infiltrated a communist cell here in the United States and was reporting back to the FBI. We'd only had a television for less than a year, and I'd seen the show several times and was thoroughly enthralled by it.

Being too young to be interested in the nightly news, "I Led Three Lives" was my single source for just how nasty and devious the communists were. It was where I learned that they were evil through-and-through and would stop at nothing to bring down the United States. I also learned that there was one simple way of sorting out the good guys from the bad. The bad guys invariably, and stupidly in my opinion because it always gave them away, referred to each other as "Comrade."

So, you see why I was concerned. Here was my teacher, a guy I really liked, being called something so evil. I let it slide the first time I heard it, but after hearing him called that another time or two, I had to tell someone. I told my mom. She laughed of course, and so did I when she told me that Mr. Porter's first name was Conrad, a name I'd never heard before.

One of the few times I embarrassed myself in school was in Mr. Porter's class. It must have been while we were studying science, because he had asked a question concerning the production of gas. Several hands shot up, including mine, but to my dismay someone else was called on to answer. When the answer was given, even though I hadn't said a word, I turned about three shades of red. It was because after hearing the answer, "the refining of oil," that I realized my confident answer of "beans" would have made me the laughing-stock of the entire school. For many years after, I thanked my lucky stars that Mr. Porter hadn't called on me that day.

I loved those first five years of school. They were years filled with joyous moments, and for the most part, youthful innocence. Naturally, as those years passed, they did become less and less innocent. A case in point—as I walked to school one morning when I was in the second grade, the patrol boy posted at the corner of Sixth and Pearl held up his middle finger and asked, "Hey kid, you know what this means?" Since I'd never seen it before, I told him no, I didn't know what it meant. I could tell he was quite proud of himself to be the first to inform me of what the sign stood for, but still I had no idea what he was talking about. Not only had I never seen the middle finger raised, I'd never heard the word he told me it represented. However, I did get the idea that it wasn't nice and I probably shouldn't repeat it.

The point is, when I started the first grade I hadn't even heard the word spoken. It was a word that I would soon realize was forbidden to say, at least in front of my parents or any other adults. But by the end of the fifth grade, I'd heard many of the bad words, had heard jokes with the words in them, had repeated the jokes to whatever kid would listen, and had laughed long and hard at the jokes, even though I had little knowledge of some of their real meanings. What was important was that the jokes had "bad" words in them, and saying them out loud to your friends somehow made you feel a little bit older, made you feel like one of the guys.

At the end of the fifth grade, now armed with the basic three "R's" and a few swear words, I was ready to head off to a new school just two blocks west, the school where the big kids went. And in the fall of 1954, I did just that as I entered the sixth grade.

# Chapter 4

# *High School*

As sixth graders, even though we were now in the same school building with the junior high and high school students who passed from class to class and had multiple teachers, we were still confined to one room and one teacher. My teacher was Lois Johnson, wife of the grade school principal, the one who made me the lieutenant patrol boy, and also my across-the-street neighbor.

The biggest change between those first five years in the elementary school building and moving to the high school building was that we lost the number one privilege that defined us as grade schoolers, a privilege we had so innocently taken for granted during all those grade school years, and the one thing that would never be given back to us. Sadly, we lost our recesses. And in my book, losing your recess was most definitely the sixth grader's number one rite of passage. So even though I was classified an elementary student, I knew my grade school days were over, and soon I began to feel a certain amount of pride in being able to attend the school where the big kids went.

I thought Lois Johnson was a good enough teacher. And as far as academics were concerned, I suppose I was probably right. She taught, I learned. But I was one of the lucky ones. Well, most of us were lucky, but at the time I never really considered the fact that there was at least one kid in the class who wasn't so lucky. Her name was Elizabeth, and Elizabeth had the bad luck to be poor and ill kept. She mostly wore clothes that looked like second and third generation hand-me-downs, ones that seldom fit her well. Her hair was not always combed, and she usually had little wads of used Kleenex either on her desk or in her hand. Looking back, I think she often had a runny nose, thus the Kleenex. Most of us thought of Elizabeth as not very clean and knew that if there was anyone who ever had "cooties", it must be Elizabeth. But the unluckiest thing for Elizabeth in her sixth grade year was that she had the misfortune of getting Mrs. Johnson as her teacher.

Mrs. Johnson had a system for encouraging good performance. Sometimes if you performed well in class or on a test, and you were one of the lucky ones, she would reward you by dipping a spoon into a can of peanuts and placing one peanut on your desk. Of course, it was not only a great treat, but also a great honor to be one of those chosen for a peanut. On the other hand, if you misbehaved or didn't perform as you were expected, you might well find yourself being quietly punished. She had several little tricks she could pull on you, most of which had to do with humiliation. But the most severe of these was always the same. If you were bad, really bad, you had to go sit side by side with Elizabeth at her little desk. And I can tell you, no one wanted to sit next to Elizabeth. In reality, this was a threat much more often than it was a true consequence, because once Mrs. Johnson threatened you with sitting with Elizabeth, you began to beg for your life.

I never had to sit with Elizabeth. I never caught her "cooties" or had to touch one of her wadded up Kleenexes. And until many years later, I never considered the suffering Elizabeth must have endured at the hands of that horrible teacher. I recently looked back at a yearbook and found that Elizabeth was no longer a member of our class in the seventh grade, so I suppose she moved away. Of course, now I'm sorry that I ever thought badly of Elizabeth or mistreated her. I never thought that I'd ever bullied anyone in my entire life, but just being a part of that sixth grade class and protesting at having to sit next to her was certainly the work of a bully. And the fact that the whole class did it, including and even instigated by the teacher, was inexcusable. If you're out there Elizabeth, I'm terribly sorry, and I hope we didn't hurt you beyond healing.

## Old Gym

The high school building was a two-story brick structure situated at the corner of Pearl and Fifth. It had two floors of classrooms, including the principal's office and a large study hall/library on the top floor. The chemistry/physics lab, music room, and sixth grade classrooms were on the bottom floor. On that level there was also a large, old gymnasium that, by the time I arrived in 1954, was no longer used as a gym. The "old gym", as we referred to it, the gym where my dad was a starter for the Covington basketball teams of 1932 and 1933, had a good-size stage with real cloth curtains that opened and closed at the pull of a rope. Off to the side of the stage were a couple of small dressing rooms. All the walls behind the stage were covered in graffiti, with mostly the names of kids who had used the stage for one event or another. By the time I graduated, my name was up there a couple of times. The old gym was used for the Spring Show, class plays, concerts, convocations, dances, after-prom parties, and as a recreation area and hangout during the school day lunch hours. For a few years, until a new cement-block building was erected between the high school and the new gym, part of the old gym was also used for the wood-shop classes. A spanking new and much bigger gym had been built and opened in the block just north of the high school a couple of years before I started attending high school, and that's where the PE classes were held and the basketball games were played. The new gym also had dressing rooms and a couple of business-class classrooms.

It was during my seventh grade year that my social life began to take on new dimensions. Previous to that year, I'd had little social contact with my classmates. Except for the normal exchanges that took place during the school days, a handful of birthday parties over the first six years, and the kids who were in my church's junior choir, I hadn't been around the kids in my class outside of school. With the exception of Bob Dicks, who was in my Boy Scout troop, I wouldn't have considered any of my classmates my real friends. That title was reserved for the neighborhood kids that I played with every day.

But sometime during my seventh grade year something new and exciting came along that began to change all of that. They may not have been anything new, really. As far as I know, they could have been around when my Dad and my aunts attended Covington High in the 1920's and 30's. What I do know is that many of my classmates and I discovered them at the same time, and they soon became our excuse to come together, have fun, and get to know each other outside of the classroom. These marvelous little events were commonly called sock-hops.

Sock-hops took place in the old gym and were held fairly often, especially after sporting events such as football or basketball games. A new genre of music was just emerging, a sound that grabbed us kids, shook us up, then set our feet to dancing. It was called rock-n-roll, a name that I always thought fit perfectly, and featured groups like Bill Haley and His Comets, Bo Diddley, Little Richard, The Platters, and any number of Doo-Wop groups. WLS radio had just switched from a country station to rock-n-roll, and Elvis was just around the corner. We had a small record player at home, and the first 45-rpm record I ever bought was a song called Lollipop by The Chordettes. I wore that record out listening to it. When the movie *Rock Around the Clock* came out in 1956, I thought it was the best movie I'd ever seen. I could barely contain myself as I watched and absorbed all that rock-n-roll up there on the Lyric's movie screen. It made me want to get up and dance in the aisles.

I guess I had the rhythm, even if I didn't have a girl to dance with. At that time in my life, and for most of my high school years, I was usually too shy to ask a girl to dance with me. I think at that time most of the boys in the class were. Thankfully, that problem was solved with the discovery of what we called the "circle dance." No one had to ask anyone else to dance in a circle dance, you just joined the circle and you were in. Many popular singing groups were creating dances to go with their songs during that time. The Twist, the Mashed Potato, and the Stroll were some of the most popular. If you didn't know how to do them, you could always watch *American Bandstand* to see how the kids in Philadelphia were dancing them. With the circle dance, any number of my classmates would form a circle, then we'd begin to sway and move with the music. There were no set steps, we each danced to our own beat and took whatever steps moved us. Then one at a time, any of us who had the urge would go to the middle of the circle and do a solo while everyone in the circle clapped and yelled encouragement. I loved taking my turn in the middle while everyone around me twisted or mashed or jumped up and down and yelled, "Go Fatman, GO!" I was in heaven.

When I told Mom about how much fun I had at these dances, I could see that she was a bit hurt that the kids called me Fatman. It had never occurred to me that it was anything but part of the fun, and I explained to her that it only happened on the dance floor, and it made me feel special. I told her that "Fatman" was actually a term of endearment, a name that seemed to fit the bill perfectly, and a name that was for me alone. I was fat, I was funny, I could dance, and the kids liked me. In the end, I think Mom understood.

Throughout the six years spent at the high school, I attended many sock-hops in that old gym. By my freshman year the circle dances were becoming too juvenile for up-and-coming high-schoolers, and they soon gave way to mostly hanging out, or if I got brave enough, I might ask a girl to dance. As much as I liked those great getting-to-know-my-classmates dances of my junior high years, I'd have to say that the dances of my senior year of high school were a close comparison.

That's because they were held after each home football game, a game that I had played in. A game where I had given my all, had gotten dirty and bruised, had blocked and tackled well, had been cheered on by my family, friends, cheerleaders, and a boisterous rooting section. I had done myself proud, and along with my fellow seniors, Bob Dicks, Ken Tuggle, Jay Paxton, John Smith, and Mike Morgan, all sporting our new "C" jackets and thinking nothing in the world could be quite as cool as we were, we stood along the dance floor basking in glory.

To top it all off, by my senior year I had a girlfriend. And not just any girlfriend, but a girlfriend who I considered to be one of, if not THE best looking girl in the entire school. Alinda was a sophomore that year, and we had been dating for about three months when my senior year football season started. Walking onto the dance floor after a football game and seeing her waiting for me across the gym was something special. Then holding her in my arms as we did a slow dance to Brenda Lee or Dion and the Belmonts, was nothing less than a rush.

One annual dance that had nothing to do with football or basketball was called the Sadie Hawkins dance. Unlike the customary protocol of a boy asking a girl on a date, for the Sadie Hawkins dance the girl was supposed to ask the boy out. Alinda asked me, of course, and I gladly accepted. What I didn't know was that you were encouraged to dress up like hillbillies. On the evening of the dance, Alinda came by my house dressed in the outfit she had made for herself, and handed me the outfit she had made for me. That may have been the first moment I realized that she was serious about our dressing up, and I was absolutely mortified at the idea. It actually upset my stomach to think that I was going to walk into that dance looking like an idiot. So we hemmed and hawed for awhile about whether I was going to put on that outfit and go to the dance or not. Finally, still grumbling, I acquiesced and put it on. The outfit, which Mom had given Alinda, was one of my old shirts that Alinda had sewn a patch on and an old pair of my trousers that she had cut off to look like high-waters. They were held up by a pair of suspenders. Still pouting about the humiliation I knew I was in for, when we arrived at the school Alinda had to drag me in. I got over my discomfort soon enough though when I saw that I wasn't the only fool in the gym, and the night actually ended on a good note. As it turned out, Alinda and I were crowned

Li'l Abner and Daisy Mae. The moment of our crowning was captured on film and became one of the published snapshots in Alinda's high school yearbook. For such a worrisome start, I'll have to say we looked pretty happy in that snapshot.

It was also in the old gym during my high school years that a Covington women's civic group, The Coffenians, began holding after-prom parties. These were really fun events and offered prom kids an alternative to the old standard post-prom activities that often included drinking and carousing. I thought the Coffenians after-prom party was lavish by Covington's standards. Decorated around a theme, it offered dancing, games, food, refreshments, and some extraordinarily nice door prizes, all for free. Over the years, the after-prom began rivaling the prom itself in fun and entertainment. My senior year I took Alinda to the prom and one of the first after-prom parties. She reciprocated her junior and senior years by taking me.

## Football

The proud "C" jacket that I wore to most of the senior year sock-hops had to be earned by playing a sport. To me that was no problem. I loved playing football and played it from my junior high years on. I was too big and too slow to play one of the star positions, but I thought I made a pretty decent center on offense and a good down lineman and linebacker on defense. I was very proud of my team during my senior season and as it turned out, we had a pretty good year.

As a kid in grade school, I loved nothing better than riding my bike down to the football field, which at that time was on the east edge of the city park, and watching the high school team practice. Some days I'd sit there a full two hours watching them. I watched guys like George Edwards, Gale

Galloway, Pete Fleming, George Copsy, Phil Gritten, Reno Crummin, and many others whom I looked up to run drills and practice plays. And I was in awe of the passion they displayed when they hit, blocked, and tackled each other. Those guys became my heroes. I remember one practice in particular when one of Ray Ferguson's teammates came down on top of him, cleats first, causing Ray's leg to bleed profusely. What was so memorable was that I couldn't believe Ray didn't cry, not even a whimper. Wow! Those guys were tough. And I wanted to grow up to be just like them. I suppose maybe I came pretty close.

When my chance finally came, I soon discovered that those August practices were not fun. I'm pretty sure I vomited the first practice of every season. This was in those years when the coaches toughened you up by denying you any water and giving you no breaks, no matter what the temperature. All the football coaches I ever had spouted the same mantra, one they repeated over and over, and it went something like this, "If you can get through two practices a day in 90 degree heat and 90% humidity with no water and no let-up, then those night games will be a breeze." I think they were right in that respect, the games were easier, by far. And if coach Sells saw that we were slacking in practice, he'd point to the marching band, which was practicing across the road, and yell at us, "If it's too tough for you over here, then go on over there and join Cramer's band with the rest of the sissies."

Even though I played each year from the seventh grade on, and loved each and every game, the real payoff didn't come until my senior year. Starting with practice in mid-August 1960, we seniors were in high spirits. Between morning and afternoon practice, a carload of us would head up to the Dog 'n Suds in Mike Morgan's car while the radio blasted away and we all sang along to "Running Bear" or "Hey Mr. Custer, I Don't Wanna Go." The Dog 'n Suds had been opened a few years earlier by Russell and Alice Bowers. Located on the east end of Liberty, it offered curb service and dished up the typical hot-dog-stand type of food. When we got there, if I could afford it, I'd get a quart carton of ice-cold root beer, a Coney dog, and a Pillsbury-like biscuit that was deep-fried, covered in powdered sugar, and dubbed a "sugar ring." Then we'd hang out, waiting for afternoon practice, knowing we were the cream of the crop and definitely hot stuff. We were seniors, and it was our turn to be the leaders, the starters, the best.

There were three games my senior year that left a lasting impression on me. One was, of course, the Perrysville game which I mentioned elsewhere, the game that I wanted to punch my teammate Jay Paxton for fumbling the football. That game was played at Perrysville, and we lost 13 to 6. Another memorable game was played against Veedersburg on their field. Veedersburg had already beaten us on our own field a month earlier, so we were really up for this one. We knew if we wanted any part of the Wabash Valley conference championship we had to win this game. It turned out to be the toughest game I ever played in. Across from me on Veedersburg's defensive line was a kid named Booe, who must have outweighed me by 100 pounds. He was so huge I simply bounced off him. But even though I couldn't move him, I discovered if I could get myself between him and my ball carrier, he was too slow to make the tackle. By the end of the game, I was hurting from head to toe and felt like I'd been in a battle with a small tank. But it had been worth it. We beat Veedersburg that night by a touchdown. Their coach was fighting mad about it too, and as we ran off the field at the end of the game he let go in a rage, yelling at Coach Sells and our whole team that we'd played way above our heads that night and by all rights his team should have won.

My third memorable game that year took place the night of our homecoming, and a truly miserable night for football it was. It had been raining all day, and at game time there was no sign of a letup. Had it been a drizzle it would have been okay, but it wasn't. It was a downpour. Of course, we wanted to have our parade of floats, the band performance, and the homecoming queen coronation at halftime. It was tradition. But with the weather as it was, all of that would have to be cancelled. When we arrived at the north end of the football field coach Sells told us to wait on the bus rather than our usual procedure of getting out onto the field for warm-ups. Our opponent, New Market, hadn't yet arrived. Coach Sells told us that when they got there he was going to ask their coach if we could possibly postpone the game until tomorrow afternoon, Saturday, so that our school and fans could enjoy the homecoming festivities.

A few minutes later their bus pulled up beside ours. Coach walked over to the New Market bus, and not a minute later, we heard a loud chant go up from their bus—"chicken shits, chicken shits, chicken shits!" Coach Sells came back hopping mad and told us we were playing tonight. The rain never stopped that night. The field had puddles of water four inches deep in spots, but it didn't matter. We were on a mission. They had denied us our homecoming fun and had called us chicken shits besides.

Lenny Smail was one of the refs that night, and as he carried the football to the tee for our sixth or seventh kickoff, he turned to Tom Hoagland and me and said, "Boys, this game is getting a little boring." We beat New Market 56-0, and I was extremely proud of my team that night.

# Classroom

As pleasurable and memorable as football and sock-hops were during my high school years, of course it was the classroom that consumed most of my time. And rightly so. What I learned there would be the key to my future. But what does a kid know about his future? Until I was faced with it, like, "Hey I'm going to graduate. Now what?" I didn't exactly dwell on what I had to do to prepare myself. The fact that I never, not one single time that I can recall, brought a book home to study attests to the idea that I was a lazy student and was willing to get by with B's and C's. I was able to get my assignments and studying done either in class or during study hall (it wouldn't be until my second year of college, after having been put on academic probation, that I finally learned to study). That being said, however, at the end of my senior year of high school, I was still classified an above-average student. That is, I was above average in a class of 65 students, many of whom were kids who never had a thought of going on to college. So it was not necessarily a grand achievement. I don't recall my ranking at graduation, but I was in the top quarter of my class. Whatever it was, I remember that I felt fairly good about myself.

Since I was not a brain, was lazy about my studies, and basically put in a minimum amount of effort on my schoolwork, it's amazing that I was ever accepted into Purdue's School of Pharmacy. And looking back now, with eyes wide open, I think I have to give a great deal of credit to Covington High School and its faculty for what learning I did absorb.

After moving to the high school in the sixth grade, where we spent the entire day in one classroom, in junior high we switched classes once or twice a day, most of them taking place in the same two rooms and taught by a couple of teachers. The most memorable of my junior high teachers was a short, white haired, bespectacled part-time minister by the name of George Beatty. Mr. Beatty was my homeroom teacher and also my English and literature teacher. In two years of Mr. Beatty's classes, I remember quite distinctly learning about the evils of dangling participles and double negatives. Oh, I know I learned tons more, but for the life of me those are about the only two bits of information from George Beatty's English classes that stuck in my mind. He harped on those two things incessantly. One problem was that Mr. Beatty was much too nice. He was so nice he had no control of his classes, and did we ever take advantage of that. His classroom was a madhouse on almost any and every given day of the school year. Instead of George Beatty we began referring to him as Clyde, as in Clyde Beatty the then world-famous Barnum and Bailey lion tamer. It fit the bill perfectly for his classes often became as loud, unpredictable, and entertaining as a three-ring circus.

Mr. Beatty was just one, albeit the first, of many memorable teachers at Covington High. There were three standouts that I felt I truly learned a lot from. Number one on my list of excellent teachers was my algebra teacher, Mr. McCormick. In those days you were taught absolutely no algebra until you were in high school, and then only if you were taking the college-prep curriculum or took it as an elective. So I entered Mr. McCormick's class never having been exposed to anything even as simple as $2X=4$. After three semesters with Mr. McCormick, I was prepared for any algebra that would ever be thrown at me, and in the coming years, first studying pharmacy at Purdue and later as I practiced it as a profession, the use of algebra would become a daily experience. Mr. McCormick had prepared me well. If you're still out there Mr. McCormick, thanks.

Mr. Bob Buser was my American History teacher. This was before he became the high school principal. It was easy to study for Mr. Buser's tests because he wrote everything he wanted you to know on the blackboard. You basically just had to copy down what he wrote and go over your notes before the tests. But what really made his class special was that as he wrote it down, he also told us the story of America as if he were reading a great novel. And I, for one, listened to him as if he were telling ghost stories around a campfire. I'd been taught history all through my school years, often disguised as social studies or geography, but I had never found any of it to be the least bit interesting. With Mr. Buser, I was eager for his next class so that the story could continue. A few years later, he became the high school principal. I didn't care much for him as a principal. I thought he was overly stringent and, to my great surprise, standoffish, nothing like his teaching days. But I couldn't have asked for a better history teacher.

The third teacher that comes to mind as outstanding was an older teacher named Sara Schwin. Miss Schwin taught business classes, courses taken by many of the high school girls but very few of the boys, with the exception of typing. And it was typing that she taught me. Miss Schwin was nice and always helpful. I don't ever recall her raising her voice to anyone, and she always had a cheerful demeanor. But those things had nothing to do with her teaching ability. The reason I thought she was an exceptional teacher is the same reason I thought Mr. McCormick was so good. When I started her class, I'd never even tried to hunt-and-peck, let alone actually type. And by the time I finished her class at the end of the year, I was probably typing 60 words a minute. With nearly unreadable handwriting, even by myself after it has sat for an hour, learning to use a typewriter was a true blessing bestowed upon me by the fine teaching of Miss Schwin.

Those were good subjects for me because I had good teachers, and I learned easily from them. Then there were a couple of classes that, through no fault of the teachers, didn't turn out so well. One of them was a required math class for those enrolled in the scholastic curriculum. The course was geometry, and it was taught to us by Mr. Don White. Now here was a case of the teacher being in a bind from the very beginning because our textbooks hadn't arrived. They didn't arrive until a month after class began. This was not a good thing for Mr. White or for me. He tried his best to teach us with handouts and blackboard instructions, but it just didn't work out well, at least for me. Maybe I needed that textbook; but most likely I just needed a kick in the rear. In any case, I ended up getting a C from Mr. White and was happy to have it.

Mrs. Cooper taught me Latin. She was older, a waif of a lady with white hair, and lacking what I would call any semblance of a personality. It was my junior year, and someone had misinformed me that since I was thinking of going to pharmacy school, maybe I should take Latin. I signed up. It was a mistake. It was without question the worst class I ever took in my beloved Covington High School. The teacher probably did her best, but a combination of my complete lack of interest, coupled with the fact that I never once took a book home to study, it became the nightmare class of my high school years. I barely passed, ending up with a D if I recall correctly, and I believe that was only out of the goodness of that good lady's heart. As it turned out, I never needed a word of Latin for my college degree.

By the time I reached high school, Harrell H. Johnson had gone from being the grade school principal to the high school chemistry teacher. This was the same man who lived across the street from us, who was married to my sixth grade teacher, and who was nicknamed Red because of his dark-red, wavy hair. He looked to me to be the redheaded brother of Arthur Godfrey, a radio and television personality of that era. I'm not sure how good Mr. Johnson was as a chemistry teacher, but I'll have to say that after three semesters of his classes, I seemed to be fairly-well prepared when I got to college.

Other than George Beatty who taught junior high, of all my high school teachers, Mr. Johnson was probably the only one I would consider to be a genuine character. I don't recall the little quirks of most of my teachers, but Mr. Johnson was an exception. The first thing I remember was that you never ever wanted him in your face because he had a serious case of halitosis. It was so bad that you did whatever was necessary to keep him at arms length, if not further. His first and middle names were something like Harrell Harel, but he was always simply listed as H. H. Johnson. It was only natural for us to dub him Halitosis Harrell.

Mr. Johnson had a most memorable way of making a point, and he used it often. While explaining whatever fact he was teaching, usually while writing it on the blackboard, he'd turn his head to look one of us squarely in the eyes. Then he'd scrunch up his face with a smile, wink his left eye, shake his curly red head from side to side, tap the chalk loudly on the blackboard, and say in his slow drawn-out voice, "And don't never fergit it!"

The crowning jewel of his class, a topic of conversation for the entire year, was what was in store for us at our final lab exam. He began warning us about it on the first day of school and reminded us of it over and over again throughout the year. He made it sound like the toughest exam we'd ever have to face in our lives, and in fact had many of us, me included, more than a little apprehensive. This exam was to consist of identifying an unknown chemical solution, one that he would provide to each of us in the last week of school. To keep us honest, none of us would be given the same substance. The deal was, if we identified it correctly, we would receive an A for the exam, but if we got it wrong we would have to keep trying. The real kicker here was that you had to keep trying until you got it right, even if it meant coming back to the lab during summer vacation. That was what scared us. It wouldn't have been so bad if he'd just give us an F for getting it wrong, but that wasn't an option, you had to work on it until you got it right. About the middle of the year, he added a new wrinkle. He started going on and on about how the front yard of his home, which was a block from the school, would be available for camping until you got your substance identified.

I thought he was kidding about the camping part. I lived across the street from him and had never noticed anyone camping in his front yard before. On the other hand, I wasn't altogether sure. He made it sound serious, and we were all nervous about it. One thing was for sure, I wanted to get that stuff identified as soon as possible so I wouldn't have to worry about spending the summer at school. Even later in the year, he shook us up a bit more when he told us about the kid he gave pure water to one year, and it took him all summer to realize there was nothing in it. That really had me worried.

In the end all the fear was for naught. During the year we'd learned how to identify a few chemicals by doing some simple tests, like using litmus paper or holding the substance over a flame and watching the change of color. When the end of the year came around and the eventful day finally arrived, I identified my substance right away when I dipped the rod into my mystery solution, held it over the Bunsen burner and watched the flame burn yellow. I had sodium. As I looked around, I saw that Mr. Johnson was right there going from table to table giving hints and pretty much telling those who were stumped what test they should run. By the end of the period, everyone had identified their substance. No one had to spend the summer camping in Mr. Johnson's front yard. It had been little more than a harmless ruse all along, but it was one of the things that made Mr. Johnson one memorable teacher.

I had coaches for a few of my classes, basketball coach Bill Miller and football coach John Kerr were two of them, but the memory of these two coaches and their classes have gotten buried in the sands of time. As teachers, only two coaches impressed me—Ralph Bunton and Bino Neves. I wasn't a basketball player, so I don't know anything about Ralph Bunton's coaching skills. Maybe they were lacking. After all, he had developed one of the finest basketball teams Covington ever produced, a team that ended up going deep into the state tournament long before there was a class system, a team that gave a school ten times Covington's size, and the eventual state champions, a run for their money. But it wasn't Mr. Bunton who led that team to glory, for he had been fired the previous year. However, as a teacher and driver's education instructor, I thought Ralph Bunton was a wonderful guy and certainly one of the friendliest, most even tempered teachers I ever had. For that reason alone, he was a bright spot in a group of coach/teachers that were otherwise forgettable.

The coach that most impressed me though was a little Hawaiian named Edwin "Bino" Neves. Bino, pronounced Beano, like the gas medicine, was the head football coach during my freshman year. He had me for freshman health a couple of days a week, a throwaway class at best, and PE the other three days of the week. In the health class, it wasn't his teaching ability that I remember him for. Bino was an all-around great guy and a friend to everyone. He was fun-loving and boiling over with a lust for life. As for his teaching ability, I can't say he really had any. The class was disorganized and chaotic. He didn't demand much from us, and we gave him little in return. After all, it was only health.

But we all loved Bino, and I'll have to say that we did learn a couple of very interesting things in his class. For starters, we learned to surf. Oh yeah, Bino would clear off his desk, jump on top of it, bend his knees, spread his arms, and show us the proper stances and nuances of catching a wave. Although I'd never been within 10 feet of a surfboard in my life, in fact, most of us had never even seen an ocean, I still remember Bino's advice, "Always keep your weight in front." On other days, we'd learn new football plays that he made up in his head then drew up on the blackboard. Then we'd practice the plays right there in class by wadding up notebook paper and pretending it was a football. He'd have the boys spread out all over the room.

Right out of Purdue, where he was a running back for the Boilermakers, sometimes when Bino had a health movie to show us, he'd also bring movies from his Purdue games and let us watch him score touchdowns. We all cheered and went crazy as we watched him up there on that little screen, celebrating each score by turning a flip in the end zone. It was, I'll have to say, the most fun, and at the same time, the most worthless class I ever took at Covington High.

There is more that I remember about Bino, namely that he was dark complected, strong, and very good looking. The high school girls went wild for him and the boys wished they could grow up to be just like him. The only thing that might have been lacking in Bino Neves was his height. I'd say he wasn't over 5'4" or 5'5" with his shoes on. But as he so aptly demonstrated to me one evening at a school dance, for a man of such stature he showed no fear of anything or anyone. On that particular evening, two of what I thought of as Covington's toughest kids, both of them school dropouts and long-time troublemakers that no one in their right mind would want to tangle with, got into a bloody fistfight right outside the high school door. Bino was chaperoning the dance that was going on inside the old gym and soon got wind of it. Out the door he flew, and even though both boys towered over him and outweighed him by fifty pounds each, I watched in frightened amazement as Bino dashed into the fray, grabbed both of them by the back of their necks and threw them hard up against the brick wall. He had his hands clamped to their necks so tight, neither of them moved a muscle until he finished with his tongue-lashing. Then he let them go, told them not to ever let him catch them fighting again, and sent them on their pathetic ways. Even though I'd witnessed the whole event, I could hardly believe the guts and power he demonstrated that night. He became my instant hero.

During my freshman year, one class honored Bino with their homecoming float. Every year in late September or early October, each class made a float for the homecoming game. This was often a week-long class project, and high school was dismissed early on Thursday afternoon so the classes would have time to finish their floats before all the homecoming activities the next day. On Friday, school let out an hour early again so everyone could participate in, or watch, the homecoming parade as it wound its way through town. Some years there was also a pep rally on the courthouse lawn. The parade went down Fifth Street from the high school to the downtown square then turned and came back on Fourth. Chuck Cramer's marching band led the parade with the floats, queen candidates, football players, and anyone else who wanted to support the Trojans following behind.

For me, the building of our class float was in itself a social event I looked forward to. We had plenty of farm kids in our class, so we always ended up building it on a flatbed farm trailer or some farmer's flatbed truck. It was important to keep it hidden from view and keep its whereabouts a secret lest another class discover it and do it damage before the big event.

In my class, it always seemed to be the same handful of kids who built the floats year after year, and I was one of them. I liked it. It was a fun way to spend an afternoon. We usually worked on them a few hours each night for about a week, but that was just an excuse to get together and have a good time. The serious work wasn't done until that Thursday afternoon when we got out of school. I have no doubt that we always spent more time having fun than we ever did building a float. And I think the results usually spoke to that fact. For a couple of years after finishing up our nightly work on the float, several of us jumped in Bill Huffman's car and hit the back roads looking for pumpkins to steal. I don't recall us actually finding any, but that didn't matter, it was just part of our being kids and a good reason for us to tear around town. Also, since many of the girls in my class helped build the floats, I thought it was a way to get closer to them. To my knowledge, none of them ever took notice. But that didn't really matter either. We were a pretty close group, were pretty much all friends, and had a lot of laughs.

Even though the floats usually turned out looking like they'd been put together by untrained monkeys, I liked being one of the monkeys. It was one of my few outlets for creativity. We always used chicken wire somewhere on the float because it could easily be stuffed with colored Kleenex (yes they made Kleenex in pastel colors back then). Even though there was no comparison, I don't think I could have felt any more creative had I been stuffing roses on a Rose Bowl float. The Kleenex-stuffed chicken wire could then be shaped and used to make footballs, giant Trojan helmets (we were the Covington Trojans), or boiling pots with dead Attica Red Ramblers sticking half-way out. It could also be used to make signs that were attached to the sides of the trailers or trucks. By stuffing the wire with two colors of Kleenex, we would spell out the float's theme. BURN THE BLUE DEVILS, SCALP THE INDIANS, and CLIP THE EAGLES were typical examples and have probably all been repeated many times over the past fifty years. If we were lucky, and didn't get too much rain and wind, the Kleenex would remain in place long enough for the fans to read it during the parade. If not, then it wasn't too hard to figure out what those cleats sticking out of a black and gold (Covington's colors) boiling pot was supposed to mean with or without the sign.

The float that honored Bino during my freshman year was built by the senior class. On the float itself were students dressed in grass skirts, wearing leis, and doing the Hula in honor of Bino's heritage. I'm not sure what else was on the float, but it was the sign that made the whole thing so memorable. In huge gold and black letters the sign read, "BINO – HE NO – SEE NO – DE FEET." Everyone thought it was great, talked about it for weeks, and in all the years I've witnessed Covington homecoming parades, I've not seen one better or more appropriate.

In my first years at the high school building, I also recall all the excitement that was generated by the approach of voting for a homecoming queen. I'm not sure what classes got to vote, maybe the entire high school, or maybe just the junior and senior classes. But a couple of weeks before the big event, "vote for" signs showed up painted on the sheds that lined Commercial Street between the high school and the grade school cafeteria. "Vote for Alice" or "Vote for Kay" or vote for someone else was sloppily applied to these mostly-dilapidated sheds with runny paint. The next year the previous year's sign would simply be painted over with another name. Since there was no cafeteria in the high school, and many kids walked or ran the two blocks from the high school to the grade school cafeteria at lunchtime, this was the perfect place to display these queen candidate signs.

I doubt that the sheds' owners appreciated this graffiti on their sheds, but to me these signs were very special. I looked up to these older students and couldn't wait until I was old enough to vote for homecoming queen or play varsity football myself. I was a dreamer, and I often dreamed of the day I could ride in the homecoming parade in the back of a truck with my pals, wearing my letter jacket for all to see. I dreamed of escorting one of the queen candidates to the dance. I dreamed of being one of those seniors who I looked up to with starry eyes. These signs merely fed that dream, even though they may have constituted little or no significance to anyone else. They simply became a part of my best memories.

## Lunch

Just as it was during my grade school years, during high school I went home for lunch on most days. Mom would have something simple prepared, so it was a quick eat and run. It was important to get back to school as soon as possible so I could spend a few minutes in the old gym playing ping-pong, or shuffle board, or just hanging out with my friends.

In my junior and senior years, after I began to earn more and more of my own spending money, I went home for lunch less often, preferring instead to buy lunch. For this, there were two choices. The cafeteria at the grade school was always a good option for what I considered a good meal. Their chili served with peanut butter sandwiches was still the best. The only disadvantage of going to the cafeteria was the two-block walk each way and then having to wait in line once I got there. All that added up to an extra ten to fifteen minutes out of my precious lunchtime. So I didn't often choose the cafeteria. Instead, I took the second choice by walking right across Fifth Street to what I called, "The Little Store". Over the years, it may have had other names, "The Trojan Store" being one, but since it was located just a block from my home, it was actually in my neighborhood, and my parents and I always referred to it as The Little Store. It wasn't really a grocery store like Meharry's, so I hardly ever went in there until I started attending school at the high school building, and then only after I could afford to buy my own lunches.

The Little Store had a reputation, and many teachers and school administrators frowned upon kids going there for lunch. Some of them preached on the subject. Lois Johnson, my sixth grade teacher, was the loudest among them. The main reasons for their disapproval were, first of all, that the meals were not healthy. A bag of chips, a hot dog, and a coke were the common fare, followed up by a candy bar or a Hostess pie, so I guess they were probably right. Secondly, too many of the school "hoods", kids with slicked back hair who carried their cigarettes rolled up in their shirtsleeves, hung out there. And finally, kids were allowed to smoke in there to their heart's content. The funny thing was, I rather liked the place for all those reasons.

I tasted my first cigarette when I was about 11 years old. It happened one summer night when I slept over in Fred Auter's tent, which was pitched in his back yard. Fred was about five years older than me so we weren't exactly best buddies, but we lived across the street from each other, which at least made us friendly neighbors. So until I reached high school age, I hung out at his house from time to time. Occasionally, when I saw that his tent was pitched, I'd ask if I could sleep over, and he sometimes agreed. On this particular night I watched as Fred snuck two of his dad's Raleigh cigarettes from the pack lying on top of their refrigerator before we headed for the tent.

Even though my dad was a regular smoker, up until that night I'd never had a cigarette in my mouth. I hadn't even thought of it. So when Fred handed me my cigarette and held a lighted match to its tip, I began to blow. "No!" Fred said. "You have to suck on it." Feeling stupid, I told him I knew that and began again. I didn't actually inhale that first cigarette, not a puff of it, didn't even know I was supposed to. But I did get plenty of that smoke into my mouth before blowing it back out, just as Fred was doing. That was all it took. I loved the way that smoke tasted from the very first puff. Still, it would be another four years before I started buying my own cigarettes and keeping them hidden from my folks.

So after football season of my senior year, not only was I a part-time smoker, but I had no fear of repercussions from coach Sells. I could eat lunch at The Little Store then light up with everyone else. There was a jukebox playing a constant mix of country music and the relatively new genre of music called rockabilly. The teachers were right when they said it was a hangout for the hoods; The Little Store was in their comfort zone. At the same time, it seems to me that it should have been outside of my comfort zone, after all, I didn't really go for country music, and I had no friends with greased back hair. Oh no, I was one of the class of 61's in-crowd. I was the class vice-president my freshman and senior years, a fair student, liked by my classmates, and figured to graduate and go on to college some day. What's more, my real friends would hardly step foot in the place. What was I doing hanging out at The Little Store?

In looking back, I guess that half hour I spent there a couple of times a week was just my somewhat repressed wild side breaking loose. I enjoyed the atmosphere, the music, and for that half hour anyway, the kids who went there for lunch. I liked it when the smoke from my cigarette rolled up into my half-squinted eyes as I arm-wrestled one of the hoods across a mustard-stained table. I liked listening to Guy Mitchell belt out "Singing the Blues" from the jukebox, a song, by the way, that's included in my I-Pod favorites even today.

I suppose it was a harbinger of the future, because in later life I discovered that I purely enjoyed an occasional night of beers at one of the local honky-tonks, singing karaoke, and hoping to see a knock-down-drag-out catfight—shades of those lunchtimes spent in The Little Store.

## Extracurriculars

Like most of the high schools in our area during those years, putting on junior and senior plays was as traditional as the school fight-song. I don't recall trying out for any particular part, but both years I ended up with one of the lead roles, and although the titles, plots, and characters have long been forgotten, I loved everything about them. I particularly liked the evening practices that started several weeks before the performances were to be given. These nights were a great excuse to get together and have a good time with my classmates, much more than they ever were to hone our parts. And after practice we'd head to Danville to cruise Marty K or get a game of poker together at a friend's house. As for the plays themselves, they were pretty much a waste of time for the home crowd. Presented on the stage of the old gym, the lighting was bad, the acoustics barely audible, and I would say those presentations had to have been quite excruciating for our friends and family. But boy, did we have a good time.

The other big production presented on the stage of the old gym each year was the Spring Show. However, unlike the school plays, which were forgotten as soon as the curtain closed on the last act, the Spring Show was not only fun, it was memorable. I had the good fortune to be in it two years. I liked to sing, so I'm not sure why I couldn't find time to take chorus for more than one semester out of four years of high school, but that was the case. I ended up in chorus the second semester of my junior year. Chuck Cramer was the director of all music in the high school, which meant he directed the marching band, concert band, pep band, chorus, and show choir. Not only was he was one of the nicest people I ever had the pleasure of knowing, but he was a great music teacher and a fine musician himself.

Mr. Cramer had to have been a very busy man, because all of his musical groups performed several times a year. The marching band, of course, marched at every home football game and in all Covington parades, besides participating in marching-band contests at various venues throughout the state. The pep band played at basketball games, while the concert band played for such events as graduation, besides putting on a concert for the general public once a year. All the band students also had the opportunity to perform at music contest as soloists and in ensembles. As for the chorus and choir, they performed for the general public once or twice a year, accompanied by the concert band. The chorus also participated in a newly organized choral contest, which took place at one of the schools in our area. It became an annual event.

But the big production for any kid who wanted to show off the fun side of his musical talent in front of a hometown crowd was the Spring Show. It was a variety show, more or less, and Mr. Cramer usually had a theme to work around. All the band and chorus members were encouraged to participate, and for those who did, it became a memory maker. The year I was in chorus, the theme was music from the Broadway show South Pacific. My big part was singing "Nothing Like A Dame" with a group of seven or eight guys who were dressed up in Army and Navy uniforms. Mom had helped me come up with some clothes that looked somewhat authentic, including some of Dad's old Army uniform pieces. I got the thrill of singing a one-line solo from that song, but I couldn't tell you today which line it was.

I didn't take chorus my senior year, but Mr. Cramer asked me if I'd be emcee for the Spring Show that year. The job consisted of telling a couple of jokes and introducing some of the acts, and I agreed. As it turned out, I was nervous that night, and I didn't think my jokes were all that funny. I'd chosen a couple of them from the jokes I'd read in Reader's Digest. The audience was kind however, and I did get some laughs. I especially remember the loud laughter from Larry Dicks, for which I was very grateful.

Of all the performances I saw during the several Spring Shows that I either participated in or attended, there was one act that stands out in my mind. I don't recall the year, but it was a trio of trumpeters who played a song that I fell in love with. I liked it so much that I keep an Al Hirt version of it on my MP3 player today. Mr. Cramer himself was one of the trio. The trumpet was his instrument, and he played it like a pro. My classmate, Tom Parke, the star trumpeter of the band in my senior year, was the second member of the trio. I'm not certain who the third person was and don't want to name someone in error. What they played that night was a tune called Bugler's Holiday, a song I had been intrigued with for years because it had been the introductory music to the Channel 3 evening news. On the news they only played a few bars of the song, and

I never realized there was actually much more to it. I loved hearing it played in its entirety at the Spring Show and came away feeling like I'd been given a great gift. I guess I was easily entertained.

I didn't play basketball, but like so many people in Indiana, I did thoroughly enjoy watching the game. And maybe more than the games themselves, I loved all the hoopla that surrounded them. After all, high school basketball was Indiana's great pastime; it even had a name—Hoosier Hysteria. In 1954 Covington played its first game in the new gymnasium. That wonderful new facility was the pride of Covington and a great venue to show off our proud basketball teams. When the new gym opened, it was the finest facility in a two-county area and soon began to host the state-sectional basketball tournaments. The tournament would start on Wednesday night with the championship game being played on Saturday night. On Saturday afternoon when the top four teams squared off for the right to play that night, you couldn't find an empty parking spot within three blocks of the gym. The town was virtually packed.

After the two afternoon games, all the fans from the two winners would spread out around town to find a place to eat and relax for a few hours, anxiously awaiting the championship game that evening, when the sectional winner would be crowned. I remember having a strange, maybe even haughty feeling in watching these groups of strangers wander around my town. I hoped that they would see Covington as I did and wanted them to wish that they lived here too. It was crazy I know, but I was very proud of everything Covington.

Unlike my junior year, when I worked at the grocery stores and couldn't attend all the games, in my sophomore year that wasn't the case, so I became one of the basketball team's student managers. I figured it was a way for me to see all the games free of charge and get a ride to the away games. Besides, I knew all the players, and those who were in my class I considered friends. There wasn't much to it really, mostly picking up basketballs and throwing sweaty clothes in the washing machine. It was just another fun activity and one I considered well worth it. Because of future work-related responsibilities, that was the only year I was able to be a student manager.

If you worked in the concession stand you also got in free, so during my senior year I worked many of the games alongside one of Covington's nicest, and I'm sorry to say, most maligned teachers. Her name was Sarabel Smith, and along with Fred Cates, Sarah Schwin, Madeline Snoddy, and Frank Conlin, she was a Covington High School institution. These people had all been teaching in Covington High since they were merely kids themselves, and by the time I was in high school they were all pushing into their retirement years.

Sarabel was a business teacher, and a good one at that. She must have been in her mid-fifties and, as far as I knew, had never been married. She went by Miss Smith. That is, she went by Miss Smith to her face. Behind her back, kids called her Sarabel if they were in a giving mood, but just as often they called her Sow-belly. That was because Sarabel was big, or more precisely I guess, you could say Sarabel was huge, definitely obese. She was one of those people who you might envision when you hear a person described as being as wide as they are tall. That was Sarabel. And to a bunch of thoughtless high school kids, the name Sow-belly did seem to fit. I'm sure she overheard the term used many times, I only hope I whispered it softly enough that she didn't hear it from me.

But Sarabel was nice, as nice and friendly as any teacher in the school when she was given a fair chance and not being looked upon as some anomaly to human nature. Sarbael was our class sponsor and also in charge of the concession stands at the basketball games. The profits from the concession stands went to the senior class to be used for our senior-class trip at the end of the school year. So by helping Sarabel, not only did I get into the games free, but I felt like I was doing my duty for the senior class.

About a gazillion other memorable things happened to me in high school, but many of them were simply moments, hardly worth mentioning. On the other hand, they were important enough to stick with me all these years later, so I'm going to touch on a few.

One day in Mr. Beatty's eighth-grade English class, Paul Hershberger walked up behind me and put a wad of chewed gum in my hair. Of course, I was immediately upset and was ready to have a go with Paul when he said he'd done it in reprisal for my putting the gum in his seat while he was up. I had no idea what he was talking about and soon found out that someone else had put the gum there and blamed it on me. Looking back now, I think that may have been the first time that I took a serious look at both sides of a situation, and even though a small harm was done to me, I understood why. As an adult, I still try to be fair in weighing many of life's conflicting issues.

Alinda and I went together during my senior year, and sometimes after we'd eaten lunch, we'd meet in the study hall to chat. One day she brought out a Valomilk candy bar and unwrapped it in front of me. Then she made the mistake of offering me a bite. Valomilks were, and I guess still are, fairly small round cups of marshmallow-cream-filled chocolate. To me it wasn't really more than a bite, so I put the whole thing in my mouth and quickly ate it up. I thought it was funny. She didn't. I'll never forget the look of disbelief on her face at what was probably the first time I ever really made her mad.

During my sophomore year, I don't recall her name or whom she was substituting for, but in one of my classes I had a substitute teacher who was obviously new and was going to be a push-over. In other words, she would have little control and we were all going to have our way. And we did. Except in my case, it sort of backfired, and I ended up living with it for the next three years.

After several of my classmates had given her their share of trouble I figured it was my turn. So when she asked the class a question I raised my hand. Referring to the seating chart, she called on me. "Yes Bob," she said. Before answering the question, I stepped up to the plate with my smart mouth. "My name's Bob," I said, "but I go by Deanie, and it sort of embarrasses me when you call me Bob." What made me say that particular thing, I don't know. As lame as it was, I guess it was the only thing I could come up with off the cuff. Actually, I was Robert Dean Dickinson, Jr. and went by Bob, or in my earlier years by Bobby Dean. My dad went by Dean. Deanie was the last thing in the world I'd want to be called. But when I told her I went by Deanie, she apologized for calling me Bob, and the whole class snickered. Wow, what a joke I'd pulled on her. I was so funny.

Within a day, everyone in the school had heard about how funny I was, and I'll have to say I was pretty proud of myself. The problem was, most of the school decided they would start calling me by my new, self-appointed name and, as much as I hated it, it stuck. I was Deanie for the next three years—my payoff for being such a smart-ass.

All in all, from the day I first stepped into the grade school, all the way through my senior year, my school days were filled with goodness. Oh there were things here and there I might have changed, given different circumstances. If I hadn't been so fat when I was 12 to 16 years old, I might have played basketball. If I hadn't had to work for my spending money, I may have joined in more organized activities. And if I had been taught to study and to strive for better grades, I might have been inducted into the honor society. But other than as fleeting thoughts, I never missed any of those things. I never yearned for anything I didn't or couldn't have. I was happy, and in that respect, I guess I was just one lucky guy.

Finally, in the spring of 1961, with eager anticipation for my coming college years, I graduated from Covington High School. My years spent in the Covington schools had prepared me in many ways to meet my future. I could never have asked for a better place to spend those twelve important years of my youth, and it goes without saying that the memories from those years will forever be among my dearest.

A few years after I graduated, the old buildings that had been the schools to two generations of Dickinsons finally reached their end. Within a few years of each other, they both were torn down and new ones erected to replace them. Where the old grade school sat is now the playground for the new school, and the high school's land became tennis courts for the newly established tennis teams. Later still the tennis courts became a school parking lot.

Those schools were a part of me, and oh, what I would give to make those one block walks down Pearl Street just one more time and see my old red-brick school buildings standing there in all their glory.

# Chapter 5

# *Neighborhood*

As warm and loving as my home was, I spent as much time outdoors as possible. After all, that's where the kids were. I don't think parents in Covington gave much thought to safety as their children freely roamed the neighborhoods. At least my parents didn't. I was probably no older than seven when I was allowed to walk almost anywhere in town by myself. By the time I was eight I was even walking downtown to the movie after dark. So I was always allowed to play anywhere in the neighborhood anytime, ever since as I was old enough to open our back door and walk out. And the really great thing about my neighborhood, there were always plenty of kids to play with.

Just in the block where I lived, bordered by Pearl, Commercial, Sixth, and Seventh Streets, there were always 10 to 15 kids living there during any given time period. Beyond that, there was Fred Auter right across Sixth Street and Dick Rowe in the block north of Commercial. Ronnie Massey lived at the end of the block with his parents, an older brother, and a younger sister. His parents, Carter and Mary Lou, were friends of my parents. One day when we were about five years old, someone, probably his brother Jim, told Ronnie and me that if we filled a Mason jar with pretty rocks, added some soap, and set it in the sun, the rocks would turn to gold. We were so excited at the prospect that we tried it that same day, expecting fully that it would work. We waited all afternoon for the magic to take place, one of us with our eyes on the jar at all times, until finally in the late afternoon we decided we'd been lied to. Oh man, was I disappointed. The Masseys moved away by the time I was seven, and another family moved in. The new family had two kids whom I seldom played with because they were too young.

Dick Rowe was probably my closest adolescent neighborhood friend. Dick lived a block and a half north of me on Sixth Street in what I recall as an old and unpainted clapboard house. His parents' names were Hazel and Henry, and they both reminded me of other people. I thought Hazel looked a lot like Marjorie Maine, the woman who played Ma Kettle in the Ma and Pa Kettle movies, who by the way, was my connection to the rich and famous. According to my Grandma Stanton, Marjorie Maine was her cousin four times removed. Henry Rowe reminded me of the pictures of the Raggedy Man in James Whitcomb Riley's poems about the Raggedy Man. I thought he was a dead ringer.

The Rowes had inside plumbing, but they also had a hand pump at their kitchen sink, which pumped water from a cistern. And even though they had an inside toilet, they also still had a useable outhouse that made for a quick stop whenever we were playing. Their backyard had no grass, but it did have one or two apple trees that dropped rotting apples on a picnic table where the Rowes often ate their meals in the summer time. That meant there were hordes of bees flying around their backyard every autumn.

Dick and I played cowboys and Indians exclusively. With other friends I played war, but with Dick it was always cowboys and Indians. Now cowboys and Indians was a rather undefined game. First, you had to argue over whether you were going to be a cowboy or an Indian, because no one ever wanted to be the Indian. Then whoever won the argument had to decide if he was going to be Roy Rogers or Gene Autry, never Tom Mix or The Cisco Kid or Hopalong Cassidy or the Lone Ranger, all cowboy heroes of my time. It was always Roy Rogers or Gene Autry. Sometimes neither of us would give in and we'd both be cowboys, so then we'd have to argue over who was going to be Roy and who was going to be Gene, that is until Gene fell completely out of favor with me when he switched from singing those great old cowboy songs like "Back in the Saddle Again" to that new little kid's song "Rudolph the Red Nosed Reindeer". Not only did I not like it because it wasn't a cowboy song, I was angry that Gene actually had the gall to make up a song about a make-believe reindeer that kids were actually going for. I knew Santa only had eight reindeer, I knew them by name. Rudolph was certainly not one of them and never would be.

The choosing was probably the most interesting part of the whole game. After that we'd hide from each other for awhile then when we got bored we'd come out of our hiding places to find each other. That's when the shooting started. You could use any stick as your shootin' iron or simply use your hand with your thumb in the air and your index finger pointing. Then all you had to do was make shooting noises with your mouth. Of course the better your shooting noise the more lethal your shot. From the straight "kapow" of the six-shooter to the "pachoo" of the carbine, I had a whole litany of shots down pat. And they were deadly. That is, unless your opponent didn't want to die and then he said "you missed", something I never understood when my stick/finger was actually poking him in the back. Of course, this could also lead to some pretty serious arguments. Too much bickering over who shot first, who hit whom, and who got missed usually signaled the end of the game.

But it didn't matter, there was always the old shed to play in, the one with a big bin filled with corncobs, or better yet the abandoned car rusting in Dick's back yard. There was no end to the things we could find to fill a day, and oftentimes it didn't come to an end until Dick's mother told me that it was supper time and time for me to go on home. And she always used that term, "time for you to go on home." I always resented her telling me that, because I knew I didn't have to go home. My mom didn't require me to go home until it was MY suppertime, so I could go wherever I wanted when I left Dick's house. But I was never so disrespectful as to say it to her.

One day when we were playing, Dick had to use the outhouse. A few minutes later he came out with tears in his eyes, and I could tell something bad had happened. It had. He had dropped his eyeglasses down the hole. Even though I felt sorry for Dick, it was one day I left his house early, right after he told his mother what had happened then came back out of the house carrying a long rope tied to a tin pail. The next time I was over he said it took awhile but he did eventually scoop his glasses out.

Dick was the only kid I ever knew to have a true phobia. This was long before I knew there was such a word, but a phobia it was. Dick was dreadfully afraid of chicken feathers. Well, any feathers probably, but chicken feathers in particular. I didn't know Dick had this fear, but I guess other kids in the neighborhood did. One day Dick and Ronnie Massey and I were playing together in Ronnie's yard when Jim Massey, Ronnie's older brother, approached us with his hand behind his back. When he suddenly brought it around in front of us, he was holding a handful of big feathers. I think they were just feathers out of a kid's Indian war bonnet, but as soon as Dick saw them, he sort of screamed and ran home. At first I was surprised, and then I was shocked. What had just happened? I soon got a half-baked explanation from Jim, which just made me angry that he had pulled such a stunt on Dick. At the same time I was naturally fascinated by what had taken place. Sometime later I asked Dick about the fear, and he explained it by saying that his sister had scared him with chicken feathers when he was younger.

The summer when I was seven years old, Dick got a new bike for his birthday. It was bright, and shiny, and beautiful, with a light on the handlebars and everything. I loved it. I didn't have a bike of my own, in fact hadn't yet learned to ride one. I don't know if I asked or if Dick offered, but Dick told me if I wanted to he'd teach me to ride it. It was a little too big for me, but in that one afternoon, I learned to ride a bicycle for the first time. Dick's new bicycle took a beating in the process, and at the end of the day it no longer looked like a new bike. As I recall, Dick's mother wasn't very happy with Dick or me.

The Rowes moved to the country when I was in the fourth grade, after that Dick started going to Rabb school and eventually Perrysville. Although I went to visit him once or maybe twice at his new home, and did think of him from time to time, it wasn't long before we lost track of each other. Of all my early childhood friends, I missed losing Dick Rowe the most.

A family named Weaver lived right behind us on Sixth Street. Esther and Johnny Weaver had four daughters, Suzy, the oldest, Linda who was my age, Julie, a couple of years younger, and Coletta, the toddler. I don't recall ever playing outdoors with them, after all, they were girls, and girls didn't have the slightest idea that a stick could be anything but a stick. They didn't seem interested in the fact that a stick could be a horse, a gun, a spear, or a killer of ants. So when I played with the Weaver girls, we played in their house. With a couple of old library stamps, a date stamper, and three or four old books, "library" was our number one game. Or sometimes, we played school with an old school desk they had in their living room. That was it. I didn't play dolls, and they didn't play war.

When I was about nine years old the Weavers moved out and the Frenches moved in. Now that was more like it. Erma and I. O. French had a bunch of kids. By the way, I say I. O. as if I knew that was right. Actually, I never did figure that out for sure. During my childhood I thought his name was "I Owe", because that's what he was called, but I think I found out later that I. O. were either his initials, or I O was actually his full name. Anyway, the Frenches turned out to have four boys and a girl. I think three other of their children had already grown up and were on their own.

Darrell was the one I played with most. He was the oldest of the kids still living at home and just a year or two older than me. Larry was about my brother John's age, so they became friends. The three younger Frenches, Sherry, Mike, and Jeff played with my younger brother Charlie and my little sisters Mary Ann and Nancy. They also had a son named Gary who was nicknamed Toby. He was younger than Larry and didn't quite fit into any of the groups that had formed between the Dickinsons and the Frenches.

One winter day I noticed that Toby hadn't been out playing for a few days. Skeeter, Darrell's nickname, told me that Toby was sick. The next day Skeeter told me that Toby had died. At first, I thought he was kidding, but he wasn't. I don't recall what Toby died from, seems I might have heard pneumonia mentioned, but I do remember that I didn't really feel scared or sad or depressed about Toby's death, and I'm not sure why. I took it pretty much as a matter of fact, which seems strange now that I look back on it. Even though I never played with Toby, why I didn't have some emotional reaction to losing a young neighbor boy, I'll never understand. Maybe I was wrapped up in my own little world a little too tightly. On the other hand, I didn't notice any of the other kids reacting to Toby's death either. We just didn't mention him again, as if he'd never existed.

Darrell and I hung together quite a bit, and sometimes, if we were feeling generous, we might include the younger kids in our games. We played war throughout the neighborhood; it was the ultimate game. Similar to cowboys and Indians, war only took two people and a couple of sticks. The biggest difference being that the guns didn't go "pow" like they did with cowboys and Indians. When you played war, they always went "uh-uh-uh-uh-uh-uh" like a sub-machine gun.

Hiding out was a great way to spend a couple of hours, even though it didn't amount to doing a thing. Hiding out could be done alone or with a friend, but the idea was to keep any of the other kids in the neighborhood from finding you. There was no real purpose to it, I guess it was akin to girls playing house. What made hiding out so much fun in our neighborhood was that there was at least one shed in every back yard. We used the French's shed most often, because it had lots of knotholes to look out of. That made it easy to check for anyone sneaking up on you. The shed in back of my house was pretty nice too, mostly because it had a loft.

The first time I realized I was big enough to move Dad's wooden ladder, I propped it up against that loft and climbed up. It was as if I'd struck it rich. Filthy dirty and covered in bird droppings, it didn't matter; it was mine. Mom and Dad said it was all right for me to go up there and play all I wanted if I was careful, but they wouldn't let the neighbors up there because they might fall off the edge to the floor below. That was okay with me because it became my own personal getaway. After a couple of months though, I got pretty bored up there by myself and soon abandoned it. Dad tore the shed down a year or so later, the same year he filled up the water cistern with ashes from the furnace. That's also the same spot where Dad built our underground fallout shelter about five years later.

Holes in the ground could be either foxholes or hideouts. Using spades, shovels, trowels, or spoons, Skeeter and I would dig a hole big enough for both of us to crawl down into. Without anything further, it became a foxhole from which to look over and shoot our stick guns or launch our walnut grenades. On the other hand, if we threw a few old boards over it, it became an excellent hideout. We worked on all kinds of schemes to cover the boards with dirt after placing them on top of us so that no one would know there was even a hideout down there.

At the opposite corner of our block lived a family named Swaney. I didn't play much with them even though two of the boys were around my age. Archie and Isabelle Swaney had four boys, and the two oldest, John and Dick, had already left home. I'd heard that one of those two liked to get into it with their fists, but that might have just been a neighborhood rumor. As it turned out though, the two who were my age were pretty tough themselves, so most of the kids on the block pretty much avoided them whenever possible. One day, however, the inevitable happened.

On the back of Swaney's property, along the alley that ran down the middle of the block, grew a big walnut tree. It hung over the alley and dropped walnuts where anyone could pick them up. One day, for a reason I don't recall, all the kids on the block decided a walnut fight was in order. And it seemed like it ought to be a fair fight because it was the rest of us against the two Swaney boys. So off the Dickinson brigade went, marching down the alley with me in the lead. In my hands was the tin lid from our garbage can, which I could use as a shield. We picked up some of the French kids on the way, and by the time we reached the Swaneys, we had seven or eight kids on our side. Mickey and Don Swaney were well outnumbered, and it took no time for the walnuts to start flying from both sides.

The battle was on, and the Dickinsons and Frenches were jumping behind trees, holding up shields, ducking, weaving, and retreating whenever necessary. The Swaneys, on the other hand, stood stock still in open ground and peppered us with a continuous barrage of walnuts. When one of our walnuts connected, it only made the Swaney boys madder, and if they got mad enough, they'd just take off after you. Then you had to run for your life.

My garbage lid shield was working well and had deflected a dozen walnuts when the end came. I saw my sister Mary Ann nearing me as she walked down the alley. I needed to warn her to get back and in doing so I let down my shield and told her to go home before she got plastered. In the instant I turned my head back to the battle, I immediately felt a searing pain shoot through my left eye. I guess it's at times like that when the old backup adrenalin system starts pumping, and without a single thought your body goes into that protective mode called fight-or-flight. I chose flight. My shield fell to the ground, my hand went to my eye, tears started falling, and my scream rose above the clamor as my legs carried me up that alley as fast as they could run. Before reaching home, I took my hand off my eye and opened it. OH NO! I was blind!

I ran into the house holding my eye and bawling like a baby. "What happened?" Mom asked.

"I got hit with a walnut," I said. "And I can't see!"

"Hit with a walnut? Well does it hurt?" Mom asked much more calmly than I thought she should have.

"Yes Mom!" I yelled. "And I can't see."

"Well, how did you get hit with a walnut?" she asked.

"What's the difference Mom! I can't see out of my eye! I'm blind!" I cried, tears rolling down my face.

"Okay, here, let me have a look," she said as she pulled my hand away from my eye and held my head back for a better look. "Hmmm," she said. "Well it's kind of red, but it doesn't look too bad," was her calm pronouncement, as if going blind was the most natural thing in the world.

This brings me to one of the main axioms at the Dickinson house, one that I've alluded to several times before, but at this point should mention again. We very seldom spent money on anything that wasn't necessary, whether it was a nickel to satisfy a sweet tooth or the money to take your 11-year-old son to the doctor because he had his eye put out with a walnut. It's just the way it was.

"Mom, I can't see. I need to see Dr. Suzuki," I begged.

"Well, it's getting late," she said, "and I don't think they're there now. I don't think it's that bad. Let's see how it is tomorrow. If it's not better we'll call Dr Suzuki."

The next day everything was still blurry, so Mom reluctantly took me to see Dr. Suzuki. He examined it, put a patch on it, and gave me some drops to use. He said I wasn't blind and that in a few days it would be much better and sent me home. I wore the patch to school for several days, proudly displaying my war wounds. When it came off, and for a long time after, I could see a crack running down everything I looked at. But I got used to it, and as time went on the crack faded away. Overall, I guess I learned a lesson from it because that was the last walnut fight I was ever in.

I wasn't a mechanically minded kid, not like Fred Auter who made his own motorbike out of a bicycle and a lawnmower engine and had rebuilt an old Model A Ford complete with a rumble seat. But two summers in a row I did build a push go-cart. I can't remember who I'd seen build one, maybe it was Fred, but I did remember how it was built, so I went to work on building my own. Over the hill towards the river from Second Street was Covington's junkyard. I don't know who owned it, but having a junk yard in town was a big plus when it came to projects like building your own go-cart. If you rooted around there long enough you'd come up with all the items you needed and for just a few cents. Sometimes they'd even give me what I needed for free. As a side note, the city garbage dump was also over the hill in the same vicinity. It was the city dump all of my childhood and wasn't moved until after it caught fire in the 60's or 70's and burned underground for months before it was completely extinguished.

For the go-cart, I needed a piece of 4x8 lumber about four feet long for the main section. That's the piece that would end up being the seat and also onto which everything else was connected. I also needed two 2x4's, each about three feet long, to hold the axles. These three pieces I could get from Dad as he always had stacks of wood left over from building projects. From the junk yard, I'd find a car steering wheel, two axles from either an old wagon or a baby buggy, and four baby buggy wheels. For the front of the go-cart, I got a wooden produce box from the grocery store, even though a nail keg would have been better. Nail kegs looked neater, but were hard to come by. A broomstick handle, some clothesline rope, two small pulleys that I usually had to buy at Faust and Frey for fifty cents each, one bolt, a few nails, a stick for the brake, and that was it. It took me a day to build it and a week of running it before it fell apart. We didn't have a hill on Pearl Street to run it down, so we had to push whoever wanted to drive it, and everyone did. We couldn't get it going fast enough for anyone to get hurt, but we tried our best to skid it in gravel and run up some curbs. The ultimate thrill was wrecking it by turning it sharp enough to flip it on its side or ramming it into a tree, so it only took a few days before things started to fall apart. That was all right, we were getting bored with it anyway. It has served its purpose, had been fun while it lasted, and I'd had fun building it. That's all that really mattered.

By the time I was in the seventh grade, I'd begun to lose interest in playing war, digging holes, and hanging out with the French kids. I was moving on with my life and had discovered a friendship with a guy a year older than me named John Mills. John was the son of Paul Mills, who was the manager of the Grab-It-Here grocery store. His mother was Mary Jean, and he had a younger sister named Linda and an older brother named Dick. I found them all to be nice, friendly people. I'm not sure how I came to know John; he lived on Seventh Street, about four blocks from my house, so it wasn't because we were neighbors. It may have had something to do with the fact that we both had paper routes in a small town. We were bound to run into each other.

There were many differences between John and myself, and maybe that's what made John so interesting to me. Like me,

John liked to have fun, but he had a more serious side than I did. He was a tinkerer and a thinker. I doubt he'd ever played war or cowboys and Indians in his life. What John liked was playing music, rigging up gadgets, and experimenting with chemicals—not as in chemicals you took to get high, but like in chemicals that made firecrackers. It really wasn't in me to be an integral part of any of that, but it was fun just being on the fringes of it all.

I was mostly an observer as John did such unorthodox things as make a bass fiddle out of a wash tub, a piece of wood, and a length of rope. It took him no time to learn to play it before he started jamming in the Mills's living room with his brother Dick, who played the sax, and some other guys. They sounded good. Also, I mostly watched as John mixed nitrates, sulfur, and charcoal together to get just the right flash point, before he rolled it up in strips of heavy paper, sealed it with some candle wax, added a homemade fuse of black powder rolled in cigarette papers, and took it into his back yard to blow a tin can fifty feet in the air. Or to work on an alarm system that was tripped whenever anyone came down to the basement and stepped on the loose step that John had rigged to send a signal to an old automobile Ooga horn. That horn would go off in our basement hideaway to warn us of an intruder. And although I was of little use in these projects, John liked my company, and we got along well.

Under John's guidance, our basement hideaway was more than what you would think of as a kid's hideout. We got the idea from our favorite magazine, *MAD*, which we both read religiously. One *MAD* issue featured a cartoon based on a real-life radio disc jockey named Al "Jazzbeaux" Collins. On his real show, Jazzbeaux's program featured not only jazz music, but a cast of strange characters all played by Jazzbeaux himself, and was broadcast from Jazzbeaux's imaginary, subterranean studio that he dubbed "The Purple Grotto"—the name of our basement hideaway. We painted the door purple and built a workbench from which we could make firecrackers and run a little mimeograph printer that John had come across, which he used to print a school newsletter. We poured cement for a built-in seat, and decorated the place up with all manner of *MAD* inspired sayings. Since John's dad ran a grocery store, he had access to all sorts of animated promotional signs, and it didn't take much for us to rig up several signs for the Grotto. The main one, of course, was a full-size cutout of *MAD* mascot and our hero Alfred E. Neuman. Alfred E's smiling face sat on the ledge above the workbench attached to a metronome-like gadget and swung back and forth with a sign that proudly announced his motto and ours, "What—Me Worry?"

John and I often talked paper routes, as that was the business we knew and the means of income for both of us. At the time John and I became friends, I had a Danville Commercial News route and John had an Indianapolis Star route. The Commercial News was an afternoon paper, which I was not too happy about. It cut into my after-school fun time. The Star was a morning route, which was much more appealing to me. Not only that, but quite a few extra people took the Sunday Star, and according to John he made a profit of a nickel for every Sunday Star he delivered. I'd never figured it out that way, but when I put a pencil to it, I discovered that he was making better money than I was making from my Sunday papers, so I applied for and got the next Indianapolis Star route that became available.

I liked having a morning paper route, that is, if I had to have a paper route at all. There was something nice about getting up when it was still dark outside and while everyone in the house was still sleeping. In a house of seven people it wasn't often that I had the living room to myself, and I found those quiet early-morning moments by myself a real gift. The bundle of papers would be waiting on our front stoop, and after carrying them into the house I folded them so they would all fit neatly into my bicycle basket. That also made it easy to toss them onto porches and stoops. Then it was off to make my deliveries.

Actually, the Indianapolis Star wasn't my first morning route. I started my series of paper routes when I was about 10 years old; my very first route was carrying the Lafayette Journal and Courier. It was not a popular newspaper in Covington so there was only one route, a route that covered the entire town. When I first started I had 11 customers, including one near the city park, a couple of businesses downtown, and a customer near Keller's Apple Orchard. That meant I was traveling to three corners of the town. It took me 30 minutes to deliver those 11 papers on an old bicycle with tires that were always half flat.

Here would be a good place to mention a little bit about Dad's sister, my Aunt Mary, and truly the nicest person you'd ever want to meet. Aunt Mary was so perpetually happy, she gushed. Nothing but a flood of pure sweetness ever escaped my Aunt Mary's mouth, even on the day of her husband's, my Uncle Allen's, funeral when she had to make certain that everyone was bearing up. She was so overwhelmingly nice that in later life my brothers, sisters, and I would sometimes mimic her whenever we wanted to feign exaggerated politeness. She was especially nice to her brother Dean's family—that was us—who I considered her less sophisticated relatives.

And so you might see why, as soon as she heard that I was delivering the Journal and Courier, she subscribed. Now that would have been great except for one thing. She lived in the ten hundred block of Liberty, which to my dismay, was the fourth corner of Covington. That one paper alone added another five minutes to my route. I'll have to hand it to my Aunt Mary though, because she made up for her unintended error in judgment with one redeeming act. Every morning before she left for work at the courthouse, and before I arrived with her paper, she set a tray of cookies and a glass of milk out for me, an act I took complete advantage of. Aunt Mary had given me an extra five minutes of work every morning, but in so doing had found the secret to her fat nephew's heart.

I made a dollar a week with those 12 papers and usually spent all or most of it on treats at Burrin's Drug Store after making my Saturday collections. My guess is, between my daily deliveries and my Saturday collecting, I worked about six hours a week to earn that dollar, but it was the first money I ever earned to be spent however I pleased. And those treats tasted mighty good. After about a year I moved up to a 60 paper Commercial News route before ending my paper-carrying career with that Indianapolis Star route.

Paper routes and The Purple Grotto were what John and I really had in common. But that wasn't enough to keep us as good friends for more than a couple of years. We were different in too many ways, and although I valued the time that John and I spent together, by the time I was fifteen we had drifted apart.

Although the Journal and Courier was my first real chance to gain some small degree of financial independence, a paper route wasn't my first effort at trying to earn something on my own. That first opportunity came in the form of an advertisement that appeared on the back of a comic book. The back covers of comic books were always covered with pictures of the great prizes a kid could earn by selling seeds. And they made it sound so easy. All I had to do was order the merchandise, sell it, send them the money and receive the great prize I'd already picked out. Amazingly, they actually trusted kids of any age to send them the money after the seeds were sold.

Studying those prizes was almost as exciting as looking through the Montgomery Ward Christmas catalog. I spent a year or so fantasizing about earning everything from footballs to roller skates, Superman x-ray vision goggles, and Flash Gordon rubber band shooters before finally, in the summer when I was nine years old, I couldn't wait any longer. There was a pair of binoculars that illustrated just how well you could spot the enemy from miles away. I had to have them. I filled out the little application with my name and address, checked the box beside "garden seeds", and sent it off.

A week later my package of garden seeds arrived along with a sampling of flower seeds. I was in business. Mom helped me decide on just how to carry the seeds so that the customers could easily see them, and we came up with a shoebox. I slipped a piece of shoestring through a couple of holes I'd punched in the shoe-box, and voila! I had a wonderful little seed display hanging down from my neck. That little shoe box seed carrier was the first truly useful thing I can ever remember making with my own hands, and I was proud of it. The best part of it was that it worked perfectly.

I filled it with my seeds, all arranged alphabetically, and off I went knocking on doors. My spiel was pretty simple. "Hello, would you like to buy some seeds today?" Some people said "no" right off the bat, but the vast majority asked me how much they were and what my name was. "A nickel a package," I'd answer to the first question and "Bobby Dean Dickinson" to the second.

"Oh, Bobby Dean," they'd say. "Let's see, you must be the mailman's boy?" Or they'd say, "Are you Dean Dickerson's boy?"

"Yes," I'd answer with a slow burn, then distinctly I'd say "DICK-IN-SON", emphasizing each syllable of the name. They seldom caught the difference. Actually, throughout my childhood, I was called Dickerson about as often as Dickinson, and even though it was one of my pet peeves, especially when my own friends said it, I soon realized that it was only a big deal to me. Still, I always corrected anyone who called me Dickerson.

"Well, let's see what kind of seeds you've got there," they'd say after we got established exactly who I was.

I'd proudly show them how they could easily thumb through the seed packets displayed in my wonderful little homemade-shoebox-seed carrier. Most of them would then pull a packet or two, say that they could use some of these, and pay me what they owed. The samples of flower seeds sold out right away, the garden seeds were a little slower. Still, it only took a couple of days to sell most all of my stock, which meant I ended up selling about $12 dollars worth of seeds before realizing that the turnip and kale seeds weren't going to sell.

The comic book seed company was good on its word. I packaged up and sent back the remaining seeds along with the money I had collected, and told them the prize I wanted for selling $12 worth of seeds. Within a couple of weeks my prize came in the mail. With reckless abandon, I ripped open the package to discover, just as they were shown on the back of the comic book, the most wonderful pair of binoculars I could have ever imagined. And when I ran outdoors to try them out I was so happy to find that, "YES!" they really did work. Err, well, sorta. Maybe they didn't work quite as well as the comic book showed. The mailbox on Mrs. Casey's porch was only slightly bigger than it looked with the naked eye. Okay, so maybe it didn't really matter that I couldn't spot the enemy from miles away. So what? At least I had some binoculars hanging around my neck, and that was more than any other kid in the neighborhood could say. I knew when they saw them they'd eat their hearts out. And they did.

Of course, it only took about half an afternoon for everyone in the neighborhood to oooh and ahhh over them, and then the excitement was over. I may have played with them a couple more times, then discovered they were not only useless, but a pain to carry around. Within a week that pair of binoculars was thrown into my bedroom's catchall-closet, never to be played with again.

Nevertheless, that didn't keep me from dreaming about earning even more and better prizes. Besides that, I sort of liked selling seeds. I was pretty good at it, a natural born salesman. So I sold seeds again the next two summers, and having learned from my first experience, both years I ordered a lot more flower seeds than garden seeds. One year I even tried selling gift-wrap and greeting cards, but that didn't go over very well. I ended up sending most of those back, having sold only enough to earn a crummy sling-shot that broke the first day I used it. Other than the binoculars and sling shot, I don't recall what other prizes I earned, but no doubt they were something wonderful that I wouldn't have had if I hadn't earned them.

I've always said that my working life started when I sold my first packet of seeds at the age of nine. After all, since then, unlike most of my friends who never had to work, there wasn't a year that went by when I didn't earn almost all of my own spending money through one job or another. After my auspicious seed-pedaling years, I went on to carry three different paper routes, worked the concession stand at the movie theater for over a year, and finally ended up working for three different grocery stores, all before my 18th birthday. And that doesn't count the lawns I mowed during the summer months while also carrying papers. By the way, when I was about 13, I went 50/50 with Dad to buy our first power mower. I don't know that we would have ever gotten a power mower if I hadn't talked Dad into it, then splitting the cost with him. But I was really getting tired of mowing lawns with an old push mower.

Would I have rather not had to work those jobs? Absolutely. If I'd thought I had a choice I would have chosen the path of most of the kids I knew, kids who didn't have regular jobs they had to go to before or after school. But I didn't fret over it either. It was simply a fact of life that I accepted and always made the best of.

# Chapter 6

# *Radio and Television*

I did earn a really great prize once, and not from selling seeds or working a job. The prize was a portable radio that I earned by collecting cloverleaf symbols from specially marked boxes of Blue Bonnet margarine. I'd never had my own radio, but it wasn't because I hadn't thought about it. We only had one radio in the house, and it was in the living room where Mom and Dad usually listened to their shows, mostly at night. Having a radio of my own would let me hear the shows and the music I wanted to listen to. And I could put it right next to my bed.

One morning at the breakfast table, Mom was taking a new stick of Blue Bonnet margarine out of its box and asked me if I'd seen this thing about a prize contest. I began reading the details along the side of the box and soon realized that I could win a radio simply by collecting the cloverleaf symbols in the upper-right-hand corner of the boxes. To win a radio I would need to collect 90 of them. That sounded to me like a bunch of margarine, and the real problem was, I only had seven weeks before the contest ended. I knew I had my work cut out for me, but it didn't matter, I was excited. I had to have that radio and would go all out to earn it.

I began by asking all my paper route customers to cut out and save them for me. I canvassed my neighbors, my barbershop, the local grocery store, and any other businesses I went into. Since this was going on during the summer, I didn't have teachers or students I could ask, but I did call a few of my school friends. I called my Aunt Mary, whom I knew I could count on, and my Great Aunt Myra. Grandma, who lived upstairs, said she'd definitely be needing a box of margarine, and of course, Mom said she'd be using a couple of boxes in the next month.

Many of the people I talked to said they didn't use Blue Bonnet. They said they used some other brand of oleo, what margarine was called back then. Parkay was one of the more popular brands people said they preferred. Others said they used butter instead of oleo. Of the ones who did use Blue Bonnet, all of them said that they'd be glad to save the symbols for me. Every week I picked up a few cloverleaves, and as the weeks went by, I was coming closer and closer to the 90 I needed. My paper route customers were the most faithful, probably because I pestered them every week when I collected for the paper. A few of them even changed brands just to help me out.

As the final weeks approached, I began to worry, and by the 6th week I knew I was in trouble. I had collected only 72 cloverleaves, 18 short of what I needed. In desperation I checked with everyone who was saving them for me and found out what

I already knew, no one planned to buy any more Blue Bonnet in the next week. My dream of having my very own radio was going to have an unhappy ending, unfulfilled and seemingly unsolvable. I was really downhearted over it, and I guess Mom could see it because that same day she got on the phone. How Mom got Aunt Mary to buy a case of 24 boxes of Blue Bonnet margarine, I'll never know. I asked, but I don't think I got a straight answer. "Aunt Mary's going to do a lot of baking," Mom told me, and that was the end of the discussion. I didn't want to say anything that would make Aunt Mary change her mind, so I kept my mouth shut. But I knew she wasn't going to do a lot of baking; she'd ordered that case of margarine just for me. I was actually a little embarrassed when I thanked her for what she'd done, and then typical of Aunt Mary, she simply went on and on about what a nice radio it was going to be.

I guess Aunt Mary knew what she was talking about because that radio turned out to be exactly what I had imagined and what would become one of my most-prized childhood possessions. Made of hard-dark-green plastic, it had a swivel handle and the name EMERSON embossed in white along its top. The day I got it, I plugged it in next to my bed and never moved it until the day it died about five years later. It was an AC/DC, but the batteries to make it portable cost about $3, more than I ever wanted to spend, so I never did find out if it was truly portable. That didn't matter, I wanted to listen to it while I was in bed, especially on Saturday mornings before I got up, when there were lots of kids' shows on.

My favorite two Saturday morning shows were *Big John and Sparky* and *The Buster Brown Show*. I don't recall much about *Big John and Sparky* other than it opened with the song *The Teddy Bear's Picnic*, a song I really liked. *The Buster Brown Show*, on the other hand, had a couple of features that I remember well and can still hear their distinct sounds as they came through the tinny speakers of my little green radio. One, was that Buster Brown Shoes sponsored the show, and the tag line for the company's radio ad was a kid's voice saying, "Hi! I'm Buster Brown. I live in a shoe. Here's my dog Tighe, he lives in the there too." It wasn't until years later that I read the ad someplace and realized that his dog wasn't named Tide, but Tighe. It was also some years later that I got a peek inside a Buster Brown shoe. I guess Philpot's didn't carry them, or they were too expensive for our budget. When I finally did find a pair, I was actually rather pleased to see that Buster Brown and his dog actually were inside there.

The other thing I remember about the Buster Brown show was a frog named Froggie. A gravelly-voiced man named Andy Devine, who in later years played Wild Bill Hickock's sidekick on television, was the host of the show. Andy would be talking to one of the other characters on the show when someone would suggest that it was time for Froggie to make an appearance. That said, someone else would then say, "Plunk your magic twanger Froggie," and from a box, or some other hiding place, you heard the "boinnngggg-boinnngggg" of a spring being sprung, propelling Froggie forth from his hiding place. The next thing you heard was Foggie's croaking-deep-bass voice saying, "Hi ya kids, hi ya, hi ya," while at the same time you heard the clapping and cheering of a very large audience of children.

After Froggie was out of his box, or wherever he lived, Andy Devine tried to continue to discuss or explain whatever he'd been talking about before Froggie's appearance, but now the problem was that Froggie kept interrupting Andy by putting words in his mouth. Andy would fall for it every time, making his sentences nonsensical and silly. For example, Andy might say, "So the boy picked up his bat and walked up to the..." At this point Froggie would interrupt him and say, "dish," which caused Andy to say, "dish," instead of "plate." This broke the audience up, sending it into absolute pandemonium. And they weren't alone. I'd lie in my bed and laugh at Froggie's shenanigans until tears rolled down my face.

There were other Saturday morning shows that I'd listen to on occasion, but I only listened to them if I was sick. After all, Saturdays were much too special to spend time in bed, radio or no radio.

Before I got my green radio, I used the radio in the living room to listen to a few shows on Saturday morning or after school. I didn't listen to them on a regular basis because I preferred to be out and about, but when there was nothing else going on, I always enjoyed the radio shows. My favorite was about a Canadian Mountie named *Sergeant Preston of the Yukon* and his dog Yukon King. Whenever Sergeant Preston was on his sled, "On King, on you huskies," was his trademark command, and "Well King, I guess this case is closed," always ended the show. My next favorite was about a rancher who piloted his own airplane, and included his niece Penny, and a nephew named Clipper. The program was *Sky King*, and I liked the idea of adventure in the wild blue yonder. I also had Penny pictured as cute beyond belief.

Seldom did I listen to radio at night with Mom and Dad. Maybe that's because they didn't listen to it that often themselves, and when they did, it was usually tuned to music instead of the comedy and mystery shows. I do recall hearing *Amos and Andy*, *The Great Gildersleeve*, and *The Shadow* a few times, but not on a regular basis.

To my dismay, because of its opening sound effects, the one nighttime show that always caught my attention was also the one that was deemed unsuitable for me to listen to. That is, until one night when I was ten years old and had finally pestered Mom and Dad into letting me stay up to hear it. The show was named *The Inner Sanctum*, although my folks called it The Squeaking Door because it started out with the very eerie sound of a squeaking door opening slowly. Until that night, I'd never been allowed to hear the entire show because it was too scary. I'd always been sent to bed when it came on. But that night, I heard it to the end and found out that the show closed with the same squeaking door slamming shut. And that was the last time I heard the door slam shut, because after that night, I was too frightened to listen to the show again. In fact, I was afraid to go to bed that night for fear a horrible man would come to my bedroom and decapitate me, just like he'd done on the show.

The adult radio show I envisioned best was *Gunsmoke,* not because of its story line, but because of its opening sound effects. I've always felt that, as a kid, I was entertained by the radio every bit as much as I was by the television after we finally got one of those, maybe even more so. With the radio, my mind had to conjure up all the pictures induced by nothing more than the sounds coming from either that little green radio next to my bed or the box-like Philco sitting on a white doily on top of an end table in our living room. Everyone had their own idea of what the scenery and the characters looked like. In the opening of *Gunsmoke* I could clearly see the cowboy, his wide-brimmed Stetson cocked to the front of his forehead, his chaps waving in the wind, and his spurs jingling as he stepped off long strides down a hollow sounding boardwalk above a dusty street. Then he stopped, drew his shootin' irons, and plugged the bad guy in a fierce hail of gunfire. It was a picture-perfect opening, and all I needed were the sounds to make it all come alive.

Dad didn't buy us a television until I was ten years old. He said there wasn't any reason for us to have a television until there was something to see on it, and he was right. Finally, in the fall of 1953, within weeks after WCIA Channel 3 in Champaign, Illinois went on the air, Dad decided it was time.

Up until then, for several months before Channel 3 came along, the only television I'd ever seen was over at the Weaver's house. Even though they couldn't get a lick of reception, they were the first family in the neighborhood to get a TV, so naturally, that's where all the neighborhood kids headed on Saturday morning. There'd be up to a dozen kids gathered around, about three feet in front of their TV, in hopes of catching even the smallest glimpse of *The Big Top* circus show broadcasting from a Chicago TV station. If it was a good morning, the show might fade in a couple of times, just long enough to whet our appetites. But mostly the picture was nothing more than what we called snow and ghosts. One Saturday the Weavers got me excited by saying they were going to turn their black and white TV into a color TV. Wow, I'd never even seen a black and white show clearly, and here the Weavers were going to have a color TV. The next week I arrived expecting something out of this world. What I saw was a three-colored piece of transparent plastic covering the screen, red at the top, green in the middle, and blue on the bottom. Some color television! In the end, I had to laugh at myself for being dumb enough to sit there and watch snow and ghosts on a rainbow-colored television screen.

It was exciting the day Dad brought home our first TV, one he had picked out at Montgomery Ward in Danville. It was a 17-inch-black-and-white Motorola, average size for that time, and I wanted to turn it on as soon as he set it up in the living room on its little stand. We had to wait though because Dad said it wouldn't work until he put up the antenna. The next day was a Sunday and Dad was off work, so he climbed up on the top of the roof and spent the entire day installing the antenna, including a motor that would rotate it whenever we turned the knob on a little device that sat on top of the TV. When he was finished that night, we all got excited again as we gathered close to the TV and Dad turned it on for the first time.

It took about 10 seconds for the tubes to warm up and then.... Whoa, hold on! What was this? I'd been hoping for something great, but deep down I had a feeling it was going to be the same old thing. Still that didn't keep me from being extremely disappointed when what showed up on that screen was exactly what we'd been watching at the Weaver's for the last six months, nothing but SNOW! Dad didn't say a thing, didn't even cuss, which surprised me. He simply reached up and turned the rotator dial to W, which I learned later meant he was rotating the antenna to the west. Then he played with a couple of knobs on the front of the TV, and.... Wait a minute! Was the snow clearing? Did I see an actual moving picture beginning to emerge? Yes, there it was! Within seconds, the screen became bright and clear and I saw my first perfectly focused television picture ever. It was someone from channel 3 announcing the news, and to me it was the miracle of miracles. I'd never seen a clear television picture in my entire life, and here was my first one coming directly into our living room. It was, without a doubt, among the most thrilling moments in my young life.

Soon stations in Danville, Terre Haute, Lafayette, and one or two more in Champaign began to show up with about every other click of the channel changer. Within a year, we were receiving four channels clear as a bell and two or three more that you had to fight with. I liked television a lot. We all did. It was so exciting to be able to bring such visual entertainment right into our living room, and what was just as amazing was that except for the cost of the TV and a little electricity, it was all free. Before television came along, you had to spend money on a movie if you wanted to be entertained by anything that even resembled television.

It wasn't long before Mom and Dad had to set rules as to bedtime. In that first year, when it was all new and exciting, if I had been allowed I would have stayed up until the waving of the American flag and the playing of our National Anthem, those great symbols of Americanism that marked the end of the broadcast day for most channels. They were followed by an all-night display of a test pattern accompanied by a high-pitched whistle. Except for Saturday nights, when stations would show a "late movie", there was no programming at all between about 11 p.m. and about 6 a.m., just the trusty old test pattern.

Being the oldest, I did get to stay up a bit later than my brothers and sisters, but still, on school nights 10 p.m. was my limit. On weekends, however, I could have at it as late as I wanted. I especially liked staying up and watching old late movies with Mom on Saturday nights.

I remember many things about those early-television years and how they affected all of our lives. In many instances, I see that our little television had a way of bringing our family closer together, mainly because all seven of us would often gather around in the living room to enjoy some of the evening programs. At the top of my evening list were westerns like *Gunsmoke* (very much as I had pictured it from radio), *The Rifleman*, *Maverick*, and *Have Gun Will Travel*. Comedy and family shows were also big at our house. My favorites were *Ozzie and Harriet*, *Father Knows Best*, *My Little Margie*, *The Phil Silvers Show* (what we called Sergeant Bilko), and *I Love Lucy*. *To Tell The Truth* and *Name That Tune* were two of the game shows we all got into. Then there were the variety and music shows like

*The Jack Benny Show, The Gary Moore Show, Cid Caesar, Milton Berle, Red Skelton, Andy Williams, Rosemary Clooney, Ed Sullivan* on Sunday nights, and *Your Hit Parade* on Saturday night, brought to you by Lucky Strike cigarettes, so round, so firm, so fully packed, so easy on the draw. The only show I ever watched during the day, and usually only if I was sick and couldn't play outside or go to school, was an afternoon program called *Art Linkletter's House Party*. I watched it only because Mom watched it, but I'll have to say, it was an hour of pretty good entertainment. I especially liked the "kids say the darndest things" segment, where Art would interview kids, usually ages four to ten, asking them innocent questions, and in return would almost always get a truthful but hilarious answer. I also enjoyed the "what's in the house", "what's in your purse", and "tell me when one minute's up" segments of the show.

There were many evening family shows to choose from, but there was one in particular at the top of my list, and I think most of my family would have agreed. It was a Saturday night show that we almost never missed, and thankfully, in those years filled with half-hour programming, this show was an hour long. It was *The Jackie Gleason Show*, and to me it was the ultimate in comedy entertainment. Since I found humor in so many things around me, and was often laughing, it was no surprise that Jackie Gleason had me guffawing for a solid hour. I thought he was hilarious. On the other hand, my Dad wasn't what you'd call a jovial person. He was too busy to be jovial. But he did have a good sense of humor, and to hear him laugh out loud was always a prize to cherish. Jackie Gleason made him laugh too, making that one hour on Saturday night well spent and very special.

The kids' shows I watched were pretty much divided up into the local live-studio shows, which the stations presented after school and on Saturday mornings, and the taped network or independent production shows that were also put on during these kid-friendly hours. Some of the taped shows were the same shows I'd been listening to on the radio, and when they sprang to life in visual form, WHOA! What a disappointment. Sergeant Preston and Sky King looked nothing like I had imagined them through all those radio years. My hero of a Sergeant had morphed from the handsome super human he-man of my mind to a skinny beanpole with a cartoonish little mustache and a funny looking hat. Only his dog Yukon King looked as valiant as I had imagined. Sky King hadn't fared much better, having turned from the good looking and daring young pilot I had pictured into a middle-aged killjoy who always dressed way too nice. Besides that, his niece Penny didn't even hold a candle to the Penny of my imagination.

Oftentimes I'd spend an hour watching television after I got home from school, before I got on with my evening activities. One after-school program I liked was a sci-fi show called *Captain Video and His Video Rangers*. It didn't have much of a story line, but I loved the ray guns they used to evaporate anything they shot at. The show I usually watched after school was a live studio show that was broadcast from the Channel 3 studios called the *Sheriff Sid Show*. It was hosted by a man named Sid dressed up in a cowboy outfit. Set up next to the Sheriff was a set of risers where approximately 20 kids could sit and watch or participate in the show. They were kids from all over the area, some of them representing groups such as 4-H or Boy Scouts, and others just because they'd sent their names in and had been selected. A few kids from Covington had even been guests over the years.

Sometimes Sheriff Sid would have some local talent to perform live, a clown or a magician, but mostly it was just Sid interviewing the kids, and showing short films or cartoons. At my age, it was the short films which mostly interested me, stuff like *The Three Stooges* or *The Little Rascals,* also titled *Our Gang Comedies* in their earlier episodes. I was thoroughly hooked on *The Little Rascals,* as were my brothers and sisters and most every kid in the neighborhood. The Rascals seemed familiar. Their antics, camaraderie, lack of money, and just the way they portrayed themselves reminded us of ourselves, right there in our own neighborhood. Oh, the Rascals may have been more organized, and certainly they possessed more singing talent than any of us had ever dreamed of, but that didn't matter, we still saw ourselves in every scene. Personally I identified most of all with Spanky, the chubby one, but I envied Alfalfa because, as goofy as I thought he looked with his one hair sticking up on the back of his head, the girls always seemed to fall for him. We were forever trying to emulate the Rascals by putting on neighborhood variety shows in one shed or another, but I think that worked out better for my siblings than it did for me. At 11 and 12 years old, I was getting a little too old to playact with a bunch of grade-schoolers.

I suppose every generation that ever grew up in Covington had a few urban legends being passed around, and in my youth Sheriff Sid's Show was the source of one of them. Sid would usually ask the kids in the studio their names and where they were from. Sometimes he'd ask them if they wanted to say "Hi" to someone. One day Sid asked a boy if he wanted to say hello to anyone and, according to the legend, the kid said, "Hi Mom. Hi Dad. And here's to you Herbie," at which point he held up his middle finger. It wasn't hard to believe, after all, in those early days, live TV meant exactly that. What happened in front of the camera went out instantly to every household tuned to the station. Did it really happen? I don't know, but it did make for a good story. When I was in college, I passed on this legend to my roommate and best friend Jack Sauer. We both laughed until tears rolled down our faces. From that point on, we referred to each other as Herbie and Herb about as often as we used our real names.

While I'm at it, there were a few other urban legends floating around Covington, one of which might have had some merit, a couple that were highly suspect, and one that was a total fabrication, although at the time every boy I ever knew wanted to believe it. The one that may have had some truth to it was about a Covington woman by the name of Hazel Rector. What I knew, because I could see it with my own eyes, was that Hazel lived in an unpainted, dilapidated, clapboard house that sat about halfway between the grade school and the high school on Market Street. When I saw her walking around town, she took long man-like strides wearing a long dress and shoes that looked like, and may very well have been, actual combat boots. That's all I knew for sure. But legend had it that on a number of occasions kids were chased all over town by Hazel because they called her Beechie to her face. Now, according to the legend, the kids called her Beechie because she chewed Beechnut chewing tobacco. Not only did she chew it, but she took it out of her mouth each night and dried it on her windowsill to be chewed again the next day. Was any of that true? I don't know. I was told the tale over and over and where there's smoke, supposedly there's fire, so maybe some, or all of it did happen. I know one thing; I never called her Beechie.

The urban legend that I sadly realized some time later was a complete and utter fabrication was one I won't explain thoroughly because of the innocent nature of this book, but it had to do with a substance that my friends and I would have given our eye teeth to have possessed a few drops of. What we knew from the legend, and were only too willing to believe, was that just a smidgen of it on the end of a pin dipped in the girl's Coke would cause her to go sexually berserk. Give her too much and she'd end up in dire circumstances. Gearshifts were often mentioned, as with the alleged girl from Hillsboro the first time I heard the story, and the poor girl from Perrysville during another telling of the story. Both girls had unfortunately received overdoses and their boyfriends had not been able to handle them. The magical substance was called Spanish Fly, and it was the source of many a graphic tale.

One legend had it that there was a girl at school a couple of years older than me who, if you accused her of wearing falsies (a padded bra), she'd prove you wrong right there in the hallway. I knew several guys who said it was the honest-to-God truth, but I, for one, never tested the legend and had serious doubts as to its authenticity.

Another was that there was a guy who lived half a block from the Covington fire station who would sometimes call in false alarms just so he could run across the street and ride the fire truck. Again, I had my doubts, but I guess it was possible.

As television became popular, it was easy to see that many of Covington's social events began to fade. I didn't see as many people at the movies. Attendance at school-sponsored events like the grade school carnival and high school concerts began to decline. Even attendance at church socials and civic group functions dwindled. People found easy entertainment in the comfort of their own homes, and it didn't cost them the price of admission. It was a social revolution, not only for Covington, but also for the whole world. Yet even as the world was changing all around me, I can't say that television really had that much effect on my own youthful social life. I still liked getting out and being with my friends as much as ever. The town was still my playground. Television was great entertainment, but if there was something else going on, I'd flip the ole boob tube off in an instant.

# Chapter 7

## *City Park*

From an early age, when my mother took me there to play on the swings, the slides, the teeter-totter, and merry-go-round, the city park was an integral part of my summer entertainment. And as I grew older, I spent more and more of my summer days there. When I was about ten years old, the city decided it was time to put in a public swimming pool. Veedersburg had already had one for a few years, and the Covington folks didn't like having to go to Veedersburg or Danville to swim. After that it seemed like half the kids in Covington spent many summer days down there, even if Dr. Suzuki did rant on-and-on about the pool being the source of Covington's annual ear infection epidemic. The fact that the pool originally had no filter was most likely the culprit. Polio was also a concern for most parents, but thankfully, we didn't have an epidemic of that dreaded disease. In the summer between my junior and senior year of high school, the summer Alinda and I started going together, the pool was common ground for the two of us.

Between the pool and the skating rink, we spent many happy hours in each other's company. I enjoyed the skating rink more so than the swimming pool because I liked the beat and sound of the loud organ music to which we skated the afternoons and nights away. Sometimes we skated arm-in-arm, performing little skating dance steps, and sometimes one of us would skate backward while the other faced forward. When I was there by myself, I joined in all the special skates like the "paddle skate", the "hokey pokey", the "men's choice", and the "reverse skate". In the reverse skate we had to skate clockwise, which was the opposite of how we normally skated. It was awkward taking the corners by crossing your left foot over your right, and caused many of us to hit the floor. I scratched a knee more than once doing the reverse skate.

The rink itself was a temporary setup and had to be erected in the spring of each year and taken down in the fall. The skating floor came in several large, wooden sections that were fitted together then supported by stacks of cement blocks. It ended up about three feet off the ground. Then the rink was covered by a huge circus tent supported by a couple of long poles that came down through the center of the floor. Unless there was bad weather, the sides of the big tent were rolled up to let the breeze blow through, and also to let the town folks, who wanted to watch the skating and listen to the music, park their cars around its perimeter. I couldn't wait for George Hershberger to put it up each spring and usually found myself at the park watching him and his crew in action. I know for at least two years I watched it being erected on Memorial Day, while they had the Indianapolis 500 race, something I never missed, blaring from a portable radio.

In the spring of 1955, a few days before my twelfth birthday, it was a beautiful sunny day as I watched George and a couple of other men put the floor together, and dreamed of skating on it the next week. The radio was broadcasting "the greatest spectacle in racing", and Bill Vukovich, my hero and the guy I wanted to grow up to be just like, was increasing his lead. That's when tragedy struck. The announcer said there had been a bad wreck on the backstretch and that Bill Vukovich had been involved. OH NO! Not Bill Vukovich! They must have been mistaken. He had won the last two years, and he was going to win again this year. There was immediate speculation on the part of the announcers as to Vukovich's circumstances, and mostly it didn't sound good. As the afternoon wore on my heart began to sink, and before the race was over they announced that my hero's car had been caught up in a wreck, jumped the back retaining wall, flipped a number of times in the air, landed on its top, and caught fire. Bill Vukovich was dead, and I went home in tears. The next week I was skating.

We didn't have a high school tennis team so during the summer months before my junior and senior years I made use of the park's tennis courts, which were located north and east of the swimming pool. The courts were lighted so we could play at night, and it was here that my folks saw me smoking for the first time one night when they came down to watch the skaters.

For many years there was a quarter-mile harness racing track at the park, grandstand and all. But by the time I was old enough to make my way to the park; harness racing in Covington was a thing of the past. While I was in junior high, the track was covered in cinders and converted to a running track for the high school track team, and about that same time the grandstand was torn down. Today there's hardly a sign that a harness racing tack ever existed. There was also a skeet shooting range just behind The American Legion cabin in the center of the track, and I always enjoyed watching the men shoot clay pigeons on a Sunday afternoon. That's no longer there either.

One year someone built and opened a small cafe just south of the tennis courts. They served sandwiches, ice cream, and soft drinks, and for several weeks it was a semi-hangout for my friends and me. It didn't last long though. A clientele of kids making a Coke last all day long while playing cards couldn't have been very profitable, and it seems to me that it closed soon after it opened.

During my later grade school years, I made good use of the small building just inside the Fourth Street entrance to the park. It had a ping-pong table and was stocked with board games and various outdoor summer-type games such as badminton, jump rope, croquet, and volleyball. I went down there several times each summer to play ping-pong inside, badminton outside, and checkers and Monopoly on the picnic tables. It was a good change of pace from playing in the neighborhood, and there were always a few kids hanging around just waiting for someone to come along and play.

One park activity that didn't turn out very well for me was Little League baseball. There was only one baseball diamond at the park at that time, and it was right across the little road from the big pavilion (where it still is today). It was on this diamond that I attempted to play Little League baseball the first year it was organized in Covington. The problem was, unlike many of the kids my age, I'd never played a game of baseball in my life, sandlot or otherwise. I'd thrown a baseball around a little, but that was it. The only thing I knew about baseball I'd learned from my Grandpa Stanton when, between the ages of five and seven, he took me to some of the Danville Dans games over at the Danville Stadium. What I learned from those games was that if I begged Grandpa long enough, he'd buy me some peanuts in the shell to go along with my root beer, and that the umpires all had vision problems.

I didn't really want to play, but Mom and Dad thought if I tried it I might like it. Foolishly, I agreed. To be part of an organized sporting activity was foreign to me and the resulting problems turned out to be numerous. First of all, most of the kids on the team were either in my class or the class above me, but none of them were my real friends. I didn't play with any of them on or off the schoolyard, so from the very beginning I felt like a stranger. Secondly, for some reason Dad hadn't mentioned Little League until they had already started practice, so I missed the first few practices, an important time when I'm sure they learned most of the rules. Thirdly, they put me on The Indians, a team full of players who'd been playing sandlot ever since they were old enough to hold a bat in their hands. I was lost from the start.

My coaches were Elmo Young and Frank Brewer, and as good as those guys were, I don't think they realized that I was starting from absolute scratch. For instance, when they talked about giving signals to the batter, I had no problem understanding that if the coach touched the bill of his cap it meant he wanted a hit-and-run. The problem was I had no idea what a hit-and-run was, and was too embarrassed to ask. By the time I started practice, the coaches already knew who the good baseball players were and who'd be out there on the field during the games. Naturally, I was relegated to the bench. In those days, they didn't have to rotate through all the players, so during the entire year I doubt that I batted half-a-dozen times. I never did hit the ball in a game, and I never caught a ball. When the Indians won the championship trophy, I felt no pride whatsoever. I knew I'd been a big fat zero to the team and was actually embarrassed when we went out to celebrate. For me it had been a miserable experience, and I was just happy that the season had finally and mercifully come to an end.

# Chapter 8

# *Buddies*

By the time I reached high school, I had grown completely apart from my neighborhood friends. I'd had years of fun with them, they'd been my playmates and best friends for a long time, but I was growing up. Besides, as I began to have less and less in common with them, my classroom friendships began to blossom. Instead of war or cowboys and Indians, I became interested in school activities. Football, sockhops, hanging out with my friends, and girls became my new priorities.

With the exception of Alinda, a friendship that didn't develop until my senior year, over the course of my sixth grade and junior high years I began to develop relationships with what would become my closest high school pals. The best of these friendships would be with four of my classmates, Bob Dicks, who I had been friends with since grade school, and had developed it even further during our Boy Scout years, plus Jim Bodine, Jerry Carter, and Bill Huffman. Even though we weren't exclusive, since we all had other friends too, the five of us did hang together a lot, and maybe the one thing that brought us together most often, especially in the early years, was that we all learned to play poker together.

I learned to play cards at an early age. Playing cards was in my blood. It was probably my parent's favorite form of entertainment, just as it had been with my mother's parents before her. She was brought up in a card-playing family. Cards were fun, entertaining, and free. Mom belonged to a bridge club that met in the various members' homes once a month and I always liked it when it was Mom's turn. On those nights, the house would be spick and span and Mom would set up card tables in the living room. She would also prepare a nice desert for the ladies, have little dishes of nuts and candy placed on the card tables, and send me to the movie. When I got home, I'd always make a trip into the living room where all the ladies, Rosie Martin, Babe West, and Gladyne Young to name a few, would ooh and ahh over what a sweet boy I was.

On weekends, Mom and Dad would often have their best friends, Jenny and Carl Bowers, and sometimes Alice and Russell Bowers, over to play cards. Many nights I'd go to bed in the next room and listen to the six of them laughing, telling jokes, and playing cards long into the night. So playing cards was second nature to me, and it didn't take long before poker was my game of choice.

Starting as early as our freshman year, my buddies and I played poker as often as we could. We didn't play high stakes of course; none of us could afford that. The most any of us would likely win or lose in a night would be a dollar, and if you won a buck and a half you thought you were rich. But we all loved the game, and it gave us something to do that many of our classmates didn't have. The games would be played in one of our homes, but most often in Bill Huffman's basement. Bill's father was the plant manager at the new Olin Mathieson cellophane plant, the plant that had brought Bill's family, Alinda's family, and a couple of hundred other families up from the Brevard, North Carolina area to settle in Covington. Bill was an only child and lived in a new home his parents had built on Orchard Drive, one of Covington's new housing developments. Several of these developments had sprung up with the opening of the new plant, and Bill's home sat smack in the middle of what five years earlier had been Keller's Apple Orchard, just on the northeast edge of town.

Bill's parents, big Bill and Nat, were very nice folks and were only too happy to have Bill and his friends playing cards in their basement. The biggest problem with playing at any of our other homes was that we had to watch our language, and just at the age when we were learning the nuances of cussing, telling dirty jokes, and just plain gutter talking. When we were older, there was also the problem of not being able to smoke in anyone else's home, a problem the smokers among us didn't have to worry about in Bill's basement.

We never played poker at my house because it was too crowded and there were just too many people to have to contend with. Neither did we play at Jerry Carter's because his parents were against card playing. We did play a few times in Bob Dicks's basement, where his dad Larry and brother John sometimes joined in. We also played just a few times at Jim Bodine's house, and it was always a hoot playing there. Jim's kitchen floor had a severe slant from one end to the other, making it way too tempting. At any given moment, one or two of us would fall sideways out of our chairs and onto the floor as if gravity had finally won out. Thankfully, Jim laughed along with the rest of us.

We usually reserved our poker playing for the weekends, when we sometimes played until early morning. I didn't really have a curfew, although until I was a senior I don't suppose I was ever out past 1 a.m. All Mom and Dad asked was that I phone them sometime before 11 p.m. to let them know I was going to be out late and where I was. They trusted me, and I never let them down by forgetting to call.

Actually, it wasn't until my senior year in high school that I found ample reason to lie to my parents about anything, particularly about where I was going or what I was doing. That's when I started a little of what I suppose would be considered testing the adulthood waters. These were typical little high school stunts requiring typical little lies. At least they were typical by Covington's standards which, when compared to what was probably going on in the bigger cities in the country, were pretty minimal. In that sense, I don't think the transgressions were what I'd call major.

It only took two warm Sterling beers to get me drunk for the first time. It happened in a ramshackle little shed along Portland Arch Road, on a hot summer night a few weeks before I was to enter my senior year of high school. The shed was owned by some relative of Ken Tuggle's, one of my classmates and the running back on our football team. It was small and unpainted, with nothing inside but three or four camp beds. We commonly referred to it as Tuggle's cabin. I don't recall how Bill Huffman got hold of the six-pack of warm Sterling beer that night, but by midnight he, Jerry Carter, and I had consumed two beers apiece and ended up stumbling drunk.

Thankfully, since coming home would have been a disaster, I'd told my parents that we were spending the night at Tuggle's cabin on a campout. That may very well have been my first pre-meditated lie to them, because I knew when I told them it was a "campout" that the sole purpose of going there was to drink my first beer. I never would have guessed how much fun or how crazy getting drunk with two friends could be, or how sorry I would be about the whole thing when I started throwing up. It was a totally new experience for all three of us, and we reveled in our inhibitions. I laughed until I cried as I watched Bill Huffman get to stumbling around so badly that he finally fell flat on his face with a cigarette in his mouth. As for myself, I fell through a bamboo curtain that separated a couple of the cots. For the first couple of hours I thought it was the best time I'd ever had, something I wanted to do many times in the future. However, by the time I'd emptied my stomach with the wet heaves, then progressed to the awful feeling of the dry heaves, I swore it was the last time I'd ever drink. The next morning the three of us looked pretty sad, but Bill was the worst because he had two big blisters on his lips from the cigarette burns he had received when he fell on his face.

Other than one other time when I went drinking during my senior year, that time with Bob Dicks and Jim Bodine, where I consumed three beers with similar falling-down-drunk results, the only other thing I had to lie to my parents about was where Alinda and I went on some of our dates. Now often-times we did go to the movies in Danville, or go to Danville to eat, or go to Veedersburg to the drive-in theater, just like I told my parents, but as often as not we'd end up going parking. Our favorite parking spot was a secluded spot up a little rise and behind a patch of pine trees just a few yards off the Sandhill road. I'm sure my folks knew we didn't spend all our dates at the movies, but they never let on that they didn't believe me. All they'd have had to do was check the mileage on the car once to find out that I'd driven it only three miles rather than the twenty that would have been required to go to Danville. If they ever did check, they never said a thing.

My pals and I all got our drivers' licenses shortly after our 16th birthdays, and that gave us a new form of freedom. I never asked for our car to cruise around with my friends. We did have a second car by then, but it was an ugly two-tone blue and white Ford station wagon that I wouldn't have been caught dead cruising in. Dad did let me borrow the nicer looking Dodge if I really needed it, especially after I started dating Alinda. But delivering mail in that car was Dad's living, so to borrow it to run around in with a carload of buddies was out of the question. So I seldom provided transportation for our gang. Jim drove us around town one night, but after that, no one would get in the car with him again. Even to us kids, who had little car sense, it was obvious that Jim was a terrible driver (Jim was the first of us to die. It was a few years after we graduated from high school, and it was the result of a car wreck in which Jim was driving). Bob Dicks drove occasionally, but not often, and Jerry drove once in a while. Whenever Jerry drove he always sat on a pillow to make himself look taller.

It was Bill who actually became our gang's main chauffeur. Right after getting his driver's license, his parents gave him a 1949 Ford coup. After that Bill didn't walk anywhere. In fact, our whole gang spent fewer hours hoofing it. Many a night we'd load up four or five of us in Bill's Ford then do nothing more than cruise the streets of Covington. From the Dog 'n Suds to the square to the park, then back to the square and on up to the Dog 'n Suds again. We might spend an entire night running this same route over and over.

One summer day, soon after Bill had gotten his car, someone mentioned that we ought to head down to the Cayuga fair because they'd heard there was a hoochy-coochy show set up. That's all it took. None of us had ever seen a hoochy-coochy show or anything resembling one, so the prospect of seeing girls in pasties and g-strings, things we'd only seen in magazines, was way too tempting. That night we loaded up Bill's car and headed south.

When we arrived, it didn't take long for us to find the tent with a scantily clad girl strutting back and forth on a small outdoor stage in front of an oversized tent. Standing next to her was a carnival barker announcing to the swelling crowd of men (and boys) that for one dollar you would be able to feast your eyes on much more of this lovely little lady when the show started inside the tent. To our dismay there was a sign posted outside the tent that said you must be 18 to enter. All of us were only 16, and after much discussion we decided that we would all stand on our tiptoes and try to fool the guy into thinking we were older. We didn't have to worry for long. Once he started selling tickets for the show, it quickly became obvious that if you were tall enough to reach up and hand the man your buck, he was only too happy to let you in. I saw boys going in there who couldn't have been over 13 years old.

I'm not going to describe the show, but let me say that I walked out of that tent another fifty cents poorer than when I walked in, and knowing for the first time in my life what a naked grown woman looked like. I'll have to say that we were all so pleased that we made a return trip the next summer.

On a Friday or Saturday night we'd sometimes head over to Danville to cruise Marty K's, one of those drive-in hamburger joints that were common in the 1950's, one of which was featured in that great teen coming-of-age movie, *American Graffiti.* Marty-K was a place where kids from towns all over the area congregated every night of the week with the main

purpose of showing off how cool they were, and of course, trying to impress the opposite sex. Being cool was the easy part for
five guys crammed into a '49 Ford. Hanging out the car windows, cussing, smoking, and waving at every car that cruised
by was all part of the ritual. On top of that, there was wink-
ing and whistling at the girls, making impromptu jokes about
everything and everyone, showing off for anyone who'd looked
our way, and challenging anyone who gave us guff. All rolled
into one, there was no better way to describe it—we were definitely cool. And we weren't alone. Adults avoided the place
like the plague, so everyone who cruised Marty K was cool. Did
our little carload from Covington actually impress anyone but
ourselves? Probably not, especially not the girls, they seemed to
shrug us off like fleas on a dog.

To anyone over 20 years old I don't suppose we were anything less than obnoxious, the whole parking lot full of us. But
we thought we were impressive, we thought we were it, and
in truth that's all that really counted. It gave us something
to laugh about, something to talk about on the way home
and for days to come, and I guess it satisfied our feelings of
self-importance.

*Mom and Me (Dad was at War in the Pacific) - 1944*

*Dad, Duke (who always followed Dad home on his mail route), and Me picking strawberries -*
*About 1956 - Dad Loved Dogs - We were Duke's second home*

*John and Me - around 1954*

*Ronnie Massey, Judy Massey, John, Me - 1951*

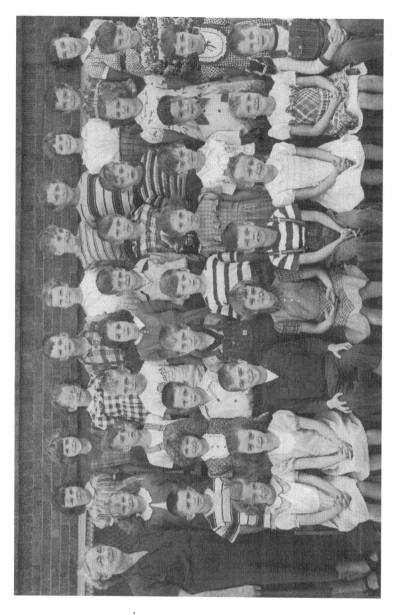

*Miss Smith's Second Grade Class 1950-51 - I'm top row, 7th from the left between Charlie Webb and Karen Keller*

*Me as a Boy Scout - about 1954*

*Covington Methodist Church - Junior Choir - About 1952*
*I'm front row, second from the right, between Dan Warrick and Karen Burrin*

*Al Harden and Me - 1951*

*Easter Morning - 1957*
*Nancy, Bob, Mary Ann, John, Charlie*

*My Family 1955 - I'm in the back*
*Front (L to R)- Mary Ann, Nancy, Mom, John, Dad, Charlie*

*1960-61 Covington Trojan Football Team*
*Front Row Seniors (L to R) - Jay Paxton, John Smith, Ken Tuggle, Bob*
*Dickinson (94), Mike Morgan, Bob Dicks*

*Alinda as Trojan Marching Band Flag Girl 1960*

*Alinda and Me at Saddie Hawkin's Dance - We were crowned
Li'l Abner and Daisy Mae - 1960*

# Chapter 9

# *Home*

From the time I was born until shortly after I turned two years old, my Mother and I lived with her parents in Tilton, Illinois. My Grandma and Grandpa Stanton had raised nine children, four of whom were still at home, if you included my mother. My cousin Bobby George was also being raised by my grandparents since his mother, their daughter, had died at an early age. I guess finding space for my baby bed was probably no big deal.

Mom had a daytime job working in downtown Danville at a business called the Earl Gasthoff, Co., where they made Christmas decorations for major department stores like Macy's in New York. During the day I was cared for by my grandmother, uncles, and cousin. At night Mom was home to take care of me. My parents had been married for a little over a year when I was born, but by the time I arrived in June of 1943,

Dad had been drafted and was doing his Army training at Ft. Leonard Wood Missouri. He got just enough leave to rush home for my birth, then was off within days to ship out to the war in the Pacific.

I was two years old when the war ended and Dad came home. I've been told many times that I was waiting on the stairs at my grandparent's house when I saw him for the first time. He came walking through the door in his army uniform, and I stood up and said, "Daddy."

My mom asked me a number of times over the years if I remembered that day, and I always answered, "Yes, I think so." However, at two years old I know it would be unusual to actually have that memory, and yet, even now, in my mind I can still see my Dad walking through that door in his Army uniform and me jumping up to say, "Daddy." Whether it was a real memory or a vision of what I had been told so many times, I'll never know.

Dad grew up in Covington, spent his whole life here. His parents, my grandfather Sam Dickinson and my grandmother Maude, along with Grandma's sister, my great Aunt Myra, moved from Decatur, Illinois to Covington in 1905. As so often happens when it's too late to ask the questions only the living can answer, I don't know the particulars of why they chose to pick up and move to Covington all those years ago. I do know that, either before or shortly after they moved here, my grandparents bought a home on Park Avenue with several acres of fruit bearing trees and bushes that became known as the Dickinson Fruit Farm.

During the great depression, my grandparents lost the fruit farm, and shortly thereafter my grandfather died. My father was an adult by that time and he and Grandma Dickinson moved to a house at 601 Pearl Street. That's the house that became our home, my home until I was grown and left Covington, my parent's home until they died, and my sister Mary Ann's home to this day.

Dad was very handy when it came to remodeling and building. In the army he'd been in the combat engineers, so when he came home from the war he put his skills to work. The first thing he did was make an upstairs apartment for my grandmother, while Mom, Dad, and I made our home downstairs. It was an arrangement that lasted for the remainder of my grandmother's life, about 40 more years. She died at the age of 96.

My first memories of Covington, actually my first memories ever, unless Dad's homecoming was indeed a memory, are, strangely, of songs and dreams. Dad usually had the radio playing whenever he was working on the house, which was often. He and Mom loved the big band sounds and loved going to dances that featured that music. So that's the radio music he usually had playing. One day he picked me up and sat me on a kitchen counter in what was our old kitchen so that I could watch him plaster an arched doorway. I must have been about four years old and as I sat there watching him, a couple of songs came on that, for some reason, caught my attention. I really liked them. I didn't know the names of the songs at the time, but they stuck with me and some years later I discovered they were, "Spring Fever" from the Broadway musical *State Fair*, plus a tune that was old, even at the time I heard it, called "The Old Lamplighter". It was a great feeling that day, listening to music that I liked and watching my dad work to make our home an even better place to live. It gave me a warm and cozy feeling.

At about that same age I had two dreams that I've never forgotten. Why I still remember them after 65 years I can't imagine, but they're the only dreams from my childhood that

I do remember, and they were both nightmares. In the first dream, I was standing on our dining room sofa, looking over the back of it through a double set of long windows. As I was looking out those windows, a ghost-like figure went skating back and forth on a pair of roller skates. It was wearing something white and gauzelike that looked like a nightgown, and its head was covered in the same material so that I couldn't see its face. I don't know if I woke up crying or not, but I do know I woke up scared. I thought about that dream for many nights to come and can still picture it quite clearly today.

The other dream was just as simple and just as scary. Part of our basement had dirt walls that ran halfway up between the floor and ceiling before leveling out and running to the end of the house, forming a crawl space under part of the house. In the dream, I was in the basement, and I could see perched on top of one of these walls a very scary shiny black animal. Again, it was a dream that woke me up with a fright. What the animal was didn't register right away. In the dream, it had two appendages that flapped together like two hands clapping. It took me awhile, but I finally figured out that the scary animal in my basement was a seal. Maybe I had just seen my first picture of a seal that day, I don't know. What I do know is that I didn't go to the basement for a long time after that night.

Mom was always the mother and housewife, staying home to take care of a husband and, eventually, five children. Later in life after a couple of us kids left the nest, she also became an Avon cosmetics sales lady. Like most men of his time, Dad was our breadwinner, and providing for his family was a responsibility he took seriously. After we got settled back in Covington after the war, Dad's first job was with the city of Covington's water and electric department.

Sometimes in the evening Dad had to check the water tower pump station, and sometimes if I was lucky he'd take me with him. That must have been where the chlorine was added to the water because I loved that smell and would ask him to take me along just so I could get a whiff. One day when Dad was working on an electric line right across from our house, Mom and I walked across the street and watched him climb the wooden power pole with special spikes that were attached to the inside of his shoes. On this day he got about halfway up the pole when the spike ripped out a chunk of the wood and down he slid. Dad was all right, but it scared me to death. I cried I was so upset. I decided then and there that I'd never have a job where I had to climb electric power poles when I grew up.

Not many years later Dad got a job with the Post Office. He started out as a city mailman, delivering mail to every house in Covington at a time when it was all done on foot. As time went on, Dad went from a city to a rural carrier. It was better money, and he no longer had to walk ten or fifeen miles a day with a twenty-pound mailbag slung over his shoulder. He started with the smallest of Covington's three rural routes and worked his way up to the longest because there was more money with each move.

As good as the postal service job was, it was still always a bit of a struggle to make ends meet around our house. With a family of seven to provide for, Dad almost always had other moneymaking projects going on. Among them were buying, then remodeling older homes to resell, building a new home from scratch, then selling it, and building and operating a cement block manufacturing company. A couple of these, including the cement block business, were in partnership with a friend and fellow mailman named Glay Abernathy.

So, when it came to household finances, it was Dad's job to bring home the money, and it was Mom's job to see that the money stretched as far as possible. They were both good at their jobs. And the kids responsibility? Well, we learned that you didn't ask for money you didn't need, and if you wanted some extra spending money, then you'd better get out and earn it. That's the way it was in the Dickinson home, and that was the way we lived our lives. The interesting thing was, I never once felt that I was underprivileged, not once in all those childhood years. And if I ever wished for something I couldn't afford, it was a fleeting moment.

By the time I was 11 years old I had four younger siblings. My brother John was born about two years after Dad got home from the war, which made him four years younger than me. He would be among the first of what became known as the "Baby Boomer Generation". Charlie, a chubby happy baby who I thought was about the cutest kid I'd ever seen, was three years younger than John, and Mary Ann, who was born about two years after Charlie was the first of my two sweet baby sisters. Nancy, the youngest, was born two years later and inherited Mom's middle name for her own, Ruth, which was also the name Mom went by. That made, including Mom and Dad, seven of us living in a five room, one bathroom house. I'm not sure how we did it. As for myself, I never saw the tight quarters or lack of bathroom time as a problem. Being a boy, I could always go outside or down to the basement coal pile to take a pee.

John, Charlie, and I shared a bedroom in what had once been the kitchen. One of Dad's earliest remodeling projects had been to build a new kitchen in what was originally a dining/sitting room, then he turned the old kitchen into our bedroom. In our bedroom there was a set of bunk beds where my brothers slept, and a single bed for me. We also had a closet and one dresser, the top of which could never be seen as it was always stacked high with dirty clothes and anything else we wanted to toss on it. Our bedroom also served as the clothes washing room for the wringer washer before Mom got a modern washing machine early in the 50's installed in the kitchen. In the winter when Mom couldn't hang clothes on the outdoor clothesline, our bedroom also served as the clothes-drying room, with multiple takedown lines running back and forth from one wall to the other.

By the time Mary Ann and Nancy came along, Dad had enlarged a tiny room in the back corner of the house that had been used for storage. So the girls had their room, the boy had theirs, and Mom and Dad had theirs, although to my amazement, it was only theirs at night after everyone else went to bed. That is to say, Mom and Dad's bedroom was the hub of the entire house. The shortest distance to the bathroom or to the girl's bedroom from either the kitchen or the living room was a beeline straight through my parents' bedroom. And to top it off, there were no doors. In fact, there were no doors on any room in the house except the bathroom, and thank goodness, Dad did put a door there. I don't even want to think of how my parents were able to have four more kids after moving into that house while sleeping in traffic central, but it's obvious they worked it out somehow and a far as I know none of us kids were ever the wiser.

As crowded as it was, I always felt good about our home. For seven people crowded together under one roof, I'd say it was pretty harmonious. There was very little anger, yelling, admonishing, or arguing. In fact, I can't remember the time I had a fight with Charlie or my sisters, mainly I suppose because they were so much younger than me. The interaction I had with the three of them was pretty much positive at all times. The thing the girls and I did most often was doing acrobatics on the floor. To do this I'd raise them up with my feet pressed against their stomachs and hold them high in the air as they straightened themselves out and did a "tah-dah." Or, they'd come up behind me and I'd toss them over my shoulder while flipping them over in mid-air onto a soft pillow. I made up words for all these tricks, and we called the shoulder flip the 'quickly-nimble'. They pestered me to do 'quickly-nimble' on a regular basis.

Mary Ann and Nancy were a set. Everything Mary Ann did, Nancy would be a step behind doing an imitation. Mary Ann was only too happy to have Nancy tagging along, so besides being sisters they turned out to be best friends. I'd say that Charlie and Mary Ann had more of an adversarial relationship, somewhat like John and I, but maybe even more intense. I didn't get to experience a lot of their growing-up years as I was off to college when Nancy was in the second grade.

John and I, on the other hand, did have our ups and downs. If I ever had a fight, it was with John, and I would have to say it was probably always my fault. When we were young, John and I were bathed together in our one and only bathtub. That was the ritual because it not only saved time, but more importantly it saved expensive hot water. Over the years, Dad came up with several schemes for saving money in the bathroom. John and I bathing together was just the first. For a short time we were all asked to flush the toilet only every other time if it was just for a pee. Then for quite a long time Dad had a brick sunk in the toilet tank so it would take up a brick's worth of water.

By the time I was in second or third grade, John and I were still bathing together, but by ourselves with no supervision. It was during these baths that I began to find perfect opportunities to tease him. I always sat with my back to the spigot (which by the way was the same position I was sitting in the bathtub 15 years later when one day Alinda asked me why I was sitting backwards in the bathtub. I didn't have a clue what she was talking about). To tease John, sometimes after I pulled the plug to let the water out, I'd pretend that I was being sucked down the drain, and told him to hurry and tell Mom or Dad. Out of the bathtub he'd jump, wet and cold, and run to Mom and Dad to save me from going down the drain. At other times we'd be playing with the soap bubbles and I'd pretend that I got the soap in my eyes and couldn't get my eyelids open. I'd ask John to help pull my eyelid open, but he couldn't do it either, so I asked him to hurry up and go get a pair of pliers. He fell for it every time.

As John got older, he became, as most kids do, afraid of bugs. One day when we were playing outside, I told him to close his eyes and open his hand for a nice surprise. I placed an ant in his palm, and when he opened his eyes he began screaming. I felt bad about that one and cut way back on my teasing after that. But still, I teased him plenty, and once in a while out of frustration, he'd take a swing at me, sometimes connecting with my arm or my chest. When this happened, I simply held him off at arm's length until he cooled down or went away crying.

John and I would sometimes compete for our younger siblings' attention by saying, "Okay, who wants to be in my Pal Club?" I have no idea where the term came from, maybe from something on TV, but it was one of our little competitions. The rules were unstated, but by default whichever one of us could talk at least two of our three siblings into being in our Pal Club was the winner. That's all there was to it. It was a game for me, I wasn't the least bit hurt if I lost. But I have a feeling it may have been more of a personal thing for John.

Many times John and I would be arguing about something at night when we went to bed, and the purpose of this game was to get in the last word. Typically, these arguments would end with something like, "No you can't," from one of us and, "Yes I can," in return. As the minutes of the argument ticked by, and both of us began to get sleepy, the words began to deteriorate to simple, "noes" and "yeses," and finally to simple grunts, "uh" and "uh." It was a given that whoever got in the last "uh" could consider himself the winner of the argument even though the other one didn't know he had lost, because he was asleep. Sometimes this would go on for half an hour or longer with each "uh" becoming further and further apart in the hopes that you would finally get in the last one and could, mercifully, close your eyes and go to sleep. I think I usually outlasted him, but in the end there was no real satisfaction in knowing you'd beaten a brother who wasn't even aware of the fact that he'd been beaten.

I loved John but I seldom showed it. Showing overt signs of love in our family was not a Dickinson trait. However, one Saturday morning I walked through the living room and saw John sitting on a short stool in front of the TV. He'd ordered a special kit that contained some markers and a piece of plastic that you could put over the TV screen. The show he was watching was called *Winky Dink and You*, featuring an animated character named Winky Dink who got into all kinds of trouble and needed your help to get him out of it. This particular morning Winky Dink had been chased to the edge of a cliff by a monster and needed a ladder to reach the bottom. "Draw a ladder for Winky Dink boys and girls," the narrator said, and up to the screen John's hands flew, drawing a ladder to save Winky Dink from dire destruction. I had a strange feeling come over me that moment as I silently stood there watching him save his little pal. I guess it was a feeling of love. It was a feeling of closeness for sure. And it seems to me that I felt a little closer to John and teased him just a little less after that morning.

Most nights all seven of us were gathered around the supper table where Mom always served up plenty to eat. After supper Dad or one of us kids would do the dishes, and later in the evening, on a night I wasn't out and about, all seven of us might be found in the living room gathered around the TV. In that room there was just enough seating to accommodate all of us, but there were only a couple of recliners, and they were prime seating. The rule was that if you got up, your seat was up for grabs, no exceptions. Those in the recliners could hold off going to the bathroom forever.

My Grandma Dickinson lived upstairs, and I had to be reminded to go up and visit her occasionally. Grandma was always glad to see me, and once I was up there I was usually glad I went. Grandma had a copy of James Whitcomb Riley's *Child Rhymes*, and when I was small, she'd take it from her bookcase and read from it as I looked at the pictures. She read the poems from that book to me many times, and I grew to love some of them. My favorites were *The Bear Story, Little Orphan Annie, The Runaway Boy,* and all the poems about *The Raggedy Man* or *Elizabeth Ann*. As I grew older we'd also play Chinese Checkers and Canasta, but mostly we'd just visit.

Grandma was a devout Methodist and a die-hard Republican, and based on these two factors, around which she shaped her life, she always had advice on how I should live mine. For the most part I agreed with her, and early on took most of it as gospel. As I grew older, however, I began to question some of her beliefs, like her obvious dislike of Catholics, Jews, Negroes, and Democrats. I never argued with my grandmother, but her seemingly blind prejudices didn't sit right with me, so I'd ask her to clarify herself. Of course she always had answers, most of which I couldn't agree with either, so as time went on I took less and less of her advice to heart.

My dad wasn't much like his mother in most ways. Oh, we were all Methodists, were baptized and members of the church at least, but unlike Grandma, who never missed a Sunday and taught a Sunday School class for decades, we made it to church only a couple of times a month. We never read the Bible at home or said prayers except on special occasions. And even though there was as much grumbling about Democrats downstairs as there was upstairs, I never heard Dad badmouth others' religious beliefs or other races. That's not to say that Dad didn't have any prejudices. Oh no. Besides Dad's constant grumbling about the weather, by the mid-1950's Dad would watch television news or read the newspaper then rage on and on about the low-life worthless hippies and America's moral decline. I tried to argue with him over these issues as I grew older, but he simply got louder. Finally, I gave up trying to reason with him at all and learned to tune him out.

I may have disagreed with his tirades of a changing America, but right or wrong, I think they were actually just one more sign that he was one of the most responsible men I've ever known. By the time I was twelve, Dad had accomplished the following with our home: dug out our basement with his own hands using a shovel and wheelbarrow, relocated our kitchen and built all the cabinets therein, remodeled two bedrooms, built a large screened-in porch, tore off the old screened-in porch, tore down two old sheds, and built a fallout shelter. Dad was also a good citizen, as demonstrated by his place on Covington's volunteer fire department. He also stepped up to help the community whenever community building projects asked for volunteers. I watched as Dad voluntarily set and detonated dynamite at the city park to remove tree stumps for the new swimming pool. In my eyes, my dad was truly what you'd call a man's man.

I'll have to say though, that Mom worked every bit as hard as Dad did. Mom was more laid back than Dad and let Dad take the lead as far as social and political issues were concerned. Whatever Dad said was usually okay with Mom, but Mom also had a mind of her own. They seldom ever argued, and never in my life did I hear either of them raise their voice to the other, but if Mom disagreed with something, Dad was the one to back off. It was Mom who usually prodded us into going to church or any other social event we might attend. Mom was also the one who controlled the household purse strings. If I needed money for something, it was Mom I had to ask, and I'd better have a good reason.

Mom loved it when she could pass along a compliment to one of her children. I could hear the joy in her voice as she described what good things someone had said about me or one of my brothers or sisters, and of course, it also made us happy. One day Mom came to me and told me how impressed my great aunt Myra Myers had been with me and what good manners I'd shown when I was mowing her yard and tipped my hat when she came out to say, "Hello." As much as I loved compliments, I told Mom that I hadn't tipped my hat at all, but that I was hot and was simply wiping my forehead. It actually made me angry and a bit embarrassed to think that my great aunt would think that I would actually do such an old-man thing. Kids didn't tip their hats. Nobody tipped their hats anymore. Maybe the Raggedy Man from a Riley poem might have tipped his hat 50 years ago, but not now, and certainly not me. I wanted to call Aunt Myra and tell her I hadn't done such a thing, but Mom said to let it lie, that Aunt Myra was just being nice and tipping my hat wouldn't have killed me anyway. A few days later when Grandma complimented me for the same hat-tipping incident, I just said, "Thanks."

Between Mom, Dad, and Grandma Dickinson, we all learned good manners as well as learning right from wrong. For myself, I felt I pretty much always had my parents' approval for my actions and mostly did whatever I had to do to maintain that approval. I guess that's why there were so few rules laid down. They trusted me, and I trusted them. It worked out well.

## HOLIDAYS

Christmastime was exciting around our house. It actually began in late November, the day the Montgomery Ward Christmas catalog arrived by mail. By the middle of December, those catalog toy pages were nearly tattered beyond reading. We kids knew not to ask for too much though. You could ask Santa for one big thing, and then maybe something small, but you better put your first choice at the top of the list because, depending on the year, that might be all Santa would bring you. There'd be a few surprises too, some wrapped gifts from Mom and Dad, a game for the family, but one big gift was the max, and if it was too big, i.e., expensive, Mom or Dad would encourage you to come up with an alternative. When I was younger, I was a little confused by this. I didn't figure Santa probably had a price limitation, but my folks seemed to think he did, so I went along, asking very few questions.

As to Santa himself, well I have two pretty good memories surrounding that jolly old elf. The first one had to do with Al Harden, a boy in my class who became one of Covington's best basketball players ever. When I was a junior in high school, Al and Bob Wallace, both classmates of mine, and three seniors named Scott Wallace, Mike (Snake) Alexander, and Larry Woodrow, along with 6th man Tom Frey, were the stars of our basketball team. That was the year Covington went all the way to the semi-state in the Indiana high school basketball tournament before being beaten by the eventual state champions, East Chicago Washington. As for Al, he ended up playing basketball for Indiana University.

So what does this have to do with Christmas? Well, I just wanted to point out that Al wasn't only a superstar on the basketball court, but once upon a time, he was also the superstar of my youth. The reason for that was that one day in the summer between our first and second grade years, I was down in Al's neighborhood on Eighth Street, along with several other kids, throwing a ball around. The subject of Santa Claus came up, and Al tells all of us that he saw Santa come down their chimney last Christmas. Of course, I was all ears and a bit skeptical so I had lots of questions for him. Where was he hiding? What did Santa look like? Did Santa have a pipe in his mouth? Al said he hid behind the living room door and watched the whole thing with his very own eyes, then went on to answer the rest of my questions without a hitch. I had no doubt that Al had seen Santa, and I was so envious of him I could hardly stand it.

It wasn't until the year I turned eight that I learned the real scoop about Santa, and the moment I found out, I was so embarrassed the disappointment didn't even register. It happened one day when Dick Rowe and I were playing in my yard, and somehow we'd gotten on the subject of Santa Claus. We'd had this same argument for years, and it was actually very simple. Dick said there was no Santa, and I said there was. To be honest, I'm not sure that Dick had ever believed in Santa. For Dick and his family it may have been easier to know the truth in order to face the fact that gift giving might be limited. Anyway, Dick and I were arguing pretty loudly when Mom stuck her head out the door and called me over. I don't remember the exact words she used, but she didn't beat around the bush or apologize for telling me straight-out that Dick was right and I was wrong. There was no Santa.

Why she chose that time to tell me I'm not sure. Maybe she was embarrassed for me, or maybe she thought it was the perfect opportunity. Neither am I sure of what my response was to her, but it seems to me that I said something like, "Yeah, I know." What I do remember for certain was that I was completely embarrassed. I had been carrying on like a lunatic with Dick Rowe, trying to get him to see the error of his ways only to learn that it was I who had no clue. I wasn't the least bit disappointed to learn the truth, but I wanted to hide under a rock for looking so foolish. When I went back out, I immediately told Dick that I had known there was no Santa all along, that I'd just been looking for an argument and that I didn't want to talk about it anymore. Knowing the truth didn't dampen my holiday spirit in the least. I still got just as much joy out of propagating the Santa myth with my brothers and sisters as I did believing it myself.

I looked forward to our Christmastime Methodist Church activities too. Since I loved singing in the junior choir, my favorite of our performances was when we sang during the December church services each year. "Away in a Manger" and "Oh Little Town of Bethlehem" were perennial favorites.

When I was older, I also enjoyed participating in the nativity presentations. One year Dick Frey played Joseph, and I played the wise man who bore gold to lay before baby Jesus. I had brought one of Mom's gold-colored aluminum mixing bowls as the golden gift, and during rehearsals Dick and I became a regular comedy team. As I approached the altar, singing "We Three Kings," Dick would lean over and pretend to spit into the bowl, at which time I would ding my finger on its bottom. The effect was like a mouthful of chewing tobacco hitting the bottom of a spittoon. Of course, that's all it took to break up the entire rehearsal, and it wasn't until we'd done it half a dozen times that it began to lose its laugh appeal. I don't believe Reverend Anderson found it quite as humorous as we did.

I don't remember my first participation in the church Christmas program; I was only four years old at the time. But Mom told me often that she was so proud of me as I stood in front of the congregation and repeated the four lines I had memorized. She told me it went like this:

I only have a little piece
It's just a line or two
So Merry Christmas to you all
And happy New Year too

Our tree always came from Kroger, and by Christmas half of its dried-up needles covered the floor and the gifts beneath it. We put it up and decorated it a few weeks before Christmas, with Dad hanging the lights and the tree topper and the rest of us putting on the balls, bells, and tinsel icicles. When we were all finished, Dad then spent quite a bit of time getting the icicles rearranged so that they were hanging down straight like real icicles, rather than draped from one branch to another. He tried year after year to get us to hang them right. "Have you ever seen an icicle hanging from the gutter sideways?" he'd ask, but it was too much trouble for us to hang them straight, so Dad continued to rearrange them year after year.

My favorite part of the decorating was setting up the little glitter-covered cardboard village somewhere near the tree. I'm not sure where it came from, I think from my Grandma and Grandpa Stanton's home, but it was already old and beginning to fall apart when I started setting it up. It had three little houses and a church with a steeple. I had to place it close to the tree because I needed to use four lights from one of the tree strands to put into the backs of the houses. When they were lit up at night, I thought they were beautiful, just like Covington at Christmastime.

On Christmas morning all of us kids gathered excitedly in the boys' bedroom before Mom and Dad gave us the go ahead to make our way into the living room. Santa always laid his gifts out unwrapped, near the tree. It was an exciting time walking through Mom and Dad's bedroom and catching that first glimpse of our presents. The tree was lit, Christmas music was playing, and Santa had eaten his cookie and drank most of his milk. With five children's gifts laid out for all to see, it was sometimes confusing as to exactly which gift belonged to whom, but Mom and Dad always seemed to know exactly which gift Santa had brought for which kid. The only time I recall picking up the wrong gift and then being a little disappointed, was one year when Santa brought a wristwatch for John and I thought it was for me. I'm sure I ended up with something that I wanted, but I still maintain that that watch would have looked mighty nice on my wrist.

After the Santa gifts came the opening of the wrapped gifts that Mom and Dad had bought for us and laid beneath the tree some days earlier. Someone was designated to play Santa and pass out the gifts, and when all the gifts were handed out, there was no waiting or taking turns, we all just tore into them simultaneously. Christmas paper, bows, name tags, and ribbons went flying everywhere, and in the end, thank-you's were said all around. The wrapped gifts were always nice but not nearly as impressive as the Santa gifts, mainly because they often contained something to wear.

By the time I was eight years old, and had started earning a quarter a week in allowance money by emptying ashes from our old coal furnace, I bought Mom and Dad each a Christmas gift every year. They never amounted to much as far as their costs were concerned, I never had much to spend. But it was important that I get just the right thing, so I carefully shopped the five-and-dimes and the drug store to find the perfect gifts. One year it was a bag of cashews from Burrin's hot nut display for Mom, another year a one-dollar bottle of Evening in Paris cologne. For Dad it was often a tool I thought he could use or maybe a cotton handkerchief. One of my favorites, however, was a wide, golden-colored necktie sporting cowboy hats and lassos. It was the most wonderful tie I'd ever seen, and I got it on sale for a dollar at the Ben Franklin. It was so nice to see Dad open it and hold it up to his neck to show me how great it looked. And I was so proud the next Sunday when he wore it to church. Strangely enough, soon after that, it somehow got pushed to the back of his closet, and I'm pretty sure it was never worn again.

One of the best things about Christmas was what we found on our kitchen table after all the gifts had been opened. It was usually a three-pound box, although one year it was a five-pound box, of either Brach's or Whitman's chocolates. And we kids were pretty much given free rein over it. Any candy at all was a rare treat in our home, but a three-pound box? Wow! Even if it was the cheapest candy on the market, we didn't know the difference, and that box sitting out there with no limits was like the icing on the Christmas cake. I guess we must have gauged ourselves pretty well though, the box didn't normally run dry until the next day.

I can remember several of my Christmas gifts in particular. One was my first bicycle when I was eight years old; another was my first, and actually my last sled, since I used it for many years, even after I'd outgrown it. I have no recollection of what the bike looked like, but I know I was thrilled with it. As for the sled, it was a beauty. Short and sturdy, a Radio Flyer that must have carried me down Douglass hill a thousand times. One year there was a miniature pool table that Santa had set up near the tree. It was one of the best family gifts we'd ever gotten because Dad got as much fun out of it as we boys did. He showed us how to put English on the ball and how to use the rails. On that Christmas we played pool all day, Dad with an occasional beer in his hand and me and my brothers with all the Prairie Farms eggnog we wanted. In my mind you couldn't get much closer to heaven than that.

I got my most exciting Christmas gift when I was eleven. I don't know why I wanted a BB gun so badly, maybe it was just a boy thing, but I'd been asking for one for a couple of years. The only previous experience I'd ever had with a BB gun had not had a positive outcome. A couple of years earlier, three guys in the class ahead of me were out riding their bikes along Commercial Street where I was playing, and they stopped to talk. I noticed that one was holding a BB gun in his hand and I asked him if I could see it. His reply was, "no" but he'd let me "feel" it. He then told me he was going to count to five, then shoot me. I didn't believe anyone would actually do something like that; I hadn't done a thing to him. I thought he must have been kidding, and then he started counting. By the time he got to "three," I took off as fast as I could run. But it wasn't fast enough. A couple of seconds later I felt the BB hit my back. Thankfully, I'd gotten far enough away from him that it only stung a little, no real damage done, but still it made me cry, not from the pain, but out of anger that someone would do that to me. I never did get revenge on that kid, but needless to say, I never liked him after that.

Anyway, the folks didn't think I was old enough the first couple of years I asked, but when they finally gave me one, I knew it was the best gift I'd ever gotten. It was a Daisy Red Ryder, and it was just what I'd been dreaming of. That Christmas morning it didn't matter that it was miserably cold out. Within minutes of snatching it up from beneath the tree, I was dressed and outside taking shots. It didn't take long before I became pretty good with it and was able to hit most anything I shot at. Within a few days of Christmas, I took the shot that every boy I've ever known has had to take with his BB gun. And I was dead on target. When I proudly told Dad I'd just shot a bird, and it had only taken one shot, I was sort of surprised that he didn't say, "That's great. Good shot son." Instead he turned to me and said, "Oh you did? Why?" I had to think about that for a second, then told him I didn't really know. He didn't scold me or tell me I shouldn't shoot birds or anything like that. My dad was an animal lover, and what he did say was that the bird probably had a home and maybe even had babies who were waiting for their mama or daddy to come home, and that maybe I'd want to think about that the next time I wanted to shoot a bird. I knew immediately he was right. Other than for my own sense of power over a helpless animal, I'd had no reason to kill that bird. I felt bad about it and that was the last animal I ever took a shot at.

The dead bird had nothing to do with the fact that I was lucky to have even gotten past my first week with that BB gun and still be allowed to have it. What happened was that several days after Christmas I set up some tin cans on the little sidewalk that ran from our back door to nowhere. It once ran to what had been a big shed on the east side of the house, but the shed had been torn down and was now a strawberry patch.

From our back door I could take aim straight down the sidewalk and hit the cans.

I liked the sound of the BBs hitting the tin cans with a ping then watching the cans jump or tip over. But I didn't hit a can every time, and when I missed I noticed that about a second later I heard a sound that I couldn't really identify. But I didn't worry about it, and I just kept on shooting. The next day Ora Van Pelt, our across the alley neighbor, talked to Mom or Dad and told them that I'd shot out his back porch windows while he was gone the day before. I liked Mr. Van Pelt, and when Mom and Dad confronted me about it, I was totally shocked at his accusation. Then I remembered the sounds I had heard. Those sounds had been my BBs ricocheting off the sidewalk right into Ora Van Pelt's porch windows. When they found out what had happened, my parents were unbelievably good to me about the whole thing. Of course, Dad wanted me to understand that I had to use my noggin when it came to shooting a BB gun, but other than that, there were no repercussions whatsoever. Mom and Dad paid for the Van Pelts' window replacement, and that was the last I ever heard of it.

Christmas afternoon always meant a trip to Aunt Mary's house. Along with Grandma, the seven of us would pack the car with a few gifts and head over to Liberty Street where Aunt Mary lived with her husband Uncle Allen and my cousins Allen F. and Dale. I liked Aunt Mary's house. It wasn't cluttered like ours. It was always so neat and clean and had a fireplace that was decorated in fresh pine boughs and displayed a stack of white birch logs on the grate. When I got a chance I'd always try to get a peek into my cousins', Allen F.'s and Dale's, bedrooms so I could see the cool swords they had hanging on their walls from their summer camps at Culver Military Academy. It was just a nice change of pace from my own home.

The main purpose of the Christmas gathering at Aunt Mary's was to exchange gift-exchange presents. A month or so before Christmas, the adults—Mom, Dad, Aunt Mary, Uncle Allen, Grandma, Aunt Marjory and Uncle Fred from California, and some of my older cousins—put their names in a hat then drew out someone else's name. Keeping the identity of the names they drew out a secret, they then had to buy that person a Christmas gift. I think the spending limit was five dollars, but as I grew older the limit was raised to ten or twenty. As neat as I thought the gift exchange was, my name never did make it into the hat. By the time I was old enough, and could afford to participate, the gift exchange had become a thing of the past.

Although we kids never participated in the gift exchange, Grandma always bought each of us a little gift. So did Aunt Mary. The difference between opening gifts at home and opening them at Aunt Mary's was that at Aunt Mary's we all opened our gifts one at a time. No madhouse there. Then we had to gush over them like they were exactly what we had wished for and thank whoever had given them to us. It was a nice Christmas tradition, but nine times out of ten the gifts were something to wear. That didn't excite me much, and I was always glad to see the afternoon end so we could go home and play with the new toys Santa had brought that morning.

The short ride from Aunt Mary's back to our home was always a little sad to me. It marked the end of Christmas for another year, and after having anticipated it for weeks on end, and having immersed myself in all its festivities, that two-minute trip home was a letdown. I just didn't want to see the day end.

Thanksgiving was another day that we normally spent at Aunt Mary's. But unlike the Christmas gathering, I looked more forward to Thanksgiving in her home. Aunt Mary had a large formal dining room with a table big enough to seat all seven of us, plus Aunt Mary's family of four, and Grandma. We arrived sometime in the early afternoon and were greeted at the door by Aunt Mary's dog Duchess. Duchess was a boxer breed and was hyper to the max. She'd go crazy jumping up on each of us, nearly knocking us over, and it didn't matter how many times the Randolphs scolded her and yelled, "No Duchess! No!" It would be the exact same scenario a month later when we came for Christmas. As much as I liked Aunt Mary's house, coming in the front door was no fun. When I was older, they actually got a second boxer, making the first few seconds at Aunt Mary's a dog-pouncing nightmare.

By the time we arrived and got past the dog, Uncle Allen was just pulling the turkey from the oven and sharpening his carving knife. The table had already been set with fine china that Aunt Mary kept in a built-in china cabinet along one of the dining room walls. She also had her best silverware placed on linen napkins beside the plates, fork on the left, knife and spoon on the right. The centerpiece was usually two burning white candles sitting on either side of a beautiful bouquet of flowers that was usually provided by Grandma. It was also Grandma who always said grace after Aunt Mary said, "Mother, will you give the blessing?" According to Reverend Miller, who praised Grandma posthumously at her funeral many years later, Maude Dickinson could pray better than any person he'd ever known. It was only natural that she be the one to say the Thanksgiving blessing before we dug in.

Manners were important at Aunt Mary's. It was a good place to learn how to set a formal table, how to pass food rather than grab for it, how to place your napkin on your lap, and to always say please and thank you and may I be excused. Not that we weren't taught good manners at home, we were, but it was good for us Dickinson kids to see how things were done in an atmosphere I always considered a little bit classier than in our own home.

I loved that Thanksgiving dinner with its variety of dishes, some of which we ate only once a year. Scalloped oysters, one of Mom's contributions, was one of my favorites, and it was definitely a once-a-year dish. For one thing, oysters were expensive, and Mom never made that dish without complaining about its price. But I loved it and looked forward to eating it year after year. To this day it's still a tradition at our Dickinson family Thanksgivings as I have inherited the recipe, the incentive to make it, and the cost. After dinner some of us would retire to the family room to watch football on a black and white television while the rest of us cleared the table and did the dishes. Late in the afternoon the leftovers were divvied up and we headed home, all to be repeated again the next year.

Easter was nice, but for me it didn't begin to measure up to Christmas or Thanksgiving. At our house the Easter bunny would deposit little nests of candy in various nooks and crannies of the living room and sometimes the kitchen. After we got up Mom and Dad would give each of us a little Easter basket, and we'd start looking for the nests. By the time I was ten, and had known the truth about the Easter bunny for a few years, I pretty much quit hunting down the nests myself and just took pleasure in watching my brothers and sisters.

Like everyone else we knew, Easter was also a time for new clothes and sunrise services, and we were no exception. It's about the only time I can remember making special trips to Danville to shop for new clothes. Even though I had little interest in what I wore, I knew that if I really needed something new, Mom was always soft around Easter time. She wasn't going to take us to church unless we looked as spiffy as everyone else, and if it meant spending money on new duds, then so be it. I'll have to admit, I always felt a bit of pride when we entered the church and walked down that sanctuary aisle on Easter morning, heads turning our way and nodding, faces smiling at us as we entered a pew and filled it half-full.

Halloween wasn't what I'd call a holiday, but to me it might as well have been. To begin with, I loved the fall and all that went with it. The excitement of getting back to school, the grade school carnival, Halloween and Thanksgiving, and the beauty of Covington in full exhibit as her tree-lined streets became a palette of glorious colors were all reasons to hold it dear. Of course, the simple task of raking leaves was ample enough reason to love the season. It was a task that usually made for a fun time, as half the neighborhood kids began to hoop and holler in the giant piles, or on a quiet day when I could simply divide the pile into rooms of a make-believe house.

Of course I loved it too when I was done playing in the leaves and finally raked them to the curb and set them on fire. From mid October to mid November there wasn't a day that went by when Covington's air wasn't full of leaf smoke, an odor I appreciated at the time. As far as that was concerned, we could smell smoke on about any day of the year, because everyone had a 55-gallon burn barrel sitting in their back yard in which to burn whatever trash and garbage was burnable. The garbage that couldn't be set on fire was placed in a garbage can for weekly pickup by a small truck with high sides. In those days before plastic bags, those garbage cans got extremely nasty in the summer time.

But fall was most importantly about Halloween. There were no rules about going trick-or-treating back then, so some years I'd go out the night before Halloween and again on Halloween night. I don't recall anyone saying, "Hey, it's not Halloween yet, come back tomorrow." I guess no one cared. I usually dressed up as a bum, although one year Mom dyed an old pair of white long-johns red, sewed on a pointy tail, and found a devil's mask for me to wear. As I recall, I made a pretty cute devil. I never went back to the same houses two nights in a row though. Not that it wasn't allowed. I could have changed costumes and gone back to the same houses again except for the fact that people in Covington always wanted you to identify yourself. Back then everyone wanted to know who you were. You had to tell them your name and who your parents were before they gave you a treat. That was part of the pre-television society.

Treats were often homemade and sometimes you paid a price for that. Popcorn made-up into popcorn balls were popular for Halloween treats, but some of them were so hard you couldn't bite into them. Others were so full of old maids, unpopped popcorn, that you nearly broke your teeth trying to eat them. You learned after a couple of years not to go back to those houses again. Others gave you an apple or an orange every year, another list of homes to avoid. But if you were lucky, you discovered a few who gave you a chocolate candy bar or a roll of Life Savers every year, and those houses went to the head of your Halloween list. Our neighbors, Lulu Bash and Ethel Casey, were in that latter category, which always made them dear to my heart.

Lulu Bash was a friendly older woman who lived directly across Pearl Street from us. She was seldom out of doors, so other than the fact that she gave out good candy on Halloween, I have only one other recollection of her, and I always thought it was pretty funny. The day after three of my Stanton uncles, Chuck, Phil, and Neil had come to visit us one Sunday afternoon, Mrs. Bash called on the phone and talked to Mom. I didn't hear the conversation, but when I asked Mom about it, she said that Mrs. Bash had heard all the laughing from our porch the day before and her curiosity had gotten the best of her. Mrs. Bash said it sounded so happy she decided to call and ask Mom what was going on, if Mom didn't mind her asking. Mom said at first she was hesitant to give Mrs. Bash an honest answer, but in the end went ahead. I couldn't believe Mom actually told that nice old neighbor lady what we were doing. It embarrassed me just to think about it. I asked Mom what Mrs. Bash had said in reply and Mom said, "Well, Mrs. Bash laughed and said she'd never been in a farting contest before, but she'd probably be pretty good at it."

Ethel Casey was another older neighbor who lived directly across Sixth Street from us, and I enjoyed going over sometimes to visit with her and her very short and very elderly mother. The strong smell of mothballs always greeted me, and it took a few minutes to get used to it, but that was never a deterrent. I knew I'd always be coddled whenever I came calling at Ethel Casey's, so I knocked on her door several times a year. Mrs. Casey always asked me in and began showing me around as if I'd never been there before. She always showed me her jigsaw puzzle, one of which was always in the works and laid out on a square card table in front of a rocking chair in her living room. Then she'd begin to show me her paintings.

Mrs. Casey was one of the artists that assisted Eugene Savage in painting the murals on the courthouse walls. She was always working on something new, and whatever painting she was working on at the time, along with her paints and other supplies, were always set up on an easel that was also in her living room. It seemed to me that most of her paintings were of flowers, so they didn't excite me much. What did excite me was what she kept on her kitchen counter in a little green glass bowl. It was filled with hard peppermint candy, and she'd uncover it and hold it out so I could dig my hand down and take a piece. Then we'd sit down on her living room couch and get out her Ouija board. With the Ouija board sitting between us, we'd both place the tips of our fingers lightly on the planchette, the plastic piece that moves around the board, although I didn't know the name of it at the time, then Mrs. Casey would ask it questions about my future. Low and behold, the planchette would mysteriously begin to move around and begin to spell out answers to her questions.

Today I couldn't tell you one thing that the Ouija board predicted for me. I know it never said anything bad, but I don't recall it saying anything particularly great either. Even though Mrs. Casey denied that she was pushing it, I never quite believed that it was moving on its own, even as we sat there and watched it answer our questions. But I think Ethel Casey may have believed it, and that was all right with me. I could see that it made her happy sitting there receiving my fortune just as I was happy to sit back on that couch and suck on my peppermint candy. I liked going over to Mrs. Casey's.

## My Last Summer

My last summer in Covington before heading off to college was good in many ways. First of all, I was lucky to have gotten a full-time summer job at the Olin plant, something I desperately needed in order to pay for my college expenses. The fact that Bill Huffman's dad was plant manager may have had something to do with that, but never mind, I was still thankful that I was among the few students who were hired that summer. Mom and Dad weren't in a financial position to pay for my college education, a fact we all recognized. Not only would it have been a serious struggle for them during the time I went to college, but it would have been virtually impossible to have followed up with four more children. So other than an occasional twenty that Dad or sometimes Mom handed me, money I told them I could do without but then accepted with great appreciation, I was on my own.

That summer at Olin was the first job I'd ever had that paid much more than minimum wage, and I was amazed to realize that by the end of the summer, along with the meager amount I had already saved, there was enough money to pay for my room, board, and tuition for the entire first year.

The second nice thing about that summer was that my family took a vacation, and I found that to be totally unbelievable. I mean, my family had never ever taken a vacation before. In my entire life, my Mom and Dad had been away from us maybe a total of three or four weeks, most of it in four and five day jaunts to visit relatives. On none of these little trips had the folks ever taken any of us kids along. So when Mom told me that they, that is Mom, Dad AND my brothers and sisters—the whole kit and caboodle—were thinking of taking a five-week trip to California, I guess you could say my chin pretty much hit the floor. Mom must have detected this chin dropping reaction, because she immediately began to apologize and second-guess their decision. She said she felt so bad that I had to work and that maybe they shouldn't take the trip after all. She said she knew it wasn't fair, that I'd never been on a vacation, but at least I was going to get to go on a senior class trip. Well, naturally I didn't want to hurt my mother's feelings, so I told her I thought it would be a wonderful trip for all of them, and even though I certainly would miss every one of them, and would miss going with them, I was a big boy now, and there was no reason to deny themselves this opportunity just because I had to work.

What I didn't tell her was that she had read me wrong from the beginning. What I didn't tell her was that my first reaction to her announcement wasn't one of disappointment at all, that my chin hitting the floor had actually been a sign of pure joy. But I know she felt bad that I couldn't go, so I wouldn't hurt her by telling her those things. I just hoped that she hadn't noticed the slightest of smiles quivering at the corner of my lips as I made every effort to look hurt.

The truth was, I couldn't believe that my family might be gone for an entire five weeks, half the summer, and I'd have the house to myself. I was ecstatic at the thought. I did everything I could to alleviate any worries Mom had about leaving me alone and assured her a hundred times that I could take care of myself, no problem. In the end, I think she quit worrying, and within a month of that conversation, they loaded up the station wagon and were off, all six of them.

There were several reasons why having the house to myself sounded so good, but mostly it boiled down to two things. First, I'd be able to have the entire run of the house to myself. I'd be able to sit in whatever chair I wanted and watch whatever television show I wanted and not have to argue with or please another soul. I could eat what and when I wanted, turn my radio as loud as I wanted, and have over as many friends as I wanted. For the first time in my life, I was going to be the master of my own castle, if only for a few weeks.

The second reason had to do with Alinda. By then we had been going together for a year, and although we'd had some intimacy, it had been little more than kissing and what I would consider heavy breathing. I thought this might be the opportunity to take things a step further. In other words, maybe we could sort of play house. But to my dismay, I never ever got to test out that idea. You see, I hadn't figured in the Grandma factor.

Grandma hadn't gone on vacation, so the idea that I had the entire house to myself wasn't exactly true. I had the downstairs to myself, but Grandma still had the upstairs. Even though Grandma was in her mid-seventies at that time, she still had the ears and eyes of a hawk. There was not one time in those five weeks that Alinda came by the house that Grandma didn't, within five minutes I swear, make her appearance. And her excuse for being there was always the same. "Would you kids like some lemonade?" she'd ask, after she made the trip down the stairs with a pitcher of lemonade and two glasses of ice in hand. Now what I thought really strange was that, until that summer, I'd never in my life been offered lemonade by my grandma. In fact, I didn't know she drank the stuff. But having never been rude to my Grandma, even though we didn't always see eye-to-eye, and not planning on starting now, of course we drank a glass of her lemonade. We even thanked her before she retreated back up the stairs to her own little castle.

The sad part was that, after each of those little intrusions, my plans always went south. On the other hand, Grandma's plan, a plan that might well have been cooked up by Mom and Dad before their departure, had worked out perfectly. Just the idea that Grandma might walk in again at any time, or at the very least probably had her ear to the floor, listening to every noise we made, sort of killed the mood. In the end, my dream of transforming my newly established castle into a little love nest turned out to be just that, a dream. And I'm sure my grandmother was well pleased with her efforts.

That final summer in Covington flew by in an instant. Besides the forty hours I spent at work, Alinda and I spent much of our leisure time together. We went to movies, swam at the pool, skated, and of course, went parking. The five weeks the family was gone felt like a week, and when they returned from their trip near the end of July, all I could think about was getting myself off to college.

I hadn't given much thought to the fact that going to college was going to change my life drastically, but I knew it was what I wanted, what I'd been dreaming of. All I really knew about college was what I'd conjured up in my mind by looking through some of the Purdue Yearbooks in the school library and watching old college movies like *Knute Rockne All American*. Pep rallies, football games, and serenading the sorority houses were what had filled my imagination for more than a year, and now the time had come to fulfill those dreams.

Looking back now, I guess I'd have to mark the last week in August of 1961 as the end of my growing-up years in Covington. That was the week I packed one bag and a cardboard box into the car and Mom and Dad took me up to Purdue. It's not the last summer I spent in Covington, that would come four years later, but it was the last summer that I still felt inherently carefree. Having set my immediate goals at little more than what I already had, it was the last summer when I was still mostly awash in innocence to the coming years of the adult world.

As I headed out the Stone Bluff road with my parents on the way to Purdue that day, out past the point and into what I would, years later, come to appreciate as some of the most beautiful countryside in the world, I didn't look back. The idea that life might not always be perfect never crossed my mind. And why should it? After all, I was heading out into the world thinking that I'd just spent my first 18 years living the best that life could ever have offered. And I'm pretty sure I was right.

# Afterward

After a twenty-year absence, along with our two children, Heidi and Lincoln, Alinda and I moved back to Covington in 1987, where we bought a large federal-style house at the corner of Seventh and Harrison. It's the place we've called home ever since. I'm glad we came back. Because to my great pleasure, I still find Covington a lovely place to live. Her tree-lined streets are as pretty as they were when I was a child, the trees lush and green from mid-April to the first of October, casting cool shadows all along her walkways. And then the magic of fall begins, bringing with it a festival of glorious color painted on every branch.

The courthouse is still city-central, although the square that surrounds it has undergone a much needed facelift, and Covington's small-town atmosphere is still small-town. I feel safe here, just as I did when I was a child, and quiet solitude can still be found day or night. Even though it's been more than 50 years since I grabbed hold of a car bumper on a snowy winter day and slid from one end of Covington to the other on the soles of my shoes, today I still love pulling on a pair of snow boots and walking those same streets.

But there's no denying it, in many ways Covington is a different town than it was when I was growing up. Her businesses, buildings, institutions, and churches have changed. Civic groups, social events, schools and their recreational facilities, sports teams, restaurants, neighbors, and neighborhoods are different. Even town pride isn't quite what it once was. And although these changes are called progress, and progress is the better alternative to stagnation, I have to tell you that I really miss the old Covington.

I miss the friendliness of the people who you'd meet on any street or sidewalk back then, people who wouldn't think of passing you by without waving to you or saying "Hello." I miss that come November you can't burn your leaves along the curb, or that seniors in high school don't paint funny things on corduroy skirts and pants and call them senior cords. I miss that a morning newspaper is never again going to sit on my doorstep before the sun comes up, and that the marching band may never lead the homecoming parade again.

I'm a little sad that I can never run up and down the stairs of those old school buildings of my youth, that there will never be another sock-hop in the old gym, or a Spring Show on that old stage. Not only do I miss my old gym, but now I have to call my new gym the old gym. I wish I could take Alinda to the Lyric just one more time, sit in the back row with my arm around her, while Dutch runs up and down the aisle with his flashlight. Then we'd go to Burrin's afterwards and share a root beer float.

Albea's barbershop, Dale Clawson's now, isn't crowded on Saturdays anymore, but at least it's still there. Smitty's, Kroger, The Green Lantern, and the food locker couldn't serve their old customers today if they wanted to; their buildings are long gone. Meharry's/Selby's/Edwards' grocery store is now a residence, Allison's gas station is a parking lot, and so are the Presbyterian Church, Faust and Frey, Paxton's, and Norma's.

Thankfully you can still bank at The Fountain Trust, but not downtown anymore, and you can still drink a beer at The Friendly, now named The Northside Pub, one of Covington's true dinosaurs. The courthouse hasn't changed much in all the years, but there's no longer a concession stand in the middle of the main floor, not since Robert Dale passed on many years ago. I miss going down to a busy square on Saturday nights, where you spent five minutes looking for a parking spot, and then you had to dodge all the passers-by scurrying along the sidewalks.

I took my granddaughters to the Covington school carnival this year, and believe me; it's nothing like the school carnivals of my days. The Covington Library looks like it did when I was a kid, but it's now twice as big. The city park still has a swimming pool exactly where it was when it was first built, and I'll have to admit it's much nicer today. I'll bet there are a lot fewer ear infections, and that would make Dr. Suzuki happy. The harness racing track at the park in now a combination of grass, walking paths, and soccer fields; the summer skating rink hasn't been put up in at least 40 years. You don't go to the park to see football anymore; that takes place in a wonderful new sports facility called the Trojan Complex.

Kids hardly ever listen to the radio anymore, and certainly not to a good old fashion radio drama. They don't play war outdoors with sticks for guns, don't dig holes to hide in, and hardly ever will you see a kid pulling a sled all over town on a snowy day. At least one church is gone and three more have popped up over the years, and trees along the main highway have been cut down and replanted in the name of progress.

The closing of the cellophane plant meant a lot of lost jobs, but I guess people found other places to work, because Covington's population hasn't changed much since it closed. We still have three active women's civic groups in town, but I no longer see signs of the Lion's Club or The American Legion.

And yet, with all these changes, I still like Covington—a lot. I like that we have a wonderful walking trail, soon to be six miles long. I like that we have an IGA that's open 24 hours a day, and a Dollar General, and a CVS. I like that Alinda and I can walk from one end of town to the other anytime and not have to worry about our safety. I like that we can walk from our house to any business in town in a matter of minutes, and at the same time delight ourselves in the beauty of the big old trees and the wonderful old homes that sit beneath them.

We've thought about selling our big house (built in the 1860's) and moving to something smaller, maybe out of town. We could build that log cabin out in the country that we've talked about a hundred times. But then where would we walk? And whom would we know? Where could we go that would stimulate so many happy thoughts with nearly every step we take?

The answer, of course, is nowhere. So I guess we'll probably just stay put. Covington's been our home for a long time. It's been good to us, and we're happy here in our old age. Maybe we'll just let Shelby's or Sunset make our next move for us. Seems like a sensible plan, and most likely inevitable. And you know what? That walk up to Mount Hope Cemetery? It's pretty darn nice most any time of the year.

# Acknowledgements

To those whose thoughts and recollections helped jog loose a memory of mine or verified a long-forgotten fact, I wish to thank Harold and Barb Hegg, Sharon Roberts, Dick Rowe, Russell (Can Man) Williams, and all who responded to the questions posed through Alinda's Facebook—Covington group. I also want to thank Jane Moore for her epic search that finally produced the picture of the Methodist Junior Choir, and my sister, Mary Ann Whitaker, for two of the Dickinson family photos. A very special thanks to Kay Hunter for her patience in proof reading my manuscript, advising me with her thoughts, and giving this project her final stamp of approval. I also owe a debt of gratitude to my daughter, Heidi, and my son, Lincoln, for their encouragement and love, and to my granddaughters, Maya and Giada, who were the true inspiration in writing this story. Finally, I must heap an entire lifetime worth of love and appreciation upon my wonderful wife, Alinda, without whom I'm certain this story never would have gotten off the ground. Because of her support, her encouragement, her patience, her advice, and the untold hours she has invested in proofing and editing this book, the final result is truly a work of love between us both.

28271079R00158

Made in the USA
Lexington, KY
12 December 2013